D0238019

SIMON &
SCHUSTER

C800373724

Also by Dr. Phil McGraw

Family First

Family First Workbook

Life Strategies

Life Strategies Workbook

Love Smart

Relationship Rescue

Relationship Rescue Workbook

Self Matters

The Self Matters Companion

The Ultimate Weight Solution

The Ultimate Weight Solution Cookbook

The Ultimate Weight Solution Food Guide

Real Life

Preparing for the 7 Most Challenging Days of Your Life

Dr. Phil McGraw

London · New York · Sydney · Toronto

A CBS COMPANY

First published in Great Britain by Simon & Schuster UK Ltd, 2008
A CBS COMPANY

Originally published in the US in 2008 by FREE PRESS,
A Division of Simon & Schuster, Inc.
1230 Avenue of the Americas
New York, NY 10020

Designed by Level C

1 3 5 7 9 10 8 6 4 2

Simon & Schuster UK Ltd
1st Floor
222 Gray's Inn Road
London
WC1X 8HB

www.simonsays.co.uk

Simon & Schuster Australia
Sydney

A CIP catalogue record for this book is available
from the British Library.

ISBN: 978-1-84737-381-6

Printed in the UK by
CPI Mackays, Chatham ME5 8TD

To my wife, Robin, and my sons, Jay and Jordan
Who have inspired me to survive those most challenging days

And to
My mother, who has endured more "challenging days"
than any woman should ever be called to do yet
never complained to any of her family

And to
All of you who have overcome and lived to
share and use your story

Acknowledgments

First and foremost, thank you to my wife, Robin, for always being there for me in my best and most challenging days. Your strength and resilience throughout our lives together are nothing short of inspirational. In your own darkest hours when losing those you loved, your grace, poise, and even your vulnerability were then and are now the emotional standard and compass for our family. I am blessed by your light.

As always, thanks to my sons, Jay and Jordan, for always believing in and supporting their dad. I hope and pray that I have conveyed to you fine young men everything that I have shared in this book, to prepare you for those days I'm sure you would rather skip. Both of you inspire me and make me proud and optimistic for the future. And to my new daughter-in-law Erica for bringing such a vibrant spirit and positive energy to our family.

Thanks to Scott Madsen, who always merits mention: as usual, you have dedicated your days, nights, and weekends when you had plenty of other places to be. When I "drop out" to write, you always cover the waterfront, and for that I give you my deepest appreciation.

Thank you also to Bill Dawson (the "Pride of Tulia, Texas") for being who you are. You are a mind among minds and a trusted and valued friend. Your support during all of my days, good and bad, over our many years has made a huge difference and inspired many of the insights in this book.

Thank you to G. Frank Lawlis, Ph.D., A.B.P.P., a fellow of the American Psychological Association and chairman of the advisory board for the *Dr. Phil* show. You have been a friend and colleague for more than thirty years, and your support, insight, enthusiasm, and encyclopedic knowledge of psychology and human functioning were an invaluable resource in the research and writing of *Real Life*.

Thanks to Terry Wood and Carla Pennington, two amazing women at the heart of my Dr. Phil team, for your uncompromising commitment to getting "the message" out there. Your passion and support for all I do make projects such as the current one possible and even fun. We are just getting started.

In addition to relying on my own professional training and experiences in formulating this book, I also relied on the valued opinions of some of the most respected experts in the world. Much appreciation goes to John T. Chirban, Ph.D., Th.D., clinical instructor in psychology at Harvard Medical School and core faculty member at the Cambridge Hospital; Barry S. Anton, Ph.D., A.B.P.P., professor emeritus at the University of Puget Sound; Susan Franks, Ph.D., associate professor of psychiatry at the University of North Texas Health Science Center in Fort Worth; Bishop T. D. Jakes, Sr., beloved pastor at the Potter's House in Dallas and CEO of TDJ Enterprises; Dr. Harold C. Urschel, III, addiction psychiatrist, The Urschel Recovery Science Institute; Beth Clay, health policy consultant; and Rich Whitman, CEO of the La Hacienda Treatment Center.

As always, a special thanks to my friend and colleague Oprah. Had she not had the vision twelve years ago and supported my work since, there would be no "Dr. Phil."

Thanks also to Carolyn Reidy, Dominick Anfuso, and the Simon & Schuster/Free Press group for always believing in the importance of my message and committing to getting it "out there."

Thank you to Michele Bender and Sandy Bloomfield, who brought their unique editorial talents to this project. Your involvement was essential, and because of your dedication and work, this book is much improved. You were true professionals in every sense of the word, and for that I am grateful.

Last but not even almost least, I have to thank my team at

Dupree Miller & Associates, Inc. Books such as *Real Life* don't just happen and require so much more than any author could ever accomplish alone. Jan Miller never gets tired, never gets off point, and never stops until the best book possible is written. Shannon Marven, whom for many years I have called my "secret weapon," is a woman of amazing depth and wisdom. Her contribution to this book is incalculable. *Real Life* was one of, if not the most challenging, projects I have ever undertaken. It simply would not have come to pass without Shannon's tireless devotion to organizing, editing, and shaping the manuscript. Thanks also to her team members Lacy Lynch, M.S., who was particularly helpful with the editorial work, and Annabelle Baxter. Both went way beyond the call of duty on the research and organizational fronts and are much appreciated for their contribution.

Contents

Introduction

If, by chance, you're one of those people who is tempted to skip ahead and read the last part of a book first, we are actually on the "same page," so to speak, because I want to work *backward* with you here for a minute. I want to tell you right off the bat how I am going to end this book. It really kind of makes sense to start this way because these few beginning pages are actually the last ones that I am writing after spending more than a year working on how best to help you, me, and the ones we love prepare for the seven most challenging days of your life.

So here's the endnote: You might expect that after being immersed so fully in the dissecting of the difficult details of days that are anything but welcome, that I might be a bit ragged or pessimistic about life. But in actuality, nothing could be further from the truth! Life can be tough, but we are not victims—at least we don't have to be! This is a book about hope, joy, personal strength, and, most importantly, peace of mind. These qualities of life can only be enhanced by doing and actively acknowledging that you have done the work needed to maintain your "life balance" and help those you love maintain theirs, in the face of the ups and downs that have always been part of life. Though they are a part for which most of us get very little preparation. *Real Life* has been written with the goal of helping to fill what I think is a real void in how we are prepped for the most challenging days of our life.

Despite the fact that life isn't always comfortable and can, in fact, be downright painful, I absolutely, unequivocally love it and cannot wait for what lies ahead in the years to come. After living in this world for more than half of a century, I have seen a lot.

Frankly, I have seen more than a lot, and, just like yours, my life hasn't always been fun. It hasn't always been easy, and I certainly haven't always had the best reactions—especially early on in my life. But all in all, I do love being in this world and feel blessed to be here. In fact, given some of the days I've had, I feel blessed to be *anywhere*!

So far, I have lived just over 21,000 days. I don't remember specifics about most of those days, but some stand out because they have been nothing short of tremendous and spectacular. Many of these really good days can be attributed to good health, a wonderful, God-centered family, and a career that is so much fun I almost feel guilty getting paid for it—*almost*!

But (and isn't there almost always a big *but*?) there have also been days that stand out because they were anything *but* tremendous and spectacular. In fact, some of those days I remember because they were among the most difficult days of my life. They were days that threatened, took away, or destroyed that which I held most dear. Some of them felt as though they were a month long and at times made me question everything I thought I knew about myself and the world around me. These were days that sometimes left me feeling inept, inadequate, and out of control—especially when they impacted or involved those closest to me. If you are at all like me, you too have sometimes wondered, in the face of those bad days, if you would ever regain your balance, your joy, and your hope and vision for any kind of future. If life can be so harsh, why am I so passionate about it and looking forward to what's coming?

Because I have come to believe that all of us, you and me included, have within us (or, if you don't believe in God-given gifts, can *acquire*) the strength and wisdom to deal effectively with every challenge we will ever face in our lives. I don't say this as a "rah-rah" platitude, and I'm certainly not saying that we have algebra or geometry knowledge built into our DNA. But when it comes to the *real* questions about life, survival, peace, and happiness—no matter how much they are threatened or challenged—I believe that the ability to get to the truth and the answers needed to meet the demands resides within us and always has. We have what it takes to make this life a huge net plus. We are beyond equal to the challenge. I know this because I have learned to step back and watch myself and others triumph in the darkest of hours. We have all seen ordinary people show extraordinary depth and resourcefulness in the face of overwhelming challenges. The hardest part in making sure that you are one of those people is overcoming all the noise, clutter, and distractions of life that may have buried and distorted the strength and wisdom you have within you and need in order to get through the toughest times.

The pace and complexity of life in this day and time sometimes make it very difficult to get back to a place in our mind and spirit where we are able to access all that we are and need to be. There is no substitute for good old-fashioned hard work, informed preparation, and clearly thought out coping strategies for difficult times.

That is what *Real Life* is all about. I want to help you access the *best parts* of who you are, especially in the *worst parts* of your life. Think about it: If you have an average life span, you will live approximately 78 years, or 28,470 days. Some (hopefully most of them) will be really good; some will be so mundane it will be as if they didn't even happen; some won't be so great; and a few (hopefully a very few) will be really tough—tough enough to affect your experience of all the other days. How much depends on how ready you are for those critical times.

You know I'm right and that you and those most precious to you are worth the time and effort it takes to prepare. In the pages that follow, I have not tried to "reinvent the wheel," and I have made a concerted effort *not* to bog you down with more information than you need or can really effectively use when facing challenging times. I could have written hundreds of pages about each of the seven days that I have chosen to address here, and in fact many experts have done exactly that and done it very well. If you feel you need more information on any of the crises I discuss here—and you very well may—there is extensive information at the back of this book. But my intention here is more focused on giving you what is, based on my experience and opinion, the *core* information that will help you manage your crisis one day at a time, without having to dig through an endless body of research (most of which was not written for real people in the real world anyway). Others might disagree, but I feel pretty strongly about what I've included here.

I have put verbs in my sentences and tried to get to the point in a clear, concise, and usable fashion. I am going to identify what some of the most challenging days are; tell you what to expect when they come so you are not surprised, ambushed, or shocked; and then suggest a strategy for getting you or your loved one back to better days. You will see that while there are some important differences, there are also some powerful commonalities in the coping strategies suggested for navigating through these tough days, so the good news is that you don't have to learn seven totally different game plans!

My hope and prayer when you have finished this book is that you feel a sense of calm in knowing that you are one of those people that are prepared for *all* that comes in this life. This preparation can yield huge dividends for yourself and even empower you to lead and help others in difficult times.

1

Prep Talk

Life is what happens to you while you're busy making other plans.

—JOHN LENNON

If we are fortunate in our lives, somewhere along the way we encounter at least a few special people who change us in powerful, positive, and sometimes unexpected ways. These individuals, although wise, are sometimes not at all persons you would consciously seek out for counsel. One such person I was blessed to have in my life was a flight instructor I met back in the sixties, a man from whom I expected to learn how to get airborne and nothing more. I could not have been more wrong, because he proved to be one of the great "gifts" in my life.

Bill was, by his own account and all appearances, just a good ol' flying cowboy without a lot of formal education who happened to love anything that had to do with flying. But his contributions to my life ultimately proved to include much more than flying, as this very book will attest.

I was just a teenager when I started taking lessons, but he "saw" into my future in that airplane. About the time I was finishing my training, he told me that I had checked all the boxes, done all the drills, met all of the requirements, and could certainly go get my license and wing happily off into the wild blue yonder. He then paused and said something that really got my attention. I have never forgotten that moment standing next to the plane on a grass landing strip outside a small town in north Texas. "Phil," he said, "you've got the basics, you know how to get 'er up and down and around the 'patch,' and frankly you ain't half bad. But I have come to know you, and I know just as sure as I'm standing here that you are going to need more than you got. You won't play at this flying stuff, you will attack it and make it a big part of your life rather than flying to Grandma's house on a nice clear Sunday afternoon. You're going to be out there 'mixing it up' come rain or come shine, daylight or dark, and that's okay, but the truth is things just happen when you mix it up. Maybe it will be your fault for being too aggressive, or maybe you will just be in the wrong place at the wrong time, but chances are that somewhere along the way this plane will carry you into a crisis. When you are airborne, all you've got is yourself. You'd have to depend on who you are, and if you aren't prepared for it ahead of time you can *die* in this airplane. So it's up to you—but know that it may come and if it does, you will be one of two types of pilots: one who was ready and survives to tell the story, or one who wasn't and doesn't."

He didn't wait for a response; he had spoken his piece and that was that. Even then I realized the significance of that exchange, mostly because he had just spoken more words than I had ever heard him say at once in the entire time I had known him. Now, you have to understand here that I was a teenager in the worst sense of the word. I suspect a lot of people who knew me then probably figured I had eaten a lot of paste as a child! Boy oh boy, did I have ants in my pants to "sky up" and go for it. Yet for some reason (and certainly out of character for me), I actually listened to his wise counsel. We weren't even *almost* done because I wasn't even *almost* prepared for when things would go wrong, and though I didn't know it then, they would in fact go wrong—way wrong.

Fast-forward four years and several hundred hours of flying later. I took off in a high-performance single-engine airplane just before midnight (some would call such behavior crazy) and on the heels of a strong winter storm that had blown through the Midwest like a freight train (some would repeat themselves). The flight started like every other I had flown, but it ended very differently. I was cruising at 10,000 feet when all of a sudden the engine just quit—and I mean *quit*. It didn't sputter, it just quit. The sky was pitch black without even the tiniest sliver of moon to illuminate it, and there were two feet of fresh snow blanketing the ground so that everything below me looked one-dimensional. I couldn't tell the difference between the houses, fields, and roads, and there was no horizon to use as a guide. The silence was deafening, making me feel utterly and totally alone. I couldn't pull over as I could if I had car trouble, and I couldn't grab a life preserver. I had just five minutes to work with—that's 300 seconds. The clock was ticking, I was going down—no negotiation, no maybe, I *was* going down. Whether I lived or died would be determined by the grace of God and what I did in those 300 seconds. There was no time to panic or call someone on the ground. Looking back, I realize that I probably went into a kind of "internal autopilot." All my training and preparation kicked in. During those additional training exercises I had completed at Bill's behest, he must have had me simulate emergency dead-stick landings dozens and dozens of times, some during the day, some in the black of night. And in that cockpit, as I quickly came to grips with my situation, I heard his voice in my mind: *Fly first, navigate second, and communicate last . . . the clock is ticking.* I felt very alone, but I calmed myself with the fact that I had prepared completely for this *exact* situation—my emergency just meant that all those practice drills were for a purpose. It was now "showtime." Let me tell you, that night I learned that there are just some things in life that come down to *you* and everything that's inside you. That's it; that's the deal.

An old joke among pilots (which wasn't very funny that night) is that any landing you walk away from is a good one. I flew that airplane-turned-glider for those 300 seconds with more purpose and focus than anything I had ever done in my life. It was a "good" landing because I did walk away. I'd love to say I swaggered away like John Wayne in *The High and Mighty*, whistling and slapping the wing as I left. But the truth is, I was so shaken and scared I was having trouble getting either one of my feet to cooperate in any way that even *resembled* walking. That five minutes of my life changed me forever, but it was all the preparation that led up to those five minutes that allowed me to make the right choices when it counted. If Bill hadn't cared enough to tell me the truth as he saw it, if he hadn't inspired and helped me get ready for what was ahead, I have no doubt I would not be here now, typing these words.

I know now that the outcome on that cold and dark winter's night was determined long before I ever took off. I survived not because I was lucky or because I was some great, macho pilot, cheating death with flair and panache. I survived because I had listened, because I had done my homework; I was prepared for the crisis before it happened. That night built into me a sense of confidence that if I prepared myself for the emergencies and crises that I would most likely face in life, I could at least influence their outcomes as well.

I hope that you never find yourself in a crisis like I was in that night. But we both know that while your crises will probably be different in both form and substance, they may already be on your schedule. The question is: Will you be ready? Will you have done your homework for yourself and those you love? Just like my night in the airplane, the outcome will probably be determined by what you do or don't do between now and then. So this is as good a time as any to start thinking about those days in life we would rather skip.

REAL LIFE BRINGS REAL PROBLEMS

Sometimes I wish I could predict, and even control, the future but I can't, and neither can you.

Nobody has a "Get out of jail free" card. Although I have identified seven of the most common crises, you may have a list of five or ten more. There is no magic number, but I wanted to focus on the ones that, in my experience, you are most likely to encounter either yourself or through a loved one. They are likely to happen whether you've got an eighth-grade education or a Ph.D. They may happen whether you walk the red carpet or clean carpets for a living. They may happen whether you're in a big city, living life in the fast lane, or in the woods, moving at a snail's pace.

That means we are left to manage, adapt to, and survive what does come. Unfortunately, some people just knee-jerk react to what pops up in front of them. Some choose to live in stark denial, deluding themselves into believing that if they just don't think about the inevitable and undeniable crises of life, maybe they just won't happen. I think Scarlett O'Hara expressed it best: "I can't think about that right now—if I do, I'll go crazy. I'll think about that tomorrow." Well, frankly, Scarlett, my dear, those tomorrows *do* come, and if you haven't prepared for them, those tomorrows can kick your butt. You will see that these strategies (or more accurately, non-strategies) can come at a very high price.

Even though we may not like to think about it, we all know that life is unpredictable. We can't expect that, just because yesterday was sunny, it won't rain today or tomorrow. A part of us always maintains a watchful eye, and no matter how well things seem to be going now, there can be the underlying nagging thought: Will the "other shoe" drop? And the truth is "yes," the other shoe probably will drop at some point. I say this not as a pessimist, but as a realist and a coach, so that you may decide to do what it takes to have the peace that comes from being ready when it does.

If I had waited until that night at 10,000 feet to make a plan, it would have been way too late. When one of these seven days does arrive, I would want you to be able to say, "This is a crisis that I have prepared myself for. I'm at a fork in the road, and I can either panic and fall apart or I can use all of my skills and preparation to manage this day. The choice is mine." Of course, the only way you can say that is if you are the person with a plan, the person who did their homework. The time to think about what you're going to do when you're in rough waters is when you are still in smooth waters, because on those seven days you'll likely be way too busy physically, mentally, and emotionally to start making a plan.

Monsters Live in the Dark

I don't think of life as being *good* versus *bad* or *fair* versus *unfair.* Life just is. I don't think the world is out to get you or me or that we should view life as a ticking time bomb that's going to blow up on us. I want all of us not just to survive these days but to come out of them with a new place to stand—with new tools, new wisdom, and a deeper understanding of how you got there, so that if it's something you were doing that was ineffective, you can change it, and if it's something that happened out of the blue, you can weather it and be stronger for it. The tools that I'll share are designed to help you do just that, as well as, in the process become more successful as an individual—a wife or husband, a mother or father, and a member of your community. It's a skill set that should be taught but seldom, if ever, is. It ought to be part of the preparation for growing up, but for most of us, it just isn't.

I want all of us not just to survive these days but to come out of them with a new place to stand—with new tools, new wisdom, and a deeper understanding of how you got there, so that if it's something you were doing that was ineffective, you can change it, and if it's something that happened out of the blue, you can weather it and be stronger for it.

My goal is not only to help you learn how to cope well but also to empower you to fill the void of information in your children's lives—whether they are still young or grown with their own families. You don't have to live your life in fear of these seven days, the "dropping shoe," or any other crisis for that matter. You don't need to live scared *if* you have a plan in place and *if* you take some time to recognize and fill any voids in coping skills—before you need them.

People who play the game with "sweaty palms" are probably scared because they should be, because they know they have a void. One woman told me that she saw herself going through life as if she were sitting at the edge of one of those stiff metal folding chairs. She feared that the second she got excited about life it would be pulled out from underneath her. I'm guessing she has a "void" in her coping skills and knows in her heart of hearts that she is not equal to the challenges that could come. She's not alone. Many of us live this way because fearing the unknown is what we do. We can't see the road ahead of us, so sometimes we just envision the worst. But what if you did think about, acknowledge, and have a sense of what's likely around the corners of your life? None of us knows exactly how our lives will play out, but wouldn't it help to know what at least seven of the most common difficult days or crises most likely to touch your life will be like? Wouldn't looking at these days *before* they hit be a lot smarter than waiting and having to struggle with the shock, distress, and confusion on top of all the stress of dealing with the event itself?

Sometimes those first moments of a crisis can be crucial. One way to explain this is to think about what happens between a mugger and his unsuspecting victim. When you're being mugged, the number one edge that your attacker has over you is those first few seconds when he steps up to you and pulls a knife, holds up a gun, or takes a swing at you. That moment of shock is a state of mind that he is actually counting on to give him the time he needs to victimize you. Now imagine if you *knew* your attacker was about to strike. If you saw him coming, he wouldn't have this advantage. Of course, you would never be totally calm in this situation or in the major kinds of crises we are talking about here. You would definitely go into high alert and arousal. But the difference is, you wouldn't panic and fall apart—not with the mugger and not with one of the seven most challenging days of your life.

I want you to feel certain that you can handle whatever comes your way and, more important, to live each day in that place of confidence. This is part of what I call your attitude of approach—something we'll talk about in detail in the next chapter. Monsters live in the dark. But once you turn the lights on, you say, "Oh, okay. I can handle this." And you can. I believe you can. More importantly, I want *you* to believe that you can.

THE 7 MOST CHALLENGING DAYS OF YOUR LIFE

For most of us, our formal education and other life experiences don't give us any information about crisis management, problem solving, or even problem recognition. Much of this book is based on my opinions and experiences of what I have seen work for people dealing with these seven days in their lives as well as in my own life. But I didn't write it in a vacuum, because most, if not all, of my opinions are also supported by the results of those studies. I also did not discover some great new information to break the "code of life," which is okay because I didn't need to.

As is my usual focus, this book is about *real* people and *real* problems of living. When I started working on this book, I was curious about what people saw themselves wrestling with in these current times. In order to get a current snapshot of what some of our friends and neighbors see as their greatest stressors and toughest days, a Web survey was conducted at www.dr.phil.com with more than a thousand respondents. We asked what they believed their top stressful events were, based on their opinion about the level of interference these stressors created in their lives according to a scale from 0 to 100 percent (0 meaning the event had no interference, 100 meaning total interference).

Ask yourself if you agree or disagree with the ratings of these various events in light of your own experiences. In other chapters, I'll discuss the relationship between stressful events, such as these and possible consequences or reactions that may be associated. Fifteen stress events that were reported to interfere at a level of at least 75 percent are ranked as follows:

Rank	Stress Event*
1	Foreclosure of mortgage or loan†
2	Death of close family member
3	Major disease diagnosis
4	Major disease diagnosis of family member
5	Severe illness (living with a chronic state of illness)
6	Death of a spouse
7	Financial ruin
8	Change in financial state
9	Traumatic legal problem
10	Separation
11	Self-identity crisis
12	Change in mental health of family member
13	Divorce
14	Severe injury
15	Death of close friend

The results of the survey were largely consistent with many of the studies that have been conducted on stress in the past. It alerts us to possible areas we need to be watchful of because—as you'll read in later chapters—these events can be linked to other physical and emotional consequences that can make a situation even worse. For example, the researchers Holmes and Rahe conducted a study with a stress scale a generation ago, and the findings suggest that interpersonal stress events, such as the death of a spouse and divorce, were the greatest stress events and furthermore could be linked to physical diseases. The data didn't answer

* As you look at these responses, keep in mind that this is an Internet survey, not high science, and even though the information is useful for discussion purposes, it has limitations from a scientific perspective—meaning that if I had conducted it for predictive, rather than discussion, purposes, I would have gone about it somewhat differently. But it *is* a "report from the field"—and as such, I think you will find it very interesting.

† Foreclosure probably rates number one more as a function of the survey being conducted in the middle of a media frenzy about the huge housing market crash rather than as a function of it really being seen as more disruptive than death of a family member or health crisis. Nonetheless, it was rated number one by these respondents.

the question about which came first, the stressor or the disease, but either way both are problems worth attending to.

Here is a breakdown of the seven days I have chosen to discuss. If you find yourself experiencing one of these days you will recognize the painful descriptions. As I have said, these seven days were selected based on my opinions and my observations of their potential for interference with your life and peace of mind, and on the commonality with which I have seen them occur in people's lives.

The Day Your Heart Is Shattered

On this day, you lose something of great value and your heart is broken. It's safe to say that none of us will escape this day, and chances are that at some time in your or your loved one's life, you have already experienced it. It's also likely that you'll go through this day more than once, and each time will be different depending on what it is that you are losing—a loved one lost to death, a marriage, a friendship, your career, or life's dream—but one common denominator is the sense of grief, mourning, or gripping pain that can bring you to your knees.

The Day You Realize You Have Lived Your Life as a Sellout

This is one of the seven most challenging days because it's the one when you realize that you are living without courage and without integrity. You finally admit that fear has been ruling your life and that almost every choice you have made up to this point has been fear-dominated. You realize that you have sold out on yourself and your dreams because you were afraid you might fail or displease those people whose opinions you value. You cannot look back on your life with a sense of pride because it's not even your own life you've been living—it's been for someone else, or maybe everyone else . . . everyone except you. You have let your "authentic self" down.

The Day You Realize You Are in Way Over Your Head

How you cope in this world is what I call your adaptability. On this most challenging day, your ability to meet life's demands has broken down. Mentally, emotionally, and physically, you feel completely overwhelmed—whether the source of your meltdown was financial or just the realization that you can't keep living as though you have everything under control because you don't. This day you are overwhelmed and feel that you are out of options. You feel as if you are drowning in demands and can't do a thing to keep your head above water.

The Day the Body Breaks Down

We hate to think about getting sick, but a health breakdown is one of the inevitable facts of life. The chances that either you or your loved ones are going to encounter a major health crisis at some point are pretty high. Even if you live a healthy and accident-free life, at some point your body will just wear out. Like all of these difficult days, the attitude of approach you take into a situation when you or somebody you love is diagnosed with a life-threatening or health-compromising disease, or experiences an injury or a breakdown, is crucial.

The Day the Mind Breaks Down

The day you recognize and acknowledge that you or a loved one's mental or emotional functioning is in trouble can be a day of pain, shame, fear, and confusion. We as a society are much less enlightened about mental as opposed to physical breakdowns, and as a result the challenges perceived in finding answers can be daunting, to say the least. Looking for answers can sometimes be as scary as the problem you are seeking help for because of the pain and fear of judgment by self and others. Amazingly, mental health is something that's still not openly discussed very much in this country, yet it's one of the most important aspects of our existence. It is something that defines all our lives in some form or another. When mental health breaks down, it can take many different forms, but statistically is most likely to be expressed as anxiety, depression, or the less frequent but more severe mental disorders that involve gross impairment of reality testing or, more simply put, an inability to distinguish what is real versus what is fantasy, delusion, or hallucinations.

The Day Addiction Takes Over

One look at the headlines, and it's clear that addiction is sweeping through this country at an alarming rate. It used to be that drug addicts were found mostly in dark alleys or other seedy parts of town. But today you might find them anywhere from the suburban bedroom to the executive boardroom. Hearing about a soccer mom or successful businessperson who's addicted to drugs isn't a fluke anymore. Part of this is how much easier they are to obtain—you can get your drug of choice with the click of a computer mouse. And it isn't limited to drugs alone; alcoholism too is occurring at alarming levels. Whether it's your own addiction or that of someone you love, it takes over your life and can easily destroy it.

The Day You Have Lost Your Purpose and Have No Answer to the Question "Why?"

This is the challenge of finding meaning for your life. It deals not so much with who you are but *why* you are. This can be a crisis of faith or a feeling of losing your compass or purpose in this life. What's the point? What's your purpose? It's that feeling of being insignificant. Time is finite, and you have a limited amount of time to make an impact. What are you going to do? If you have lost your connection to meaning in your life, you need to examine this area and get plugged in to something that will stabilize you when nothing around you makes any sense. This could be anything from a new foundation in your faith to devoting yourself to a cause you have always wanted to join to just being the best dad, mentor, employee, daughter, or friend that you can be.

When you face your challenges on these seven days or on others that may come into your life, and you watch yourself come through to the other side, you can be exhilarated and empowered by it. You can hold your head up even when everything around you is falling down.

LIFE IS NOT A SUCCESS-ONLY JOURNEY

The fact is that despite our best-laid plans and deepest desires, real life isn't always easy. It isn't a success-only journey for any of us. Going through life can at times feel like going through a wind tunnel. Sometimes life comes at you in a steady breeze; other times it's like a category five hurricane. The storms of life may not always have happy endings, but they can at least be dealt with and sometimes even put you in a better place on the other side. What's at least as important is that you will be able to be in a position to lead your family—to be calm in the middle of the storm.

If you live a faith-based or spiritual life, you may say that you will pray to God when a crisis hits and He will save you. That makes perfect sense, but you also have to get busy yourself. I can tell you that as somebody who embraces a faith-based life, I am also very active in using all of my resources to help myself. I figure that's why God gave them to me. My point is that no matter where your strength comes from, your job is to kick, fight, scratch, and claw for your best position in this world. Whether you think you got them through the DNA chain or as a gift from God, you have resources that are going to be called into play especially on those seven days, and what I want you to do is learn how to mobilize them.

HOLD YOUR HEAD UP

We are all products of our learning history, and if there were never any challenges, we wouldn't develop mentally, physically, emotionally, or spiritually. I've always said that if you face adversity in life and you don't learn from it, it's a penalty. If you learn from it, at least you can consider it tuition. I'm not saying that changing your attitude of approach or having an action plan is going to keep you from having problems or keep you from the challenges that life is going to serve up. It won't. I'm not saying that it's going to prevent these seven days of your life. It won't. You may still hit the same bumps on those seven days, but now you can react differently.

The way you walk through this world is going to be different. It's sort of like this: Imagine someone who is a black belt in martial arts walking down a dark alley late at night. Then imagine someone who *doesn't* have that training going down that same alley. The difference in their experience of that walk is huge. Ultimately, my goal with this book is to equip you to walk with confidence and power, not based on a false bravado, but based on readiness.

2

Attitude of Approach

Pray to God, but continue to row to shore.
—RUSSIAN PROVERB

No one can fix your life—because it is something that is managed, not cured. Hopefully, your life is, for the most part, working *okay*. But you can always become better equipped to manage it. When you finish reading this book, chances are you will have most of the same problems you had before you started reading it. If you had a bad marriage when you started this book, you're going to have a bad marriage when you finish it, maybe even worse. If you were in a dead-end career and were overweight before, you're going to have the same career and same body after. Moreover, you almost certainly had some if not all seven of these days ahead of you when you began reading, and you still do. Reading this book may not change the problems you already have or enable you to avoid what may be coming.

What's going to change is far more important than any one situation or problem. What's going to change is *you:* your ability to manage your life and to put things in the right perspective, your understanding of why you're doing the things you do and the things you *don't do*, and where it's all getting you. And most importantly, you're going to examine and make a conscious decision to embrace or change the attitude with which you approach your life. And that is huge because it is this attitude that can determine how your life turns out.

You're going to pick up some new and important skills so that you can *work* the problem, not *be part of* the problem. Instead of focusing on, or even obsessing about, things you can't control, you're going to gain the understanding that will help you avoid feeling like a victim, even at those "intersections" in life where you feel as if you have been broadsided in a hit-and-run. My hope is that you will understand that it is not what happens in your life that makes you feel the way you do but instead how you *choose* to respond. I'll talk more about that later; for right now, I want to make it clear that I'm not saying that pumping yourself full of sunshine will make a problem like one of the seven days disappear. I wish it were that easy, but it's not.

So let's talk about your personal and unique "attitude of approach." Everyone without exception, whether they know what it is or not, has one. You have one even if you aren't consciously aware of it; I am betting that if you really think about it, you will quickly see yours, because it is such an important part of who you are. Different people simply approach the world and their life in different ways. Some people are victims and some are hunters, some people are givers and some are takers, some people are passive while others are very aggressive. The categories, descriptors, and dichotomies are endless.

I start here because if your "attitude of approach" is not working for you in calm waters, you are going to be in a real mess when one of the big seven hits. So the important questions are: "What is your attitude of approach, and is it working?" "How would those who know you best describe your approach?" "Is it generating the results you want, or is it getting in your way and keeping you from creating what you most want and need?" "Where did it come from, and when was the last time you tried to change it?" Your attitude of approach affects everything you do and feel, and it is a filter through which you view the world; it is the sum and substance of the strategy with which you take on life. It also can powerfully influence how other people respond to you and define your place in this world. You get what you give. If you've never sat down and asked yourself what your philosophy of life is, what your strategy is, what your unique approach is—now is the time.

In the Eye of the Beholder

I believe that there is no reality, only perception. There is no good news or bad news; it is only your interpretation of the news that makes it "good" or "bad." It is a function of your point of view, your perception, and your interpretation of how any event you experience impacts you.

My point is that you make a choice, sometimes very habitually, about how you interpret and react to the events of your life. Maybe your habitual pattern is analytical, maybe it's emotional, maybe you personalize almost everything from a traffic jam to a rate increase on your electric bill. Your reactions and interpretations come from someplace, and they influence the running conversation you have with yourself about what's going on and how you're going to feel about it. The fact is, how you react today to

Knowing where your choices come from, and being able to anticipate how you'll react to a situation, can help you understand and acknowledge your "patterns."

people or events is probably shaped to a great degree by outdated information that you need to examine in order to make sure it is not obsolete and secretly sabotaging your best-laid plans. It is all a choice. Knowing where your choices come from, and being able to anticipate how you'll react to a situation, can help you understand and acknowledge your "patterns." And that's what I want to talk about here—how those filters that have been put into place over the years have resulted in your interpreting certain words, gestures, actions, and events the way you do.

So how did you develop your specific attitude of approach, and how do you become consciously aware of what it is? (And, if necessary, how do you change it?) Your attitude of approach is maybe one small part inherited tendencies and many parts the cumulative and ever-evolving result of events, experiences, and consequences in your life and how you've learned to react emotionally to and interpret them. A big component of your attitude of approach is emotional. Your emotions don't just happen automatically or by magic. It helps to understand what my predecessors in rational thinking have termed "the anatomy of an emotion."

The Four Basic Parts of the Anatomy of an Emotion

1. *An event takes place, and you* perceive *it in a sensory way—using your sight, hearing, smelling, touching, and maybe even tasting abilities. The same event can be perceived 1,000 different ways by 1,000 different people, which is why police investigators will tell you that multiple eyewitnesses to the same event seldom give consistent or accurate reports. They are all looking through different filters (past experiences).*
2. *You label it by using your filters to place meaning on the event—this could mean seeing an authority figure as threatening because of an abusive father, or, on the other hand, using pleasure points like that "warm and fuzzy" feeling we get when we enjoy a birthday cake or the smell of the ocean because you spent blissful childhood summers at the beach.*
3. *You have an emotional reaction based on what you say to yourself about the event, your internal dialogue—which is the nonstop conversation you have in your head. Your internal dialogue can become so well rehearsed and so deeply entrenched as to become automatic and operate habitually without your conscious awareness.*
4. *You respond behaviorally in a way that flows from the emotions you have chosen by your internal dialogue.*

The anatomy of an emotion is complex. Let me show you how it comes together in the following real-life scenario: Ann's father walked out on her family when Ann was just three. (The beginning of the "event.") With no support from her husband, Ann's mother could barely make ends meet, so for the next five years Ann bounced from one foster home to the next. Unfortunately, each one was worse than the last. She slept on a bare cot in a room filled with other foster children, had few personal belongings, and, at some homes, had to fight for basic things like a hot meal and clean clothes. If she complained or questioned anything, Ann was punished with physical or verbal abuse. She switched schools so frequently that she could never make any real friends, and her mother came in and out of her life in an unpredictable pattern.

Ann applied meaning to each of these events, forming "facts" about her experiences as she went along. (The second part of the anatomy: labeling and "filing" each event for future reference.) These facts would shape her future views and expectations of how people will treat her and how she must behave in order to escape the negative treatment. Ann's lack of a stable routine and steady, nurturing caregiver in her life—on top of the harsh treatment she received early on—set her up for future intimacy and relationship issues. Although she had occasionally encountered the truly devoted loving and caring foster parents that typify most of the "saints" that sacrifice personally for children in need, her early experiences had already put many of her filters in place. She made emotional judgments about people because of the things that had happened to her, which caused her to maintain a safe distance from others as she tried to make her way through life.

Not surprisingly, Ann grew up feeling like the only person she could depend on was herself. (The third part of the anatomy: with her internal dialogue running daily on the same tracks, her childhood judgments continued on into her adult life.) She knew if she needed something, it was up to her to figure out how to get it. She also decided that she needed to stay in control of her world so she would never again be subject to the whims of other people. As a result, right out of school she took a sales job in the field, where she would not have to deal with the typical pressures of office supervisors and rules. (The final part of the anatomy of an emotion, where the internal dialogue fuels the emotions, which results in the behavior that completes the cycle.) Her performance became her currency (that which she valued)—she learned she could let her sales numbers do the talking, which, in certain ways, worked for her. She was a real go-getter, and it won her the respect and admiration she felt she deserved. But what it did *not* win for her was the love and trust that had been violated as a child, which she was actually craving all along underneath her self-reliant exterior. Her career kept her busy so she always had excuses to pull back when relationships started getting too serious, and she never learned how to partner with others or to give and receive love in committed relationships. Ann is finally living the successful life she always dreamed of, yet she still feels emotionally crippled because she is living through the same filters of her childhood. Because she never went back to reexamine and correct old information about the unreliability of people and the pain they would cause her, she has no one to share her deepest joys or heartaches in life.

As I said earlier, the anatomy of an emotion is not a simple process. Ann's attitude of approach was created by many different factors, and if her reactions to her earlier perceptions had been different (meaning, if step two had taken a different turn), her experiences could have created a response from the other end of the spectrum. She could have interpreted her foster-care events to mean that if you're the "good girl" and don't complain or make waves, you won't be hurt. If she had chosen this response, her attitude of approach would probably be one that was more passive rather than driven. Either way, she would have serious baggage to deal with. Ann's filters are directly related to how she learned to process her childhood experiences, attaching meaning to the events that took place and establishing an internal dialogue that supported her views—no matter how false or incomplete—until they became her chosen reality. The good news is that no one has to live with the consequences of old information and dirty filters: you can choose to identify the source of your conflicts and to challenge the "facts" you may have accepted as truth for so long.

This is a good place to briefly discuss something I've written about before, called the Litmus Logic Test—a simple set of questions you can apply to any thought or belief to see if it might be poisoning the "well" of your internal dialogue. Maybe it's a judgment or idea that has followed you from past situations or events or has just attached itself to you somewhere in your journey. Wherever it came from, you should be the only one deciding if it should go forward with you. Challenge your thoughts on a regular basis and make sure they can pass this four-point test:

- **Is the thought or belief a true fact?**
  Remember that a fact is different from an opinion that you may hold. For example, no matter how much you want to believe or tell yourself that downing a box of 12 glazed donuts every week won't affect your health, the fact remains that it will. You need to line up with the truth of the matter if you're serious about making any kind of lasting changes in life. In other words, you need to deal with the truth in order to be healthy.

- **Does the thought or belief serve your best interest?**
  Is your best interest served when you prioritize this matter? In other words, is putting it high on your list actually giving you true satisfaction? If you have trouble saying, "No," as many people do, you may be telling yourself things that distort your perception of the world. You join committees that you don't really want to be on or do things for friends that you don't have the time—or desire—to do. Why do you do these things that aren't working for you? Because somewhere in your internal dialogue you are loading yourself up with "shoulds" and "musts." That kind of thinking poisons your internal dialogue. It may lead you to make choices that are based on a fear of rejection that are clearly not in your best interest.

- **Does the thought or belief protect and prolong your health?** Does making this matter a priority compromise your health in any way? For example, does worrying about it create chronic stress, which can cause a physical breakdown in your system and eventually lead to a major illness or even death? How does your internal conversation affect you physically? If you are obese, is your denial about your condition placing you at risk of heart disease, diabetes, or cancer? If you call yourself a "failure" or "worthless," are you allowing yourself to live a stress-filled life because you don't believe you deserve better?

- **Does the thought or belief get you what you want?** Is this behavior working for you? Does your internal dialogue help you achieve your goals, or has it negatively impacted your ability to pursue things that you want in life? For example, if your mother often said that you'd never be as good as your sister, you may grow up telling yourself that you're unworthy. Even though you're now an adult, you still hear your mother's words in your head. *You're not good enough, you're not worthy of love,* and—as a result—you live in fear about losing your job or spouse. Though these fears are unfounded, you spend a lot of time and energy trying not to lose things, instead of working toward the things you really want in life.

It's important to give yourself this Litmus Logic Test often so that you don't slip into bad patterns or filters.

PRIORITIZING CONSISTENT WITH A HEALTHY ATTITUDE OF APPROACH

Your attitude of approach is directly linked not only to your daily life, but also to the highly significant peaks and valleys throughout, which include the seven most challenging days of your life. To develop a plan that will help you survive those days intact, you need to understand the importance of perspective, accountability, and taking action to create the experience you want in life. Once you have these in place, you're on your way to establishing an attitude of approach that will work for you.

Living with Perspective

People always say, "I never met a man on his deathbed who said he wished he'd spent more time at the office." Why? Because when you're down to those final moments of your life, you realize what really matters. You have the ultimate perspective. Unfortunately, at that point it's a little too late to do anything about it. You see executives who are so busy trying to make money that they burn through a great marriage and a set of kids before they realize that they were already rich. They had what really matters in life, but they squandered it because they didn't have the right definition of currency. Their "income" was monetary instead of familial.

My father told me just before he died that one of life's greatest lessons would be the wisdom to recognize critical moments and decisions when they *happened* instead of at the end of your life—when it's too late to do anything about it. He told me if I wanted to really make a contribution to people's lives, helping them see those critical, life-changing moments when they occurred rather than after the fact would be a great place to start.

Having perspective is critical to a productive attitude of approach. It puts a frame around your problems and creates a context. I see people who *think* they have problems because their kids didn't get into the right preschool or a coworker was talking behind their back. Then their husband or wife is diagnosed with cancer, and now they *really* have problems. Now they don't care quite so much whether or not their child got into the "cool" preschool or who is gossiping about them around the water cooler. Those things don't matter anymore because their life has been forced into perspective for them. What I want to do with your attitude of approach is visit that on you *before* you get hit over the head and discover you aren't ready.

To be ready, you have to decide what your life is *really* all about.

You have to decide what your priorities truly are—what it is that is truly important to you. What does success look like to you? What do you really stand for and where do you spend your time, energy, and money? In chapter 10, there is an exercise that may help you delve into this further. These things have to be clear in your mind and heart so that you have your feet solidly on the ground and your compass sensitive to the direction you really want to go if one of these seven days hit. If you aren't already clear about who you are and where you want to be, it may be awfully hard to keep your balance once the crisis hits.

To be ready, you have to decide what your life is *really* all about.

For example, among the things I value most in my life are my personal relationship with Jesus Christ; providing for, protecting and nurturing my family; my health; and being a responsible and contributing member of society. After that, I value my career and dealing with important life issues for people who also care about them. My point about perspective is that if a camera breaks in the middle of the show or a guest doesn't show up, I put it into a bigger framework. Were my wife and kids healthy before that camera broke? Yes. Was my home warm and dry? Yes. Was I proud of the contribution I am making to society? Yes. So in the grand scheme of things, a broken camera may provide a moment of temporary frustration, but it is ultimately not that big a deal. But you have the ability to look at it that way only if you have an attitude of approach that includes a balanced perspective.

Words Are Very Powerful Because You Believe What You Say to Yourself

Words are very, very powerful, and the language you use plays a major role in your ability to put things into perspective and therefore your attitude of approach. This is important to note in regard to your conversations with other people and your internal dialogue. Words are emotionally laden; for every thought you have or word you say, you have a physiological reaction. Your words cause a visceral reaction in you, especially negative ones, which seem to scream louder than positive ones. And the more extreme the negative language, the louder it screams. So if you say that a movie is the worst one you've ever seen, you will feel more strongly about it than if you just said, "That movie was bad." That also means that if you say, "This is the worst thing that has ever happened to me," you will be more affected than if you said, "This is bad but not the end of the world." What I'm getting at here is that you do not want to have a melodramatic, histrionic, and overreactive way of talking to yourself about life.

For example, I try to never use words like "horrible," "disastrous," or "catastrophic" to describe a flat tire or sitting in endless Los Angeles traffic when I'm in a hurry. Sure, those things are annoyances. They're irritating and inconvenient. However, they're *not* catastrophic. They're not disastrous. They're not horrific. But I often hear people use words like those to describe things that don't even *almost* qualify for that level of crisis, and they do so because they don't have the right attitude of approach. I have known couples whose weddings went awry—one groom drank too much, one bride tripped on her long veil, and a third couple's bus full of wedding guests broke down in the pouring rain. They described these events as "devastating," "a nightmare," and "the worst moment of my life." Admittedly, their weddings were not fairy-tale perfect and I am not trivializing the fact that they wanted this special day to go well. But "horrible" and "devastating" are words that I used to hear in the burn unit of a hospital during my training. They're words that can describe Hurricane Katrina, 9/11, and a multitude of other tragedies. They aren't appropriate descriptions of a melted wedding cake, tipsy groom, or rain-soaked guests. Those things pale in comparison to what is really important in life, and if these kinds of events are truly the "worst moments" of your life, you have hit the lottery! Again, if you are saying these things to yourself, you have a lack of clear, realistic perspective.

Do Not Give Your Power Away

One of the most burdensome attitudes of approach that you can have is letting your self-worth and your choice of what matters be determined by, be a function of, or be greatly influenced by what others say and think about you. Why? Because if you give your power away to an employer, mate, family member, friend, or anyone else you interact with, then you put yourself in a highly vulnerable position. How well *you* feel about yourself is going to be a function of how secure that person is. If they are insecure and can only feel good about themselves by putting you down, then you're doomed to be judged and criticized independently of what you do. If you let that affect you, then you're giving your power away to somebody whom you don't and can't control.

For example, imagine you are driving to work, enjoying the sunny morning with your coffee and a favorite song playing on the radio. Suddenly, a guy whips up next to you, gesturing and yelling angrily as he makes sure you know that you're not moving fast enough for him. You had noticed someone riding your bumper but didn't realize how upset he was until he was in your face, ranting and raving. Then, just like that, he's gone. Although it all happened in less than a minute, you spend the rest of the morning thinking about the guy and being upset. Why did he do that? Why didn't he just pass you without making such a big deal? He didn't have to be so mean. What was so terrible about your driving anyway? It's not as if you were creeping along—or were you? You waste hours dwelling on something that occurred in a moment with someone you don't know and you will probably never see again. Even worse, you've let him affect how you feel about yourself. So just think: if you're that blown away by something as small as a stranger's reaction, imagine what will happen when a real crisis comes knocking on your door!

Now, if you're secure and know who you are, that rude driver's behavior will still be an annoyance. But it will also be irrelevant. You'll be able to shrug it off and say to yourself, "He must be a really miserable human being." After that, you won't give it another thought. You'll go on with your day because your self-worth, self-esteem, and what matters to you are self-determined.

And "self" is the key word here. Although we will be discussing your "authentic self" in the context of a fear-based life later on in chapter 5, I want to bring it up here, because how you view yourself makes all the difference in how you relate to your world. If you have never heard me use this term before, in brief, your authentic self is the *you* that can be found at your absolute core, in contrast to your "fictional" self (who the world has told you to be). It is the part of you that is not defined by your job, function, or role but is the composite of everything unique in you. Having a clear understanding of what really matters to you and who you are is like being inoculated against the negative messages of the world. You say, "*I* am going to decide what matters in my life. *I* am going to decide what is important. *I* am going to decide how I feel about me!" You realize that you don't have to be liked or included to feel good about yourself.

I'm not saying this is easy. It's not. It's a tremendous thing to strive for, but it is one of the most freeing experiences you can have in your life. Think about it: if the only person you have to control to feel happy, secure, and accepted is you, then that sure simplifies your life. Yes, it's okay to want people to like you and accept you, but there is a huge difference between *wanting* that acceptance and *needing* it. In your approach to life, you need to sort out the wants from the needs. You need to prioritize the things that are truly consistent with your values over the things that are just preferences. Please don't sabotage yourself by thinking it is selfish to press your own agenda for you. You aren't pressing it onto anyone else. If it does involve others, be sensitive and negotiate to be sure everyone's needs are respected. There is a difference between being aggressive, which protects your interests but at another's expense, versus being assertive, which protects your interests but not at another's expense.

I work really hard not to give my power away, which is one reason why I don't play the game of life with sweaty palms. Acceptance by everybody in the world is just not a high priority for me. I couldn't do what I do and take on the topics I do if I didn't have that in perspective, because I have a lot of critics. If I let the critics determine how I feel about myself, I would withdraw and spend the rest of my life apologizing. I don't do that because I believe in what I do. If you let your self-esteem be determined by your critics (and we all have them), you will spend a lot of time sitting life out. You have to decide that everyone doesn't have to like you, understand you, agree with you, or want you to succeed in order for you to be okay. And unless you can really take that attitude of approach, you are vulnerable. If other people think they can control you, they will. People debate me all the time on the show and my website's message boards. They say things like "Dr. Phil, you're an idiot. Where did you get your degree? Sears?" I don't mind if people criticize me, but that doesn't mean I'm going to substitute their judgment for my own. I know my values. I know what I believe and what I stand for. That's what matters.

You need to prioritize the things that are truly consistent with your values over the things that are just preferences.

You have to decide, "I accept myself—flaws, fallacies, and all. I don't have a gap that must be filled by your approval. I believe in who I am and what I do. If I don't, I need to change it, but I sure don't need your approval to be okay with me." Just imagine that freedom. I promise that getting to this place will be very, very valuable when you are in the middle of one of the seven most challenging days of your life.

Accountability Counts

Another critical element of your attitude of approach is being accountable. You cannot dodge responsibility for how and why your life is the way it is. If you don't like your job, you are accountable. If you are overweight, you are accountable. If you are not happy, you are accountable. You have to take ownership over any situation if you're ever going to be able to change it.

In life and in the middle of a crisis, the best way to take control of a situation or challenge is to stop blaming others and stop playing the victim. Until you acknowledge that you are not a passenger in your own life and take responsibility for what's going on, you're going to be looking for excuses instead of solutions. You will not move forward but will remain stuck. When you play the victim, you waste precious time thinking, *Why did this happen to me? What did I do to deserve this?* You can't fixate on *why* it is happening to the exclusion of dealing with the fact that it *is* happening. As you know, I have learned the hard way that if I'm piloting a plane that is going down, it's not going to do much good to sit there just wondering why the plane is going down. Unless it directly impacts *how* to deal with the fact that it *is* going down. The seconds will tick away and I will get closer and closer to the ground whether I dwell on life being unjust or whether I get busy and fly that plane. Which one I choose determines how that plane hits the ground and my chances of survival. The same goes for you when you hit a bump in the road of life. You have to take action and think about what you're going to do *now.* When you have this attitude of approach, you stop waiting for someone to fly the plane for you.

Until you acknowledge that you are not a passenger in your own life and take responsibility for what's going on, you're going to be looking for excuses instead of solutions.

If you want change, and you want to endure the marathon of life—whether it's a divorce, the loss of a loved one, a financial crisis, or any of the other seven days—you have to realize that you create your own experience. You have to look to yourself for the explanation of why your life is where it is. When you are accountable, you understand that the solutions to life's challenges lie within you. Even if you feel angry, hurt, or upset, you own those feelings. You are responsible for their presence in your life. You need to see that no one but you is going to help you get out of any situation and say, "I *do* have the power and therefore the responsibility, so I need to grab the laboring oar and get busy creating what I want."

One of the biggest obstacles that people face when it comes to accountability is denial. There are very few people who don't lie to themselves; we lie by either omission or distortion, both of which are a huge problem because we can't change what we don't acknowledge. If you panic or pretend that a situation isn't happening, you won't take responsibility and you won't take action. But if you stop denying it, and feel the pain, then you'll do something. If you were victimized as a child, your accountability for that is zero, but how you react to it and respond to it once you are an adult *is* your responsibility.

The following are important questions that can help you determine how accountable you are in your life and what your attitude of approach is. Think about your answers in terms of a situation that may have already happened. Be honest. Your answers are for your eyes only.

- How often do you find yourself thinking that a situation is unfair? ______________________________
- When and if someone else gets credit for your efforts, what do you do? Do you sulk, try to undermine that person, or find some level of satisfaction for what must have been some very good ideas? ______________________________
- What have you done with unfair experiences or events from your childhood? Have you brought that resentment to relationships in your adult life, or have you been able to create value from those experiences? ______________________________
____

- If you are in a bad situation, such as being married to someone who is abusive or working a job with a boss who is unfair to you, what do you do? Do you sit back and wait to be rescued by Prince Charming? Do you hope and pray that the other person is going to change? Or do you figure out a plan to improve the relationship or leave? ____________

  ____

- Imagine that you have invested a major part of your life in a career that you no longer enjoy, but doing anything else would cost you a lot of time and/or money. Do you stay in that profession until you retire and look for a hobby that you like, or do you study and prepare for another field? ________

  ____

TAKE ACTION

One of my core beliefs is that you create your own experience in life. I say it often because I truly believe it. If you're in a car going down the highway at 90 mph and you sit there with your hands in your lap refusing to take the wheel, things are going to go badly for you. I don't care how well intentioned you are, I don't care how pure your heart is, you're going to come to a sad end. It's the same way on the highway of life. If you won't take the wheel and you won't be proactive, you're going to wind up with a bad result. You have to decide what matters and behave consistently with that. *Do* something with it. I am not saying that this is easy, but if you do nothing, you get nothing. Life rewards action.

When developing your attitude of approach, you have got to be proactive. My father used to say, "You should spend 5 percent of the time deciding if you got a good deal or a bad deal and 95 percent of the time deciding what you're going to do about it." It's true. When you come up against friction, you shouldn't spend a lot of time asking "why" questions, you should be asking "what" questions. What can you do to make what you want happen?

What actions can you take? What triggers can you pull? If you want different, you have to do different. If you're unhappy in your career or marriage, you are probably in some emotional pain. The only way to stop that pain is to get busy. You have to be willing to get out of your comfort zone and reach for something other than what you have. There's that old expression that "time heals all wounds." Not true! That is a big oversimplification because time itself really heals nothing. It's what *happens* in that time that heals. If you want to reduce your stress level, if you want to have a winning record in dealing with the crises of life and those seven days, you're going to have to be proactive.

I believe that I'm this way partly because I grew up very poor. I had a small paper route where I got paid about ten bucks a week. It sounds like a small sum of money, but the difference between that few dollars and no money at all was huge, because sometimes it was the difference between whether I ate that day or went to bed hungry. There were times when there would be a freezing storm, with sleet and winds blowing thirty-five miles per hour. My mother would say, "You're not going out to do your collections tonight, are you?" You bet I was! Everyone was home on a stormy night. I'd get them at the front door and they would pay me. And I would get to eat that day. I had to be results-oriented; you can have all the good intentions in the world when you're dirt poor, but you can't go to the grocery store and say, "I'd like some food, but I don't have any money. I meant to collect my pay tonight but I didn't." Nope, I had to perform. I had to be pragmatic.

When we get to the seven days later in this book, I will tell you the helpful action-oriented steps you need to take. However, just reading them or thinking about them isn't going to help you. It's a start, but it won't get you out of a crisis. What *will* help is actually *doing* those things now. Intentions won't take you very far when you find out you have a life-threatening disease or you're drowning in debt. Intending to get a second opinion on a cancer diagnosis is not the same as actually making an appointment and going to see the second doctor. Intending to create a budget is not going to help you pay your bills when you're neck-deep in debt.

The collection agencies don't care that you "really meant to send them a check." They don't care that you were thinking about it. They care that you do it. No matter what the problem, crisis, or challenge, it's not going to resolve itself or get better based on what you intended to do. It will get better or resolve itself only based on what you *do*.

Living with this attitude of approach also means that you don't waste time worrying about things you can't control. The Serenity Prayer that's used in Alcoholics Anonymous pretty much sums it up: "God, grant me the serenity to accept the things I cannot change, courage to change the things I can, and wisdom to know the difference." In my opinion, too many people spend too much time focusing on things that they can't control. As a result, they don't enjoy life on days when friction is low and they decrease their chances of survival when they're face-to-face with a crisis.

YOUR ATTITUDE CAN CHANGE YOUR LIFE

I can't predict anything in your life, but I can tell you one thing for sure: with the right attitude of approach, you will change your life. You will change the outcome of those seven most challenging days and in turn change the other days in between. You will be more prepared for what's to come and feel safer and more secure day to day. As a result, your relationships with everyone and everything around you will change. If you *do* different, you will *get* different. Your actions will be rewarded. You will gain momentum. You will begin to find new solutions to the problems and challenges you face, and instead of being swallowed up and spit out by life, you will confront it and get through it. It will shape you rather than demolish you. You'll live differently day to day. You'll have a sense of peace, calm, and confidence that's just amazing. And I'll bet you'll react differently when any of those seven days arrives.

3

Stress

The Days Between the Peaks and the Valleys

Life is hard. After all, it kills you.

—KATHARINE HEPBURN

Real life is stressful. If it does not exact a toll on you as you move through it, then you aren't really living. There are days where the intensity can spike to the point that it dominates your thinking, feeling, and behavior completely and totally. These are the seven most challenging days of your life. But before we get there, I want to talk about the days *in between* those seven days. Why? Because even when your life is *not* in crisis mode, it can still be very demanding mentally, emotionally, and physically, thanks to two things, *stressors* and *stress*. It is important to realize that there is a distinction between these two words. Let's be sure that we are using the same words with the correct definitions to talk about this. *Stress* is your body's reaction to the demands. *Stressors* are the things that you deal with along the way. In order to manage both stressors and stress, you must understand the difference.

WHAT IS A STRESSOR?

Stressors are things that drain you, wear you out, pressure you, and impact you. They put a demand on you mentally, emotionally, and physically. A stressor can be a combative marriage or pressure from in-laws. It can be the constant battles with a difficult boss or the worry of financial disaster looming just around the next corner. It can be noise from a screaming kid or screaming vacuum cleaner. It can be traffic or driving a carpool for hours on end. I'm listing just a few here, but there are an endless, endless number of stressors that can create problems. My point is that it's not always some "big-deal" crisis that breaks you down physically, mentally, and emotionally; it can be the relentless barrage of life's smaller demands, or stressors, that are constantly coming at you. We've all heard stories about water torture. One drop of water is nothing, but if drops just keep pecking on you and pecking on you and pecking on you, pretty soon they feel like bricks hitting you on the head.

Besides external stressors such as your boss, marriage, kids, and financial situation, another one can come from right inside of you and your own internal dialogue. Yes, we can be our own worst enemies! This is where our self-esteem issues and negative self-talk come into play. You may often hear me say that there is no reality, only perception. If your perceptions are based on a core set of irrational beliefs that you have picked up along the way or had pounded into you over the years, then you can be in a lot of trouble. This is because you are "pecking" at yourself from the inside—and believe me, that can be a *huge* stressor. That's why I talked about your attitude of approach and irrational thinking.

Some early influences in my training in the cognitive behavioral area were experts who held that there are certain irrational beliefs that can lead to a lot of stress in our minds and bodies. The good news is these beliefs are learned and can therefore be unlearned, but you have to know what you're up against.

Here are some common thought patterns that many people find themselves stuck in, as outlined by Albert Ellis and Emmett Veiten.[1]

1. *Musterbation: "I must succeed and obtain approval."*
2. *Awfulizing: "I did _____, isn't that awful?"*

3. Low frustration tolerance: "I can't do ______, it would be too hard for me."

4. Rating and blaming: "I'm worthless because I made a mistake" or "The world's a rotten place to live in."

5. Overgeneralizing: Having an "always" or "never" attitude. "______ is good for everybody, it worked for me" or "_______ is lousy, I tried it and it didn't work."

I'm guessing you are already adding to the list by recognizing additional ones that sabotage you personally. If so, write them down because it helps to see them on paper, staring right back at you!

Your own thoughts may not seem as harmful or powerful than if the same messages came to you from someone else, but they are. Our bodies respond the same way to stressors that come from the inside out as they do to stressors that come from the outside in, because we typically believe what we tell ourselves. A stress-producing internal dialogue and labeling system can become a way of life—one that can drain every ounce of your energy.

WHAT IS STRESS?

Stress is the body and mind's reaction to all the demands put upon you by stressors. The more stressors you have in your life, the higher your stress reaction can be and the more your body is drained of important energy. If you're in this state too often, you might even start noticing the toll it is taking on you: *mentally* you can become inefficient, *emotionally* you can become very volatile, and *physically* you can become more susceptible to disease. Remember, I am not even talking about the big crises yet. I'm talking about the small stuff that can accumulate day after day after day. It can be like a small hole in a boat that is constantly accumulating water in the bottom. At some point, that hole will eventually sink the boat.

You need to manage your stressors and stress so that you're not behind the power curve when a crisis hits.

Picture a two-by-four-inch piece of wood that's ten feet long and resting on two sawhorses. Then you load cinder blocks on the middle of it. When you do that, the two-by-four starts to bend, but if you remove the blocks shortly after loading them, that board will go back to being straight as string. It's not a problem. It snaps right back. But if you leave the blocks on the wood for a week and then take them off, you'll have a warped board. Put cinder blocks on top of that warped board, and you'll start to hear some internal cracks as some of the wood's fibers give way. It has not broken in two, but it has been compromised and cracked by the chronic load as well as these acute spikes. It's not as strong as it used to be. Still, the ability to rehabilitate that two-by-four even after it is warped but before it's cracked is pretty good. However, once it cracks and eventually breaks, you can't fix it. Those cracks are the wood breaking down under demand. Your body is the same way.

Even if you don't have major stressors that you can point to in your life, such as those difficult in-laws or a constantly ringing phone with bill collectors on the other end, your basic day-to-day activities (even those that you enjoy) are stressors and can cause stress. I once asked a woman I met where she lived, and she said, "In a white Chevy Suburban." When I asked her what she meant, she said, "I've got three kids in three different schools. One's in choir, one's in dance, and one's in football. I work as a realtor, so I'm either racing from property to property with a client or racing to pick up one kid and take him somewhere before rushing to pick up and drop off a second kid. All the while, I'm on my cell phone with clients." She went on to tell me how, after a day like this, she'd crawl into bed and have a hard time sleeping because she was busy making tomorrow's to-do list. I would venture to say that many of you are living similar lives that make balancing on a high wire seem easy compared to the balancing you're doing daily.

Just producing the energy to maintain this lifestyle causes a huge physical stress reaction in the body, and over time it takes its toll. Think about a hummingbird. It has the highest energy expenditure of any warm-blooded animal, with a heart rate of up to 500 beats per minute. It flaps its wings around fifty times per second, so all we see is a blur when one flies. In part, because it has to produce a lot of energy to keep up this pace, it lives an average of only six to twelve years. Compare that to the giant Galapagos tortoise, a very slow animal that ambles along at a pace of 0.16 miles per hour and has a heart rate of 6 beats per minute. Because it has very little energy output, this tortoise has a life expectancy of 177 years! Now, we may not be whizzing through life at a hummingbird's pace, but our energy output does have a huge impact on us.

If you don't release this stress and let your body go back to its normal state, you could be putting your body and, consequently, your life at risk. Not only are you more revved up and tense day to day, but all these cumulative stress reactions can impact how you survive and manage the stress spikes that occur on those seven most challenging days. I guarantee you that when you're in this chronically aroused state and something big does come along, you're going to give way a lot faster than a fresh board that hasn't been stressed for a period of time. You need to manage your stressors and stress so that you're not behind the power curve when a crisis hits. You have to get yourself as strong and ready for the storm as you can.

Your Body on Stress

Animals have to have the ability to "ramp up" in the face of threats, and humans do too as we attempt to face life's challenges. It ensures that our brains and bodies garner all of our resources—our best thinking, our physical strengths, and all of our focus—at once so that we can survive. This response is not meant to be "left on" like a burner under a pot of water. It's often called "fight or flight," and a good way to understand what happens when you have a stress reaction is to think about a rabbit and a wolf. Imagine that the rabbit is sitting there nibbling on grass when suddenly it realizes that a wolf is approaching. It knows that if it doesn't react quickly, it will be the wolf's dinner. Suddenly, there's a shift in the rabbit's physiology as its body prepares everything within it to deal with this threat. Its heart beats faster, its blood pressure and muscle tension increase, and its body releases a cascade of energizing hormones. Its lungs get ready to take in more oxygen. Other systems in its body that are not needed—such as digestion, reproduction, and immunity—shut down in order to conserve every ounce of that rabbit's energy so it can run as fast as it can. Its brain narrows its focus totally onto the foe, completely eliminating sensations of pain and extraneous matters. Thanks to this stress/arousal response, it can dart to its rabbit hole, where it is safe from the wolf. Once it's there and knows that danger has passed, its physiology returns to normal.

In this situation, the arousal is a good thing as it helps spur the rabbit into action. An acute, stimulating energy or arousal can mobilize you the same way when you need to rush your child to the emergency room after an accident, run away from an attacker, or even head down an exciting yet challenging ski slope. In fact, there is a point to which the stress reaction is actually invigorating and a positive reaction. We all experience it as we juggle our busy lives involving family, work, recreation, social calendar, and on and on. You may love what you do for a living and get excited about being involved in fun activities or projects at work, church, or the community center—and that's good. Having nothing to do would be a toxic stressor that could generate stress as bad as or worse than an increase in demand. However, there's a point where too many stressors, even the fun ones, tip the balance and put you into danger. If it sounds odd to think about positive activities causing an accumulation of toxic stress, just think about how many times you have gotten back from a vacation or Christmas at Grandma's house with all the extended family and said, "Whew, I'm glad to be back at work so I can get some rest!"

The body's reaction to stress, especially if it's chronic, isn't something to be taken lightly. It can take years off your life. It can even kill you.

Going back to our rabbit-and-wolf example, what would happen if you trapped that rabbit so it couldn't escape from that wolf? Knowing that the wolf was nearby, the rabbit would be in a state of perpetual stress. This means that the physiological responses we just discussed don't subside, and prolonged exposure to them can cause serious damage to the rabbit's body and immune system. Our bodies and brains react the same way under chronic stress. Even at low levels, persistent stress can cause all parts of the body's stress apparatus (the lungs, brain, vessels, muscles, and heart) to become chronically over- or underactivated, leading to all sorts of mental, emotional, and physical problems.[2] It can make you moody, cynical, and depressed,[3, 4] any of which can affect your relationships.[5] It can make you chronically tired, disrupt your sleep, affect your memory, and cause you to carry muscle tension that leads to headaches, back pain, muscle spasms, and cramps. Many scientific studies show that your body's reaction to stressors can impair your immune system, impact your fertility and sexual function, disrupt your digestive system, increase your risk of glandular problems, obesity, hypertension, heart attacks, strokes, osteoporosis, ulcers, cancer, multiple sclerosis, lupus, respiratory problems (such as asthma), and aggravate pain in conditions like arthritis. The list of stress's negative impacts can go on and on.[6, 7] But hopefully I'm getting my point across: The body's reaction to stress, especially if it's chronic, isn't something to be taken lightly. It can take years off your life. It can even kill you.[8]

THE STRESS INDEX

You probably don't need me to tell you that high levels of stress are not good for you. But just because you *know* doesn't mean you *do* anything about it! I've witnessed this connection between stress and physical breakdowns countless times in the years that I've spent working in the field of human behavior, so I know how bad it can be. In fact, as I mentioned earlier, I did an Internet survey to see how people would respond when asked to name any specific stress events that had occurred within five years before a disease was diagnosed. After looking at all of the responses, I found that those who had experienced a significant stressor in their lives had a higher incidence of a number of physical problems such as cancer, heart disease, strokes, diabetes, and multiple sclerosis and were more likely to have had a substance addiction, severe car accident, or severe accident at home. Does this mean that stress caused these diseases and problems? Not necessarily, but it may have been a contributor, along with other factors such as genetics, exposure to environmental toxins, or other life events.

Now, this group of people may or may not be representative of the population at large, and in no way does this survey meet the rigors of a scientific study, but the results were definitely interesting to me. They were also consistent with a large body of research, beginning as far back as the 1900s, as well as common sense. The results showed that people who live with high stress levels are more susceptible to physical breakdown than those who don't. It's not possible to share with you all the reams of research on the subject (nor would you want to see it all), but I would like to give you a very broad overview just to elaborate on this point.*

Below, I talk about three categories of stress that have been studied repeatedly, with substantial results. These include social disconnection stresses, performance stresses, and pessimistic stress.

*The Internet survey mentioned was all self-reported data and was not confirmed. It is not considered to be predictive of your life but is offered as food for thought and further evidence that your body's having a high stress reaction could leave you more vulnerable to physical breakdown.

This may sound boring at first, but take a look at some of the study information I've summarized; I bet it is going to be a huge wake-up call for you and those you love. I promise there is no pop quiz coming.

Social Disconnection Stresses

When I talk about the stresses of social disconnection, I'm talking about the stress reaction that results from things like marital discord, divorce, and strained relationships with friends and family. The studies conducted in these areas have shown them to be correlated with a shorter life span[9] and common disease diagnoses such as asthma, hypertension, ulcers, and rheumatoid arthritis.[10] It has been my experience that women seem to be more sensitive to the stresses of social disconnection, although men have more dramatic consequences. The relationship between these factors can be influenced by such things as the quantity of conflict and the sensitivities of the person involved.*[11] These findings were also reflected in the survey that I conducted showing that certain stressful events such as death or separation from one's spouse were correlated with a higher incidence of diseases within the following five years.

I have to say that I'm not really surprised by any of these findings because I've witnessed this link between social disconnection stresses and disease in many people over the years. Does this mean that if you have experienced any or all of these life events that you are doomed to a future of poor health? No, it does not. But it can mean you may be at a higher risk level and in need of some very purposeful stress management.

If you are interested in more information about the connection between stress and physical breakdown, there are more details in

*Furthermore, the clinical studies, especially those related to marital disruption, tend to have a very specific physiological correlation to lower immunity markers, which have an impact on a wide range of illnesses.[12]

the Resource Guide as well as the Notes, but I'm betting you are getting the point.

Performance Stresses

This stress category includes work and academic stress in which people report being pressured to have high productivity and to meet time demands. It can also refer to work in the home when a stay-at-home mom is trying to juggle too many activities and feels that her performance is being criticized. An estimated 1 million people call in sick to work each day due to stress![13] There has also been a large group of studies showing that workplace stresses lead to increases in rates of diseases such as flu, heart disease, metabolic syndrome (obesity), and high blood pressure.[14] One study found that those who experienced job burnout were almost 1.8 times more likely to develop type 2 diabetes,[15] and another found that people who had previously suffered a heart attack and then experienced chronic work stress had twice the risk of having a second such attack.[16] Aside from all of that research, it just makes common sense. You can even see how people who have reported stress in dealing with their bosses and coworkers age more quickly. Just take a look at most U.S. presidents, who I think have a very high-stress job. Look at them in a photo from their inauguration day and then again on their last day of office four or eight years later, and these men seem to have aged twenty years.

When it comes to academic stress, studies show that students who are preparing for exams for which their careers may be at stake, such as medical and law students, have higher instances of herpes simplex, depression, and hepatitis B.[17] Again, these results don't surprise me because people in such situations tend to lose sight of how important it is to take care of themselves.

Pessimistic Stress

By pessimism, I mean an attitude in which you don't have any faith or hope, you tend to deny the resources that are available to you, and you do not make plans for success. I'm talking about people who view their futures as being set with only negative consequences. They're suspicious of their friends, government, and workplace and have a very dim view of their environment and themselves. This attitude takes a physical toll on the body because of the biochemistry that comes with it.

Pessimistic stress is a broad category of thinking patterns based on hostility, resentment, and despair. It has been correlated to various kinds of diseases, especially cardiovascular disease. For example, a study of men ages 40 to 55 showed that those with high levels of hostility had a 42 percent higher risk of death than those who didn't have high levels of hostility.[18] Other research looked at people who had experienced one cardiovascular event and survived over a ten-year period. They found that people with negative affect (a spectrum of negative emotions) were more likely to experience another cardiac event than those with a better outlook.[19] Further studies for pessimistic stress have included HIV patients who had highly correlated viral infections and advanced disease progression.[20] My interpretation of this research is simple: bad attitude, a "chip on the shoulder," and high stress levels equal higher risks of physical breakdown.

I've seen and heard about this often in the psychological community in several patients whose negative thinking appeared to contribute to compromising their own physical destiny. For example, a colleague of mine told me about Julie, whose mother and grandmother had each died at the age of 60 of a heart attack. Julie believed that she would suffer a similar fate, regardless of any other information about their differences. Her lifestyle of alcoholism and poor diet contributed to this lack of perceived control over her destiny, so she never made an effort to break the bad cycle because she believed it was out of her hands. She died of a heart attack on her sixtieth birthday. I guess she proved herself right.

Now, again, does all this mean that you are going to have these diseases if you've had one of these events in your life, experience these stressors yourself, or walk around with a negative attitude? Not necessarily. But there's enough suggestion here to tell you that stress can impact your life in more ways than you might think. You may want to think about whether you need to focus on reducing the stressors in your life to protect and prolong that life.

The Velocity of Life

Compared to just a couple of generations ago, the velocity of life today, and the friction generated by it, have skyrocketed. So have our stress levels. If you feel this way, you're not alone. Not by a long shot. A recent survey by the Anxiety Disorders Association of America[21] found that close to half of U.S. employees say that they experience persistent and excessive stress or anxiety in their daily lives. It makes sense; I'd venture to say that we're living in one of the most stressful times ever, at least in the speed of life category. Our pace and hurry-up lifestyle have been observed in New York City, where people walk 10 percent faster than they did ten years ago[22] to try to meet appointments and schedules—a real sign of a stressful society.

Why now, more than ever before? Today, we're bombarded with more information, more data, more decisions, and more options than ever before. The benefits of these things are obvious; the detriments to our society may not be. Our wireless world is good for business and helps far-flung families stay in touch, but being connected 24/7 via BlackBerrys and the Internet isn't always healthy. It makes us feel we need to be in touch and plugged in at all times, leaving us feeling anxious when we actually have to turn off our electronic devices. The other downside to technology is that it has conditioned us to want everything in seconds, and when that doesn't happen we feel stressed. Admit it, when your computer takes minutes rather than seconds to download a file you get irritated, and when your supermarket's express line is slow, your heart rate quickens.

You may not think your life is stressful or that this is a big deal, especially if this is the only life you've known. We have accepted these things as a reality of life and are so used to the white noise of stress buzzing in the background that we don't even notice it anymore. But what I'm trying to show you is that you don't have to accept that as the way things will always be. You may live in a household where the kids are always screaming, four or five televisions are always blaring, the dogs are always barking, the bills are always piling up, and your husband is drunk half the time. Maybe you are forty pounds overweight, and that's just the way you live! Well, that's crazy. I promise you that these irritants and stressors are changing the quality of your life.

In psychology, we talk about a concept called reflexive fighting in response to aversive stimulation, which is the immediate, involuntary aggression that occurs when humans or animals are stressed. An example of this is if you have a mouse cage that comfortably holds ten mice but you put twenty mice into it. Because of this crowding, normally docile animals will suddenly become aggressive and start biting each other. Add a lot of noise to the overcrowding, and this aggression and the biting get even worse. The reflexive fighting behavior is instinctive, meaning that it happens without you thinking about it as an automatic response to a situation. The same thing can happen to you when the white noise of stress is humming in the background of your life. You feel irritated and fatigued. You don't think as well, and your problem-solving skills and ability to communicate are compromised. You snap at your spouse and raise your voice with your children. I don't think the high divorce rate in today's world is a coincidence, since divorce can be a direct result of stress. It's like having a bad sunburn. Somebody can come by and just brush up against you, and you scream and jump. It's not because what that person did was so terrible, but you are hypersensitive because you've run to the end of your rope, coping-wise.

Assessing Your Stress

I have always said that you can't change what you don't acknowledge. To help you evaluate how much stress you're experiencing,

I've developed the following audit. Take a minute or two to check off the level of stress you may be having in the present time.

1. **How often do you feel that you are not coping well with the demands that are placed on you?**

   All the time __ Most of the time __ Some of the time __ Rarely __

2. **Do you have problems falling asleep and/or staying asleep?**

   All the time __ Most of the time __ Some of the time __ Rarely __

3. **Do you find yourself withdrawing from friends, family, and colleagues?**

   All the time __ Most of the time __ Some of the time __ Rarely __

4. **Do you feel you are working harder but getting less done?**

   All the time __ Most of the time __ Some of the time __ Rarely __

5. **Do you find yourself afraid to make decisions?**

   All the time __ Most of the time __ Some of the time __ Rarely __

6. **Are you feeling anxious?**

   All the time __ Most of the time __ Some of the time __ Rarely __

7. **Are you feeling tense?**

   All the time __ Most of the time __ Some of the time __ Rarely __

8. **Are you feeling nervous?**

   All the time __ Most of the time __ Some of the time __ Rarely __

9. **Are you jumpy and unable to relax?**

   All the time __ Most of the time __ Some of the time __ Rarely __

10. **Do you feel hostile and become angry about minor things?**

    All the time __ Most of the time __ Some of the time __ Rarely __

11. Do you blame others for everything?

All the time __ Most of the time __ Some of the time __ Rarely __

12. Are you critical of others' efforts?

All the time __ Most of the time __ Some of the time __ Rarely __

13. Are other family members having stress problems, and do you think that you might be responsible for them?

All the time __ Most of the time __ Some of the time __ Rarely __

14. Are you finding yourself unable to have conversations about stress issues with family and friends?

All the time __ Most of the time __ Some of the time __ Rarely __

15. Are you having fights with people about "everything and nothing"?

All the time __ Most of the time __ Some of the time __ Rarely __

16. Are you sharing fewer satisfactory moments with family and friends?

All the time __ Most of the time __ Some of the time __ Rarely __

17. Are you sad and feeling "down" for no reason?

All the time __ Most of the time __ Some of the time __ Rarely __

18. Are you experiencing physical signs of stress such as high blood pressure, tense muscles, and fatigue?

All the time __ Most of the time __ Some of the time __ Rarely __

19. Are you not taking the time to relax and let your body and mind restore after stress?

All the time __ Most of the time __ Some of the time __ Rarely __

20. Are you aware that you're experiencing stress, and that it is affecting your life negatively?

All the time __ Most of the time __ Some of the time __ Rarely __

Scoring

If you marked "All the time" or "Most of the time" to more than five of these questions, you are likely dealing with too much stress.

If you marked "All the time" or "Most of the time" to at least one, you need to start doing something about it before it gets worse, because it likely will.

If you don't manage your stress over time by unloading the burden and allowing yourself a chance to spring back, you are likely to become more susceptible to breaking down. You can become distressed if you don't de-stress! You can lessen that toll dramatically by doing some maintenance along the way to shut the noise off, unload the bricks, and let yourself snap back on a regular basis. The key is to attack the problem on two different fronts. First, you have to reduce the number of stressors you are exposed to, and second, you have to manage your stress reaction. Unfortunately, not many of us were taught skills for coping with stress in school or by our parents as we're growing up. I find that rather amazing since it has the most critical impact on our health today. Now, I don't want to be guilty of shouting "fire!" without handing you a fire extinguisher, so here are a few ways you can stop stress in its tracks. Make this your to-do list for the next week or month. Write down what you did and how it made you feel afterward.

You can become distressed if you don't de-stress!

STRESS-FIGHTING STRATEGIES

- **Forgive yourself**

  Stop wasting time beating yourself up for past errors. Every mistake is a learning experience. Learn from it, then move on. If you ever hear successful professional athletes talk about their defeats, you'll hear them say that they learned something and are using it to improve their game going forward. They don't beat themselves up or let the defeat derail them (if they did, they wouldn't be pro athletes for long).

- **Conscientiously manage your reactions**
  Categorize and prioritize things so you make sure you're not having a big reaction to a small problem. We don't react to what happens in our lives; we react to what values and what filters we use in perceiving what's happened As I mentioned earlier, I believe there is no good news or bad news, just news. It's up to the receiver to decide. Taking a minor annoyance in life and catastrophizing it through your perception can turn it into a bigger issue than it should be, and that can send your stress level soaring. Again, the words you use also affect your stress level. If you say, "A catastrophe happened at work" or "My life is a nightmare," your body may react to it that way. You heighten your stress level because, as I said earlier, we tend to believe ourselves.

- **Exercise regularly**
  According to the Centers for Disease Control and Prevention,[23] regular exercise means at least twenty minutes of vigorous-intensity physical activity per day, three times a week, or thirty minutes of moderate-intensity physical activity per day, most days a week. Exercise releases "feel-good" hormones called endorphins into your bloodstream, lowering blood pressure, relaxing your muscles, and clearing your mind.[24] Plus, if stress-induced eating has caused you to put on a few pounds, exercise can help you burn off the extra calories.

- **Practice relaxation techniques such as visualization and progressive muscle relaxation**
  Most people find it helpful to listen to a relaxation CD because it can help you move through the muscle relaxation technique. It can be easier to have someone's voice guiding you through the exercises than having to remember all the steps yourself.

This takes concentration, but with practice you'll find it getting easier. For example, here is one way to start the process:

Focus on your feet and relax each toe, each muscle letting out all of the tension you are holding in your feet. Breathe out the stress and begin to feel the tension leave your feet. Now focus on your legs and let all the tension leave your legs as you let out your next breath.

Now focus on your hips and let go of any stress, pain, or discomfort that you have there. Breathe out and let go as you relax deeper and deeper . . .

A lot of people develop their own scripts to help them relax, and that's great, too. The key thing for you to know is that doing this type of of relaxation exercise for even fifteen minutes a few times a day may cause you to operate at a lower stress level. You may think, "Okay, I'll feel good for that fifteen minutes, but what about afterward?" The answer is that the effects of the relaxation can last for hours. It is like emptying a bucket that you put on the floor to catch water from a drip in the ceiling. When the bucket fills up and you empty it, it takes hours before it is overflowing again. The same thing is true with stress. When you empty your stress bucket, it can take hours for it to fill up again.

- **Breathe deeply at least once a day**
Often, this is easiest if you can put your hand on your abdomen and feel the rising and falling of your stomach—a sign that you're breathing deeply enough to let go of stress. One of the best techniques to learn effective breathing for stress inoculation is to count to seven each time you breathe out and each time you breathe in. Steady breathing on a regular pace will help your body and mind to position themselves into a stress-resistant basis. Repeat this process for at least fifteen minutes. One of the signs of stress is the "rabbit breathing" mentioned earlier, which actually sends stress messages to the brain. By breathing in regular breaths, you send a message to harmonize

the body instead. Studies show that this breathing pattern can increase the healing of patients from surgery.[25]

- **Repeat a powerful affirmation to yourself several times daily** Positive affirmations can combat the negative self-talk that tends to be a hotbed of growing dissatisfaction and stress. If you don't pay attention to all of the wonderful things in your life now, you will have an even harder time remembering them when bad things happen. This can lead you to feel isolated and sorry for yourself, creating a lot more stress. I recommend that you come up with your own selection of affirmations, but some of my favorites are "I can handle anything" or "I am enough" or "I am ready." Find a phrase that works for you and repeat it to yourself at least 100 times a day, and you may find your stress level decreasing.

- **Avoid excessive amounts of alcohol, caffeine, fats, and sugar** These things help create stress in your metabolic system and send your energy level and mood on a roller-coaster ride.[26] Maintaining your energy level and having the strength to keep your attitude positive and your stress under control rely greatly on putting good fuel into your body. Protein and complex carbohydrates are the best stress-combating foods.[27] Fish and eggs have been shown to improve individuals' abilities to deal with stress,[28] while water is an essential nutrient for good thinking. Fruits and vegetables are loaded with vitamins and nutrients that can also help you handle stress better.

- **Get high-quality sleep** When you're well rested, it's easier to focus and have the energy to accomplish all that needs to be done. Start a routine where you get at least seven hours of shut-eye each night. If you have trouble getting to sleep, look at what you're eating before bed or see if there is too much noise or light in your bedroom (amazingly, even the light from a digital alarm clock or VCR can disturb sleep). But most of the time, problems going to sleep are the result of poor relaxation skills and an inability to let go of the stresses of the day. Again, you might use a relaxation CD to help relax your body or practice your own method of letting go. Consult a psychologist if your stress still keeps you from drifting off to dreamland and staying asleep. It may be necessary to consult a sleep expert to find out if physical issues are the cause of your sleep problems.

- **Acknowledge and celebrate a goal you've accomplished at least once a week**
  I think this is critical to maintaining a positive sense of self. Too often we remember only the mistakes we make, and many of us have a mental resistance to celebrating ourselves. Even if no one else sees your achievement, you still need to tell someone about it and create a healthy response to it. That way, you start inoculating yourself against accumulative stress and boost your self-confidence.

- **Laugh at least once a day**
  Research shows that laughing can lower your blood pressure and help you relax.[29] See a funny movie, visit a comedy club, or just spend time with your kids. Make time to fit laughter into your life, and you'll be amazed at how much better you will feel. Research shows that people have healed themselves from serious diseases merely by watching hours of funny movies and television shows.[30]

- **Take a hot bath**
  Saunas and thermal baths have been used for centuries to help resolve stress. So sit in a hot tub, take a warm shower, or go for a swim.

- **Recognize what you can control and what you can't**
  Work to accept that some things are just not within your power to change. It is a waste of time to focus on or obsess about

people and events over which you have no control or maybe not even any influence. For the things you *can* control, such as your internal responses and your actions, rational focus is a powerful and effective choice to make, since your stress reaction is an internal reaction and often the product of what you are saying to yourself about the world and your life in it. You have tremendous power to change yourself by being aware of your internal reactions, so work to improve that. Once you do, other people and events will start seeming less overwhelming.

Some of the suggestions I have just made may lack what is called "face validity." That means you look at them and say *Nah, no big deal. That is a bunch of simplistic stuff. I was looking for something new and exotic, maybe a miracle drug or something.* If that is what you're thinking, trust me, you are wrong. Stress management really can begin with these simple steps. The beauty is that they *are* simple and doable and *not* something difficult, exotic, or expensive!

FINAL THOUGHT

I chose to talk about general, cumulative "daily" stress and stressors before dealing specifically with the seven days for a very important reason. Anytime you step up to face a major challenge, you want to be in the best shape, in the best state of mind, and in command of the most available resources that you can muster. But if you are allowing an endless string of daily stressors in your marriage, family, job, finances, and overall lifestyle to wear you down and deplete you, you will already be way behind the coping curve when you wake up to one of these seven days. On the other hand, if you actively manage your life, dealing with demands head-on while also taking the time and energy to nurture your mind and body, you will be strong and vibrant when one of the seven days challenges you. Take care of you now, because you will need all of you then!

4

Loss

The Day Your Heart Is Shattered

Do not measure your loss by itself; if you do, it will seem intolerable; but if you will take all human affairs into account, you will find that some comfort is to be derived from them."

—SAINT BASIL

In its simplest form, loss is when something you truly value, something in which you are deeply invested, is taken from you. The first thing most of us think of when we hear that word is death, but the loss of love and security through a divorce or other attachments in which you are passionately intertwined with someone or something can also rank right up there on this day where loving, investing, and losing can hurt so much. Loss can shake you so deeply because you are so heavily invested and the gravity of everything that happens is magnified by that investment. Further complicating matters is the reality that our self-worth is often tied up in our relationships, careers, and social acceptability; if we lose on any one of those fronts, it can be extremely devastating.

Perhaps one of the saddest realities is that this heartbreaking day is likely to repeat at different times and different stages of your life. Unless you die very young, you cannot escape the day your heart is shattered. The more people you love in this world and the more causes you are passionate about, the more places you are vulnerable. As a result, you'll probably go around this track more than once. So the question is not *if* you will lose, because you will; the question is how you will handle it *when* you do.

At the risk of stating the obvious, that old saying "None of us is getting out of this alive" is absolutely true. Everyone who is born dies. I have yet to see any different, and still we want to deny that fact as long as we can because it is such a painful reality. Look, I know that no one likes to talk about losing someone or something they love. It's not fun to think about this stuff, and it's much harder to talk about. After all, who wants to do that when you could be reading the latest Harry Potter novel, taking a jog, or throwing a ball with your kids? Most of us would probably even enthusiastically choose an hour in the dentist chair over a conversation about losing a loved one or something we deeply value. But unfortunately, it's a fact that many things in life, including life itself, do not last forever. Life is finite. So it stands to reason that loss is one of the steepest hills we're ever going to climb.

You can love, lose, and survive.

Nothing I can say in this book can derail this inevitability, but with some thought and planning you can get through it with much more grace and balance when it does come. You can love, lose, and survive. You can fall to your knees and cry in pain. You can feel a horrible, crippling emptiness, yet recover and fill yourself up again. We all seem to survive it—at least most of us do. But what I want to do is help you prepare so you can even be able to help your loved ones when they, too, have lost someone or something dear to them.

WHAT IS LOSS?

Regardless of the specifics of your loss, this is a day when your heart is broken because someone or something you deeply cherish in your life is lost. One way of understanding the inevitable pain (although an unusual way of thinking about it) is to recognize that in a way loss, even the death of a loved one, feels like a rejection, something the majority of us fear most in life. Although we might agree in theory with the quote by the English poet Alfred Lord Tennyson, "It is better to have loved and lost than never to have loved at all," in reality, we usually do all we can to protect our hearts from the pain of disappointment and loss. In fact, I always seem to hear that said by someone who is trying to comfort someone *else's* loss. I seldom hear that from the one who just suffered a loss.

Still, I believe in Tennyson's quote. To me, the most tragic life you could ever have would be not caring enough about anyone or anything to hurt if it is lost. One of the greatest victories in life is to be passionately involved with and connected to someone or something. If you are successful in doing so, that passionate connection and investment can be deep, broad, and almost to the level of defining in part who and what you are. Such an investment can be one of the greatest high points of your entire life, but as with all things there is also a huge downside. The higher you go the further you have to fall: if you love deeply, if you invest passionately and the object of that emotional investment is lost, you will suffer, plain and simple. Not a good day by any stretch.

Doing Your Best to Prepare for the Worst

Naturally, no one can keep your heart from skipping a beat the night your teenager is out with friends and the phone rings at 1:43 a.m. with a stranger on the other end asking, "Are you the mother of . . . ? " Or when a siren screams nearby and your husband is already an hour late for dinner, or when you hear of a plane crash, a ten-car pile-up, or a local gas station robbery, and the people you love are anywhere but right there in front of you. I think everybody has felt that knot of fear in their stomach, and probably more than once.

But what's amazing to me is that despite the fact that we may spend a lot of time and energy worrying about these things, despite the fact that loss is one of the biggest challenges we'll face, and despite the fact that it's part of the natural cycle of life, most of us never really prepare to actually *deal* with it. It's one of the things we're least ready for. I strongly believe that we need to open the dialogue on loss, because right now it is almost a taboo. We need to think about the unthinkable. Part of the problem can be handled before it happens.

Violated Expectations

One of the hardest parts about all these days we're talking about is that they violate our expectations. If you expect A and you get A or you even get close with B or C, you aren't thrown off as much. You still have rails to run on even though you can't control the painful event. You can say, "Okay, I knew this was coming, I knew this was what to expect, so yes, it hurts. But I'm not going to panic. I will survive and get through this. It may get worse before it gets better, and frankly it's even worse than I expected, but I'm not totally in shock, so I can believe I'm going to be okay." But if you expect A and get Z, you are likely to have a difficult time knowing where to go next.

I will never forget the situation of an acquaintance of mine. Charlie had just gotten home from work and knew something was wrong when he opened the door and smelled freshly baked cookies. He walked into the kitchen, and, sure enough, there was a letter leaning up against a plate of his favorite sugar cookies: "Don't go into the bathroom. Just call 911. Then, sit and wait. I'm sorry. I love you."

He didn't call 911. He didn't call a neighbor. He called me. I could barely understand the words as his voice choked and cracked with fear and panic. He couldn't catch his breath. "My wife has done something horrible, I just know it. I don't know what to do. I don't know where to turn." And he was right. His wife of twenty-seven years had gone into the bathroom of their beautiful California hillside home, wrapped a towel around her head, and put a bullet through her brain.

The horror of that moment was only partly why this was one of the days that shook Charlie's life to the core. He had to deal not only with the shock of the violent and unexpected suicide but also with the long, cold, and relentless reality of the death and the absence of his partner in life, the mother of his children, and the woman he'd envisioned growing old with. He took her back east to her birthplace for burial, and after the funeral he remained with her family for a few weeks. When I left him at the cemetery, I feared he was in trouble, but at least he would be with family for awhile. But because he was not equipped to navigate the terrain of the shock of that moment or dark days ahead, Charlie immediately spiraled down into a black hole of grief and depression. He experienced a storm of anger, confusion, guilt, pain, and remorse. When I saw him two weeks later, two weeks in which he avoided calls from me and many other concerned friends, I *knew* he was in trouble. We all tried to pull him back up, to help him get through the nightmare, but it was too late. He was already gone. He fell so deeply into depression, shock, and panic that it was like talking to a wall. He stopped all contact with me, his family, and his friends, and he quit his job. He withdrew from his children, leaving them reeling as well.

I remember how helpless I felt as I watched this man—someone I greatly respected—slipping further away each day. It was then that I swore to myself that if I ever got the opportunity to prepare people for any kind of devastating loss and tragedy before they got into it, I would.

And Then It Was My Turn . . .

I have personally experienced this day several times in my life, but never more powerfully than twelve years ago when my father died. To be completely frank, I thought I was ready. I thought I was prepared. I was not. Sure, it's somewhat expected that you'll bury a parent, but when it happens, logic doesn't really matter. It is still terribly painful, surprising, and hard to accept. It can be just as hard if you are not particularly close as it is if you are, maybe more so, because if there was distance between you and the one you lost, there may be a lot of unfinished emotional business. My father and I had had terrible ups and downs, but none of them seemed to matter when this reality was visited upon me. In fact, sometimes this kind of loss hits harder when you've had a difficult relationship with the person who passes away, especially if it's a parent. Even though it is the cycle of life when you lose a parent, you may have just lost the person who was always yelling the loudest in the cheering section of your life, one of the few people who could tell you, "It's okay," and you actually believed them. When my father died, I remember thinking that there was one less person in this world who thought I was a champion.

I have often counseled people to make certain that they have left nothing unsaid and left nothing undone between them and the people they love. I do so because I know that we so often take for granted our existence and that of the people we love. Somehow or other a mechanism in our brain defies logic and makes us think that we have them forever. I knew better. My father was diagnosed with a heart defect, and we knew that he would soon be passing. I think I actually started grieving his loss before he was gone because I knew it was imminent. Taking my own counsel and what I had taught people so often to do, I made sure that there was nothing left unsaid between us. Interestingly enough, that included both negatives and some positives. Life always seems to have a certain symmetry to it. He had not been a perfect father, and I absolutely had not been a perfect son. He had spent many years of his life drinking hard, as only a chronic alcoholic can do, and this had put a lot of distance between us. I needed to tell him about things that he had said or done that had caused me pain, and, just as much, I needed to tell him how much he had contributed to my life and how much he meant to me. I also needed *him* to tell *me* the frustrations and pain that I had caused him along the way, his hopes and dreams for me, and his vision for the rest of my life. We laughed, we cried, we talked, and we listened.

I thought I had been a good "emotional soldier." It did help. It was important work. I would love to tell you that doing this is the magic answer to soothing the pain of loss and that it was enough. But it wasn't. I had not prepared myself for what would happen after the moment of his death. I had cleared the air between us, and we had closed the gap of communication and sharing. He and I had done that *together* as father and son. But after he took his last breath, I was alone. I had not thought far enough ahead in the process to acknowledge my own vulnerabilities and feelings about being in this world for the first time ever without a father. Now without our patriarch and as the only boy in our family, all of a sudden I had a whole new set of jobs and responsibilities. I experienced a whole new emotional "gravity" later that day at the funeral home. My parents had been married for fifty years, and my mother and father had been inseparable from the second grade on. My mother had asked for some alone time in the room where his body was being housed. I was waiting outside in the corridor when all of a sudden she opened the door and came stumbling out, leaning against the wall and looking at me in the most confused and perplexed state I had ever seen. She was crying and kept repeating the same sentence I'll never forget; "He won't wake up. He won't wake up. He won't wake up." I have to tell you that I sure didn't feel like I was in control at that point. I didn't know what to say, I didn't know what to do as I watched my mother falling into a state of shock, denial, and pain. I had not seen that one coming. As I stood there in the corridor watching my mother tearfully repeat those words, I realized that I had not prepared myself as well as I could have and *should* have for what we all knew was coming—and coming soon. Again, for probably the thousandth time in my life, my wife, Robin, stepped in, intuitively knowing that I was in way over my head.

Was my counsel to others and to myself—about not taking life for granted, and not letting the sun set another day with something left unsaid or undone—bad counsel? Absolutely not. It wasn't bad advice. It was just incomplete. I suppose this chapter is my attempt to tell, as Paul Harvey would call it, "the rest of the story."

How to Support Grieving Friends and Family

When a loved one has experienced a loss, it's hard to know what to do or not to do. Here are some tips that may help you lead a loved one through this difficult time.

- *When appropriate, talk about their loss. You may think it's better to avoid talking about it—possibly because you're uncomfortable—but discusssing their grief may be just what they need.*
- *Be a good listener.*
- *Check in often by phone or e-mail.*
- *Support them nonverbally—hold them, listen to them, or sit with them in silence. Just knowing that you're there can help.*
- *Let the other person feel sad. Don't dismiss their pain or minimize their grief by telling them to "get over it."*
- *If it seems appropriate, share your own experience with loss without losing focus on the person who is suffering.*
- *Take action. Huge gestures are not necessary. In fact, it's usually small tasks that they need help with, such as picking up children from school, going to the supermarket for them, and household tasks like taking care of their pets.*

More than One Way to Lose

Now, I wish that the only difficult and paralyzing pain came from the experiences of death in the cycle of life—after all, that hurts enough. But unfortunately, death is not the only way to lose those you love. It can happen one night while you are sitting at dinner with your husband. The kids have already finished and are playing in the yard or doing homework. You get up to clear the table just as you've done every night for the last ten years. But this time, as you reach for the silverware, you hear words coming from your husband that you never expected to hear in a million years: "I want a divorce. I don't love you anymore. Actually, I *never* loved you." Suddenly, there is a crack in your universe. Then again, maybe things between you and your spouse have been rough and rocky for years. You've tried to work things out together. You've read self-help books and spent time in personal therapy and/or marriage counseling. But after a lot of thought and effort, you've decided to separate. Just because it was a conscious decision that you made together and just because it may turn out to be the best outcome for the two of you and your family doesn't mean it will be any less painful. Suddenly you don't have that partner for life, that person you thought you'd be rocking on the porch with when you are old and gray. Your vision of your life has changed. Though it may be for the best, the uncertainty of what lies ahead and the gaping hole in your life can leave you shaking in your shoes.

As I said earlier, divorce and death may be the big ones, and the first many of us think of when we hear the word loss. But, unfortunately, there are many, many other ways that people's hearts can be shattered. There are also rejection, failure, exclusion, and isolation. But you have to remember that there is no loss that you can't recover from. If you have lost something that can be replaced, such as a job, you can in time (and perhaps with help) devise a strategy to re-create that which has been lost. If you have lost something that you *can't* get back, your challenge involves folding that truth into your reality and learning to live with the permanence of that loss. In any loss situation, though, you need to learn how to focus on the things that remain in your life before the loss.

I had a friend who had been at the same firm for a decade. She had a corner office and fancy title that she had worked quite hard to achieve. Then her company announced that all executives at her level had to take a test to get their Series 7 license (for securities trading) or risk getting demoted, transferred, or even fired. Suddenly this woman's life was thrown into turmoil as she spent day and night studying. Finally test day came, and just minutes after taking the exam, she found out that she had failed. She was shocked and devastated. In just a few minutes, the score on this test, at least in her estimation, had wiped out all her years of experience, success, and hard work. She felt as if her world had been turned upside down—and unfairly, to boot! My point is that there are lots of ways to lose, too many to list in fact, but they all connect to things we treasure in life.

What It Is Not

Now that we have talked about loss and, more important, what your reaction to loss is likely to entail, I want to talk about what it might feel like. Everyone responds to loss differently, and there is no right or wrong way to behave. But I want to stress a few things that your reaction is not so that you don't add to difficult times by mislabeling or misjudging yourself or others.

- ***It is not psychosis.*** *You are not going crazy, even though it may feel as if you are. You are in mourning. You are grieving, and all that you may be experiencing is part of that process. You may be out of sorts and not making contact with others, but this is the nature of the human reaction to loving, investing, and then losing.*
- ***It is not necessarily the beginning of long-term clinical depression.*** *You may have symptoms of depression such as change of appetite, trouble concentrating, sleep problems, loss of interest in things you used to love, fatigue or low energy, and irritability. However, these are the elements of a reactive depression related to a specific event—your loss. If those symptoms persist for more than a few months and you begin to experience marked functional impairment, a morbid preoccupation with worthlessness, thoughts of suicide, or psychotic symptoms, you definitely should seek professional help and support.*
- ***It is not a particular defect to experience, whether two weeks or even two years later, continued feelings of anger, sadness, and an array of other emotions.*** *That is normal. There is no timetable for when you'll feel ready to*

step back into your life. Each one of us is unique and has a different set of barriers to go through to adjust to loss. You are not only entitled to hurt and cry or have other pain responses, it is actually healthy to do so. Many people call it "catharsis," the discharge of pent-up emotions that may result in a lessening of emotional pain.

- ***Grief is not a pain that will likely stay the same for the rest of your life.*** *It is not a life sentence (although, at times, you may feel that it is). You have to believe that you will get through this paralyzing time and maintain a hope that the pain will evolve and lessen. You must be patient with yourself while at the same time recognizing that you are the one who must ultimately choose to stand up for you and the rest of your life and make the conscious choice to put one foot in front of the other and move on with your life. You must hold yourself accountable for embracing people and the other parts of your life that you cared about before your difficult loss.*
- ***It is not a punishment from God or the Devil.*** *It is not personal. Loss is a natural part of the cycle of life. It happens to all people despite their race, religion, and education, and it happens all over the world. This is exactly why every culture has created special rituals for loss associated with death. Loss from rejection and failure is sadly also universal and again not personal.*
- ***Loss doesn't have to be just an end, it can also be a beginning.*** *It may be hard to see now, but once you get through or at least adjust to and accept your loss, whether it involves death or rejection or failure, you will realize that there is much more to your life still ahead.*

As I discussed earlier, while all losses have some commonality in terms of pain, there are clearly differences in at least the magnitude of the impact and gravity of different losses. Therefore there are also some differences in the strategies for getting back to better days. When we face death-related losses, our challenges may be to accept, heal, and find the strength to go on. For losses of material things, lifestyles, and positions, the strategies may involve regaining or replacing that which was lost or resetting your compass and goals toward differently defined successes.

WHAT TO EXPECT

There are so many feelings and emotions that you can expect when you experience any significant loss, and I'm going to talk about several of these reactions now. Some of these emotions, such as anger and panic and fear, hurt deeply. But—and this is a very important "but"—as much as you can expect all these difficult or painful feelings initially, believe that there is a day in your future that may hurt a little bit less. Regardless of the specific loss you're going through, expect that the day will come that you will begin to see hope again. You *can* survive. You *do* have the strength to get through this. Expect that you can lose someone to death without their being gone from your spirit and soul. Expect that you can experience failures in life and regain your momentum and pride of accomplishment.

If your loss involves the passing of a loved one, know that death is a change and not an end. I strongly believe that your relationship will change from the physical to the spiritual. To me, this is a truth and not just a platitude that is tossed at you to make you feel better in the moment. You may still "hear" your deceased father's laugh when something that he would have thought was funny comes through your world. You can "speak" to your father or mother just as you would if they were physically here. You may feel their presence and hear their wisdom in your head. You have your loved one—be it a parent, child, friend, or other relative—inside you. You have that person's spirit and presence in you and your memories. You will learn to "hear" differently. You will learn to relate differently. Will you miss that person's physical presence, the warmth of their hug? Of course you will. I'm not in any way trying to trivialize the loss. But you must also challenge yourself to "embrace" what you do have, despite the fact that it is not *all* that you would wish for. As bereavement counselor (and psychiatric nurse for more than thirty-five years) Martha Tousley so eloquently puts it, "Grief is like a long, winding tunnel whose entrance is closed behind you and the only way out is through it."[1]

If you are faced with a loss that does not involve death, expect that you may experience the searing rejection and despair from a divorce, failed dream, broken friendship, or other loss. But you can survive. It may seem shallow at first, but you need to remind yourself that you have made it this far and will make it to tomorrow too. You must acknowledge that there is hope as long as you are alive and kicking. As the old saying goes, "It ain't over till it's over."

It's important that you label how you're feeling and thinking as "what people do in this situation," rather than labeling it the beginning of the end.

Whatever your loss, I want you to know as much about what is coming as is possible so that when it does happen you can say, "This is exactly what Dr. Phil told me in that book. This is pretty much what he said the experience would be like. *I'm not losing it.* I believe that however much it may not feel like it now, this pain and confusion will get better and I can get through this." Does this mean that your loss isn't a problem? No. But at least it will allow you to say, "I don't have to question me. I don't have to wonder if I'm being weak or whining or if I'm crazy or flawed." That last point is key. It's important that you label how you're feeling and thinking as "what people do in this situation," rather than labeling it the beginning of the end. It is not. It is the beginning of a difficult but much needed grieving, healing, and recovery process. And, yes, you can "grieve" the loss of a career, lifestyle, or marriage. Again, the gravity is different but it is painful just the same.

Many experts have labeled reactions to loss (particularly when involving death of a loved one) as "stages of grief" and there are various theories as to how many stages there are. But we are unpredictable beings, especially when it comes to our emotions. Although the experience of grief in some form or another is universal, our reactions within the overall process vary widely. Newer research and my own experience tell me that, really, there are not "stages" of grief but an array of feelings that arise.[2] They don't pop up in a specific order, and it's rare that one set of emotions ends completely before another begins. More likely, you'll experience a number of emotions—perhaps one at a time, perhaps three at a time. There's no formula, though it would be easier if there were. But the reality is that there is no "normal" way to grieve. We each have our own timeline and reactions. Let me repeat that because it is so very important: *We each have our own timeline and reactions.* You are not on a schedule, and you will not earn a prize if you push for a record recovery time. Actually, you may even impede the process by rushing it beyond its natural resolution, and many experts suggest that great good can come from fully experiencing the grieving process.[3] Is six months enough time after becoming a widow before cleaning out his personal things or perhaps starting to see someone else? There is no right answer. You must be real and honest with yourself, and you will then know when it is right; right for *you.*

Loss from Death

The death of a loved one is horrible. It is gripping. It has such a sense of finality. There's an overwhelming realization that you can't get a redo with death. You may want to say, "Let me explain. Let me talk my way out of this. You can't do this." You may experience a sense of panic because you're not prepared for the finality of death and everything feels as if it's tumbling down. It knocks you back, and it's as if you have a thousand-pound weight on your chest and can't get up from under it.

Initially, you may feel as though you're living in a fog, simply going through the motions of day-to-day life as if on autopilot.

When friends and family ask you questions about arrangements to be made for your loved one, even the smallest decision may be hard to handle, especially when you can barely concentrate or focus. You may wonder if you're in the midst of a nightmare that's never-ending. When my mother-in-law passed away at mid-life, it was totally unexpected. I remember waking up the next morning and wondering for those first groggy minutes if this painful reality was just a bad dream.

You may cry so much that your eyes feel parched, or be surprised to find that you're not crying at all. Neither reaction is right or wrong, it just *is*. If the latter is the case, you may feel a surge of guilt wondering why you can't even eke out a tear for someone you cared about so much. The spectrum of emotions that you may be experiencing is huge. It can range from shock and numbness to fear and panic to anger and resentment. The last may be a surprising emotion—especially toward someone who has died—but it's quite common to wonder, "How can you leave me? How can you abandon me?" No matter which end of the emotional spectrum you're on, the pain runs deep.

As I said, sometimes this can be magnified if you have unfinished emotional business with the person who died. You didn't get to say what you wanted to say or you didn't hear the "I'm sorry" or "I love you" that you desperately needed to hear. Or maybe your good-bye did happen, but not the way you'd planned. Many of us think we'll have this profound last moment where we'll express our feelings for the other person and have closure. But wrapping up a relationship with a neat and tidy bow before someone dies is more Hollywood than reality. As I said, my father and I had some really intense conversations before he died. We probably thought that we said 110 percent of what we wanted to, but after he died I realized that we probably only got through about 80 percent. We did a pretty good job, but still the permanence of death is so hard to grasp. With my dad, it was hard to wrap my mind around the fact that I would never see, touch, argue with, hang out with, or laugh with him again.

On this day, you may find yourself thinking similar thoughts.

It's hard to accept that a future without your loved one is your new reality; the mere thought of it can make you feel amazingly empty and alone. The yearning for their presence may feel as if it is going to consume you. As a result, you may refuse to get out of bed or want to go off alone somewhere to lick your wounds. Even if you can't literally drop off the face of the earth or stay huddled under the covers, you may try to go off by yourself emotionally by pushing others away. You may think being alone will ease the pain, but it rarely does.

You may feel a sense of spiritual emptiness or feel that you were betrayed by your faith or experience feelings of bitterness, anger, and disappointment in your religion. After all, if the God you believe in is so good, how could he take away something you loved so intensely? How could he allow a senseless or violent death to occur? This is painful and confusing and something many, many people experience—especially when innocent children are the victims.

You may think being alone will ease the pain, but it rarely does.

As the days and weeks pass, don't be surprised if you feel stressed and anxious and if your relationships with friends, family, or coworkers feel strained. When your nerves are frayed and you feel emotionally drained and are trying to grapple with this loss, it can be hard to relate to others around you. No matter how good their intentions, their words or actions may really upset and irritate you.

Imagine Judy, a mother who lost one of her thirteen-month-old twin boys tragically because he drowned in a baby pool. Friends and family kept trying to console her with comments like "At least you have another child" or "You're lucky you're young enough to have another baby." She knew their intentions were good, but she couldn't help feeling anger and pain inside every time they tried to comfort her that way, because to Judy it seemed as if they were saying her precious son could easily be replaced.

Couples Who Have Experienced Loss

If you're married, experiencing the loss of a loved one can weigh heavily on the relationship, and reactive marital problems are actually very common. Though some tragedies may bring you together, others may pull you apart, especially if you have different ways of grieving. The loss of a child is one that can be especially tough on couples, as one spouse may blame the other or they may have different reactions to a child's death—something that's senseless and hard to grasp in the first place. As we discussed earlier, when you have two or more human beings that are under stress, they tend to attack each other instinctively, known as "reflexive fighting in response to aversive stimulation." Therefore, it becomes very important in situations like this that both parties consult an independent mental health professional in order to create and maintain a high level of communication and to help prevent damage to the relationship.

You may notice that the people in your life—from close friends to mere acquaintances—may offer their advice, opinions, and counsel without your asking. Some of their counsel may help, but just be aware that others may place their own timelines and expectations on you and try to shoehorn you into *their* definition of "appropriate" for a given situation. Employers may be sympathetic but think that you should get over it in the three days to a week that you get off for a death in the family. After that, the grace period is pretty much over—some people may expect you to snap out of it and get back to work. That's much easier said than done, so don't put that kind of pressure on yourself. You have to understand that your emotionality may be uncomfortable for others, and to be frank it is probably, well—*inconvenient*. I know that sounds harsh, but it's true.

When people approach you after the death of a loved one in your life and ask, "How are you doing?," one of the most common answers you can give is "Fine." But I've often wondered how those same people would react or what they would say if you replied by asking, "Compared to *what?*" or, "Measured by *what* yardstick?" I bet you that most people would not have an answer for you. Now, I'm not suggesting they don't really care how you feel, but I think that oftentimes people equate the answer "Fine" with the notion that you are not particularly emotional. On the other hand, *I* might define "Fine" as you screaming at the top of your lungs and crying until the snot runs down your face and getting all of your emotions out in a healthy and cathartic way. Of course, that type of reaction would certainly be inconvenient for a lot of people, but how *you* feel and what *you* do is *your* unique choice and you are entitled to make it. The only boundary or caveat would be that you not choose anything that is self-destructive, dangerous, or unhealthy. I'm not really suggesting that you go out of your way to be rude to people who check in because, most likely, they *do* care very much about you and are probably just trying to help. What I *am* suggesting is that you choose your own emotional place to be in and the time to be there.

The day you face your most personal loss may certainly qualify as one of the loneliest days you will ever experience. The loss of a loved one can be a very private pain. To add to the feeling of isolation, don't be surprised if, at some point, it feels that those closest to you seem to withdraw. You may even feel after a short period of time as though you have been abandoned by friends and family. They may "unplug" from you gradually or all at once, not because they don't care but because they don't know what to say or what to do. If they do see you they don't know if they should bring it up or not. They may worry about whether to say the person's name or if doing so is a "dagger" to your soul. They may fear that if you seem to be having a good day they will remind you or bring you down by a reference to your loss. They may not realize that mentioning the person is an honor to their memory, or that even an unrelated act of kindness, rather than an act of avoidance, can help to heal your heart. They may underestimate the importance of dropping off a cooked meal or offering to drive car pool for a week, which can make a big, big difference in lightening your load.

Getting Distracted

Often we try to distract ourselves from the pain at hand by shifting the focus. One way you may do this is to spend hours wondering *why* someone died, or what you did to deserve this. Maybe this means focusing on the intricacies of their illness or obsessing over all the details of an accident. You may be replaying the movies of these horrid scenes over and over in your mind, torturing yourself with the gruesome and painful images.

After a long illness or suffering, there could be a sense of relief when your loved one passes away. That was the case for Maddy when her mother was in hospice after battling cancer at home. It took a lot of Maddy's time and energy to care for her mother. It was also an emotional burden to watch someone she loved so much and someone who had once been so strong, independent, and vibrant suffer and waste away. Once her mother died, she felt relieved—both that her mother was not in pain and that she no longer had the difficult job as caretaker. This filled her with tremendous guilt. How can you feel happy that your mother, husband, child, or friend died?

Guilt may also come up a lot in the weeks and months after a loss—guilt over being unable to save your loved one or about just living your life. At some point you will likely catch yourself laughing or relaxing. It's natural to actually start to feel better at some point after grieving a loss. It's also natural to feel guilty about it. You may think, "How can I stand here enjoying myself when my son is dead?" If you realize that a day went by when you didn't think about your loved one (which may or may not happen in time), you may feel guilty that you're "forgetting" them.

But the fact that you recover from a loss doesn't mean you only loved a little. The depth, breadth, and longevity of your grief are *not* a reflection of how much you cared about the person. There is no one-to-one correlation here. People often think, "If I really loved Joe a lot, I'd suffer long(er) and hard(er)." That's simply not true. It is just plain wrong to think that if you hurt for two years instead of one, that means you loved the one you lost more. It just doesn't work that way, and most likely, Joe wouldn't want you to spend time pining away over what can't be changed. Instead, he would want you to remember him and celebrate all of the days of his life instead of obsessing about the one day when he died.

Loss from Divorce

When you're going through a divorce, you may experience many of the emotions I just talked about in regard to death. After all, your relationship has died, and you may now be grieving it. You may find intense anger bubbling up inside you, which is one way we tend to express hurt, fear, or frustration. Anger can be a protective mechanism when you feel vulnerable because if you're on the attack, then at least you're not being rejected. If your spouse cheated on you or is leaving you for someone else, saying that you'll feel betrayed is an understatement.

Expect that you may feel total shock. Imagine how Shari felt when her husband announced that not only was he leaving her, but he was leaving her for another woman. She couldn't believe what she heard. His lips were still moving, but it was as if someone had cut the sound off. Shari looked at him blankly, still stuck on his opening bombshell: "Now that the kids are gone, I want to move on with my life. Brianna and I love each other." What clues had she missed all this time? She fought the nausea as this brief two-minute confession turned her twenty-two-year marriage into a sick joke. Whether your story is filled with drama or ends with little more than a note or a phone call, you'll probably still feel as if someone has punched you in the stomach when you learn that life will change, starting *now*.

In a divorce, feelings of rejection may run high because we often measure the results of our efforts in terms of whether or not the world accepts or rejects us. Sometimes, another person's reaction can be a barometer of our very worth and value (at least in our minds), and when the love of our life leaves us, any past rejection issues can be magnified. We may feel unworthy, not good enough, and less than. This may be even worse if your partner is leaving you for someone else. Sometimes, this can turn into a sense that you are "damaged goods" and that if this one partner didn't love you, no one else will either.

You may feel as if you're branded and that something is wrong with you because you couldn't make your marriage work. If you come from a family that prides itself on not having divorce in its history, the extra pressure of "dropping the baton" may be intense.

A staggering number of women have told me that it would be much easier if the husband who left them had died instead, so don't be surprised if you have similar thoughts. After all, if your ex had passed away, you wouldn't have to see him with someone else or deal with him again. Especially if children are involved, regular contact is inevitable, and it can be like dying a thousand deaths and reliving the pain of your loss for months or even years to come.

Fear may overwhelm you, and you may experience a fear of being alone—especially if you've been in the relationship so long that you can't remember what it was like to be on your own. This may be even worse if you have children, as endless questions about your new life run through your head: How will I play both mother and father? How will I support them? Who will they live with? How can I get them through this so they're not emotionally scarred? The thought of raising and supporting them by yourself can be frightening; if they won't be living with you, it can be extremely painful to go from being a family to being a single person again.

To go from the noisy, bustling home that's par for the course when you have kids to living by yourself is difficult. To go from big family meals to cereal for dinner and a mere quart of milk and stick of butter in your refrigerator can be tough. It's also scary to know that your financial situation is likely to change. All that you have may be divvied up—and, for some couples, how that will happen may be a source of contention and a long-drawn-out battle. There's often an inequity between the standard of living of one partner versus the other; women tend to suffer more economically than men do.[4]

Children: Casualties of Divorce?*

Life after divorce isn't easy, and often your children pick up the tab. To minimize the price they have to pay for this, it's important to understand and meet your children's biggest needs at this time. The top ones include:

- **Acceptance and approval.** *This will be your children's greatest need—especially if they are very young—since their belongingness to your family has been shattered. What I am talking about here is that the children need to feel acceptance and approval from both parents and be given the time to accommodate to the new lifestyle of parents no longer residing in the same home.*
- **Assurance of safety.** *Your children's lives have been shaken to the core, so it's key to let them know that the protection their family has always provided will remain strong despite this major life change.*
- **Freedom from guilt.** *Children often blame themselves for the dissolution of their parents' marriage. They may think that they're being punished for some bad behavior, so it's crucial to assure them that they are not to blame.*
- **Structure and rules.** *Make sure to maintain regular schedules and patterns and stick to your rules. Now more than ever, your children need sameness in all aspects of their lives.*
- **A stable parent who has the strength to conduct business.** *You may feel anything but brave and strong, but you have to do your best to appear that way to your kids. They're worried and scared, so showing them that you can still take care of things will be reassuring.*

Your children should not be given the job of healing your pain. Don't burden them with situations they can't control, and don't ask them to deal with adult issues. But don't forget to deal with them about their issues. They can perceive your emotionality, your anxiety, your pain, your fear (whether the loss has been death-, divorce- or career-related). Talk to them about any feelings that may be associated with yours. It doesn't mean you should "dump" or "vent," but be sensitive to where they are emotionally and help them deal with that.

* Dr. Phil McGraw, *Family First* (New York: Free Press, 2004).

Riding what I call the "bitter bus" is pretty common for many reasons. You may be bitter that your spouse tore down that nice picket fence and ruined the perfect-family ideal you believed in. You may be bitter that he threw your life into turmoil and, if he is leaving you for someone else, that he is moving on with his life while you're struggling to hang on. If you're a stay-at-home parent, maybe you'll be forced to get a job and resent the fact that you can't be home with your children. Just the thought of going back to work can be terrifying if you've been out of the workforce for a while. Can those office skills from years and years ago still earn you a living, or are they obsolete?

There may also be the feeling of loss over everything you had as a couple. This includes your friends—you may lose some when you split. Finding out which friends side with you and which don't can be shocking as you sift through the rubble of your relationship. In fact, some of your own family members may be less than sympathetic, which can be especially upsetting.

You may also develop what I refer to as "selective memory" following a divorce. It's just all too easy once you separate from an irreconcilable situation to remember and focus on only the good things. After all, with a little time and distance, you may forget their irritating habit of not paying bills or lying to you and choose to selectively focus on only the good and sweet things they did for you, however rarely they may have occurred. You may think about the early days, the good times, or even imagine your former spouse as you wished he or she had been (rather than who he or she actually was). By doing this, it's very easy to fool yourself into wishing that you were back in the relationship and rationalizing that things actually weren't that bad. But in reality, it is unfortunately more likely than not that nothing has happened to heal the situation or fix the true problems since the breakup. If you were to reconcile with your spouse without serious work being done with professionals on both sides, it would likely be because you are moving *away* from loneliness instead of *toward* someone you really miss. It is quite likely that you could move back together and within a few days you might be saying "Oh, yeah! That's why I wanted to gag him every day of the last three years!" The point is, don't go back in a weak and lonely moment. Whether it was you or your spouse who left, once you are out, stay out, unless one or both of you *earn* your way back in.

Loss Comes in Many Forms

As we all know, there are many losses in life that, while maybe not as painful as losing someone through death or divorce, can hurt and hurt plenty. The loss of a friendship, the loss of custody of a child, the loss of a career or dream, or the loss of social acceptance, to name just a few, can hit you so hard that they take your breath away. Because of this, many of the emotions that you may experience are quite similar, at least to some degree, to what I've already talked about.

Many of these losses in what I'm calling the "other" category are those in which you may have no control, and may leave you feeling hopeless, helpless, and confused. In some cases, you may experience feelings of injustice. You may feel totally powerless, victimized, and angry at anyone who seems to be in control of this terrible situation, such as a judge who didn't grant you custody of your child or a friend who has inexplicably betrayed you. You may feel that you're at their mercy and don't know the next step that you're going to take. The future looks dark and uncertain because you feel so out of control. The bottom line is, we can grieve all kinds of losses, some more than others, but the pain can seem relentless. But as I've said before and as I will say again, those feelings won't last forever. Whatever situation you are in, you do have control over one thing: how you let it impact your life.

For more information about grief and loss, please see the Resource Guide at the end of this book.

GETTING BACK TO BETTER DAYS

One of the most important points I want to make is that hope really does spring eternal. There is always another day. As I said earlier, you must be patient with yourself. Give yourself time to accept what has happened. Choose to stand up for you and the rest of your life and choose to move on. Sometimes we just have to get through "now." We don't necessarily have to answer the question about how we can get through the rest of our lives. We just need to get through this moment and stay alive, stay in the game, stay focused on a meaning and purpose to exist.

The sun *will* come up, and it *will* shine on your face. You will begin to breathe easy again. You will survive because you always have, whether you have acknowledged it or not. You made it this far because you can. Based on results, you have been given the strength to face challenges. I personally believe it was in you the moment you were born. Your answers and wisdom have allowed you to make it this far, and you will make it further. I don't want you to be robotic. I don't want you *not* to cry. I don't even necessarily want you *not* to hurt. I would expect you to be down or even depressed. What I *do* want you to know is that all those things are normal. Despite them, you will survive this. And although hard-earned, you will probably be wiser and stronger for it. But you need to keep putting one foot in front of the other. You can't just go into the fetal position and expect to emerge a year later all better. You have to get up, you have to take a shower, you have to fix your hair. Put on your makeup or shave. Go to work. Go to church. You have to continue carrying on with your life, because going MIA from your routine and support from friends and family will only magnify the grief you feel.

The sun *will* come up, and it *will* shine on your face. You will begin to breathe easy again.

I'm not saying the loss you're going through is easy or that the suffering is in any way a fair price to pay for whatever you might learn from the experience, but since you can't avoid it anyway, you might as well gain something from it. Something that you can use to better cope with loss not if, but when, you experience it again. Something that you can pass on to your children so that they can better survive this most challenging day when it pops up in their lives.

So let's discuss your action plan and how you are going to navigate the rocks of this whitewater experience and move on the best that you can. As I said earlier, you can be part of the problem and choose the victim role, or you can be part of the solution. Here are eight basic action steps that you need to follow to do the latter:

Action Steps

- **Adjust your expectations**

  I have told you some of what you're likely to experience as the result of a loss—you may cry and feel blue, tired, lethargic, and angry. Your next step is to accept that these things are a natural part of grieving. Experiencing death, divorce, or other loss that makes you feel rejected and alone isn't a life sentence of grief, and, yes, you will emerge. But don't put generic expectations on yourself and don't let others do so either. Again, just accept that you may first go through these difficult emotions and that it will take time. You may be surprised that although you loved deeply, you have an inability to cry or feel anything but numb following the death of a loved one. You may feel completely disconnected from your emotions, and then suddenly, at a seemingly unexpected, ordinary moment, you come unraveled. Again, remember that grief from any loss is not a linear process with a beginning, middle, and definitive end. You will begin to move on in your own time; just be sure it is before you totally lose your way.

- **Accept what you cannot change**
  One of the most frequent struggles you may face when someone you care about dies or leaves, or when you have your heart shattered from any other kind of loss, is a sense of being out of control. We want control of how people and things exit our lives because we want to maintain possession of those things that are most important to us. Even though we can't even *almost* have that control, we are not victims—or at least we don't have to be. There is a point in this process where you can and must choose to take a stand for how you are going to react to this hard hit. It certainly may not be what you wanted, but you have to actively, consciously choose to focus on what you can change. You can choose your reaction now *and* how you will think, feel, and live in the future; and, just as important, consciously choose to accept what you can't change. This means mentally, emotionally, and spiritually accepting the reality of your loss and letting go of a past that you cannot bring back or alter.

  You may not like the fact that you've lost someone or something you loved, but unfortunately, *you don't get a vote.* Like it or not, most things in life—no matter how much you enjoy them—don't last forever. And like it or not, death is probably the only thing that's certain in this world. Nobody gets to live forever, and we don't get to pick when it's our time.

  Taking that stand also means that you are going to make the choice to embrace those things that are left in your life that you value. Timing can differ, but it will ultimately be up to you to accept and move on. The philosopher Friedrich Nietzsche observed, "Growth in wisdom may be exactly measured by decrease in bitterness."

- **Find strength in others**

In addition to what I said above about accepting reality sooner rather than later, and also holding yourself accountable, it is also appropriate to find strength in others. Although it may feel as if you're all alone and no one else can relate to what you're going through, try talking to someone else who has experienced a similar loss or someone whose presence is a source of comfort and strength. Sometimes a compassionate person may be of great help even though they have not been through a similar loss. The very fact that they haven't been down that road may bring some much-needed objectivity to your dark hour.

And please remember to be patient with others who haven't been through what you're going through. As I mentioned earlier, some people, no matter how well intentioned or how close you are to them, will say insensitive or inappropriate things such as "It's for the best" or "You can start another business." Try to take a deep breath and remember that most people just don't know what to say. Their words may be downright irritating, but their intention was probably to show you that they care.

- **Don't get stuck**

It's easy to get "stuck" in this negative experience and all the emotions of it. Do what you need to do to help you get unstuck. This is different for everyone, but it could mean giving away what you need the most, such as being there for others, for example, helping with disadvantaged children or the elderly. It may be as simple as finding a new interest, taking up a new hobby, getting counseling, or talking to your doctor about treatment options such as antidepressants or anti-anxiety medications. Some people shy away from medication for fear that it will change their personality or be something they need to be on forever. However, your grief may cause you to be biochemically unbalanced, and medication may be the short-term jump start that you need to move forward if in fact you are stuck. You can also help yourself by focusing on all of your reasons to get up tomorrow and be who you were before your loss. Sometimes it can help to remind yourself of your purpose by saying: "I'm not going to lose *me* because there are a lot of people who depend on me, not just the one I lost." I have had so many situations when mothers have come to me who have lost a child. They are often understandably robotic or even zombielike, but the problem is that they have other children. Those children are being robbed of their mother. You can't do that. You have to fight to find a balance; sometimes you just have to get unstuck because you are needed, and that's a good thing.

You can also help yourself by focusing on all of your reasons to get up tomorrow and be who you were before your loss.

Sometimes trying something totally new can also help begin and mark a new era. Maybe it's reading poetry, exercising, seeking spiritual support, listening to music, joining a support group, or going on a trip you always dreamed of. Just make sure that you find healthy ways to soothe your pain. Also know that you're in a vulnerable place right now, so beware if you've had an addiction in the past. Don't reach for alcohol, drugs, or food to soothe your soul. They won't. Don't fall back on addictions. Be aware that you are extra vulnerable to these things now and divert yourself if you see you're going down that path. If you need help, enlist a counselor, friend, or support group to help you quell any destructive desires. Accountability can be your greatest protection during times of crisis.

- **Recognize that time is finite**
Most of us don't think about that every day. Instead, we have a sense of timelessness and immortality. We think love is forever

and people die or leave us only when they are old. Not true. There's wisdom in that old saying about living every day as though it were your last. It doesn't mean you should be reckless or careless, blow all your money, and not plan for your future. It just means that you can't take the attitude "Those things happen to other people."

Often, people don't nurture what they love when it's right in front of them. The Harry Chapin song "Cat's in the Cradle" states it pretty eloquently. The father didn't have time for his son when he was little, and then the son grows up and doesn't have time for the dad. You have to wake up and understand that you can't go through this life numbly thinking that the unexpected won't happen to you. You have to see time as currency that you need to spend now, not wait for a day that may never come. Instead of thinking "I've got next year, I've got next summer," why not take that vacation, coach that team, go see your parents *this* Sunday? The most common thing I hear from people who lose loved ones is "There's so much I wanted to say. There was so much I wanted to do." You are not here forever, and neither is anybody you love.

- **Create value from this experience**
This is probably the last thing you want to think about right now, but it's important to ask yourself what you learned from going through this experience. Maybe you feel closer to God or your family; or you appreciate each day more because you know how unpredictable life is. Maybe you are able to break out of patterns and limitations that have held you back. There is value in all experiences; it just may take a closer look or a little time to see what it is. Part of getting your mind around this inevitability and what you don't control and can't change is making sure that you maximize what you *do* control—and part of that is focusing on what you can gain from this experience.

- **Think about how you will prepare for your own death when you're in calm waters**
I think it is very hard to have a family discussion about death. But it is a necessity. I don't know if I will be alive at the end of this sentence. I get that. I really get that. I expect to be alive and I expect to die old, gray, and in my bed, but I realize that may not happen. That means it's important for me to plan for my family and to make sure that they are provided for financially and that my two sons are prepared for life. My father didn't do anything like that. He got caught unaware and could have been better prepared on many different levels. It taught me an important lesson, and I started planning for the inevitable twelve years ago. As a direct result, I have extensive planning in terms of a will and financial details, but I also have planning in other aspects. As morbid as it may sound, I have actually created videotapes for my wife and two sons that they will not see before the right time. I have changed the tapes as I get older, and frankly I have more to say. It's not fun to make those tapes. Not at all. But I think I owe it to my sons to make them because they are about preparing my boys for life after I'm gone, whenever that may be. I talk about what I see in each of them, what my hopes and dreams are for them, what kind of men, husbands, and fathers I hope for them to be, what kind of citizens in life I hope for them to be. I talk about how I want them to take care of their mother. I want them to be able to deal with these things in my absence. I have said much of this to them already, but I want them to be able to hear them again if they need to. I guess it's my way of "haunting" them after I've gone!

You may also want to prepare your family for a time when you're not here by focusing on the spiritual aspects of their upbringing. In that case, you should decide what you believe. Do you have faith? Do you believe in an afterlife? I didn't push my faith on my boys, I just led by example, and it is all they have ever known. I have made sure that they have an active spiritual life and an active conversation through prayer with their heavenly father. I believe that having a relationship with the heavenly father can keep children from feeling completely alone when they lose their parents because they feel watched over, cared for, and protected. This way, though my sons may lose their worldly father, they will never lose their heavenly father. I always knew that my boys' relationship with Him would be a reflection of their relationship with me. If I define our relationship in such a way that they can come to me in times of need and trouble and speak to me openly about it, that would then prepare them to go to their heavenly father in times of need and trouble and, through prayer, tell Him what was going on. I'm just a transient stand-in for the real father. That is their strength and somewhere for them to turn in that time of loss.

And that can be somewhere for you and your family to turn, too. It doesn't really matter what your religion is. In one form or another, all religions embrace the concept of a supreme being that is not finite. And that can be another layer of strength and comfort for you. If you do believe in a higher power of some sort, then you understand that you are doing it for a purpose—you are not just going through the motions of being respectful. I look at this as a place of comfort when I'm gone. That has been my philosophy; if you do not have that philosophy, then this is not going to be one of your tools in managing this. I'm certainly not trying to force religion on you. I use this tool to prepare for my ultimate demise, but if this is not your belief system, then okay, move on to the next item.

- **Celebrate life**

As I briefly mentioned earlier and want to focus on again because it is so important, when someone dies, it's a tragic injustice if all you do is focus on the day you lost your loved one or their illness, accident, or death. The same goes for the loss of a dream, friendship, or other similar experience. Not only is it painful, but it doesn't get you any closer to healing and moving on. Yes, you can and need to mourn their passing, but don't do that to the exclusion of celebrating their life.

There is no doubt that each individual's life should be honored for what he or she contributed to the world and to us personally. Surely their lack of presence will be noted and grieved. This process will take time for adjustment. However, life does not stop and I seriously doubt that anyone's last wishes would be for those left behind to close up shop. It is the purpose of everyone's life for those loved ones to continue in a more prosperous and generous way. For what other purpose can there be?

FINAL THOUGHT

The past is over, and the future hasn't happened yet. Adopt an attitude that says, "The only time is *now*—I need to live in the moment. I have to deal with my children, parents, and marriage so that I'm always reminded that if I neglect or take any of it for granted or do not pay attention—it can go away. My feelings can go away, their feelings can go away." Things change. People die. Don't take them for granted. You also have to ask yourself, "Have I said and done the things that I would wish I had said and done if I lost someone I loved?" Why? Because if the sun sets on you today, leaving certain things unsaid and undone, you are not protecting yourself, your sanity, or your future. If you have suffered a loss, let it emphasize the importance of the relationships you have with yourself and those who are still with you in this physical world.

5

Fear

The Day You Realize You Have Lived Your Life as a Sellout

If you do not express your own original ideas, if you do not listen to your own being, you will have betrayed yourself. The opposite of courage in our society is not cowardice, it is conformity.

—ROLLO MAY

You may be surprised that I have defined one of the seven most challenging days in this way. But when I say "sellout," I'm talking about the day you realize that you, like so many others, have been allowing fear—a powerful force that can dictate so many of the choices you make every day—to dominate how you live, why you do what you do, and even where you do it. Obviously I'm not talking about day-to-day fears such as getting squeamish over spiders, heights, and public speaking. I mean, we *all* experience fears of different kinds that remind us that we're human. Some fears are good and exist to protect us; for example, fear can save your life by keeping you from going down a dark alley in the middle of the night or taking risks that are emotionally, financially, or physically reckless. No, the day I'm talking about now is much bigger than that—it's the day you are hit with the stomach-turning realization that fear has been, and is, dominating your life. That just about every major decision you've ever made has been to please, appease, or somehow meet the needs of everyone—*except yourself.* It's the day you realize you have sold out yourself, your life, and your dreams because you were afraid you might fail or displease those people whose opinions you value. It is the day you finally admit that you have put yourself, and your needs, on permanent hold.

If you have allowed fear to dominate your life, and now admit it, you will have to acknowledge many of the following scenarios. Let's take a look to see if the shoe fits. You may find that you have made decisions because you're scared to death of what might happen if you don't take the safe way out. You may have settled for what you *don't* want instead of what you *do* want because you are afraid that you might not get it and of how much that would hurt. You may be afraid that if you don't settle for a "bird in the hand," you may never get the two in the bush. I'm talking about the fact that you may be telling yourself "no" over and over again because you don't want to face the risk of falling flat on your face and thus allowing people in your life to say "I told you so!" Rather than possibly standing alone (or having to fight) for what you truly wanted or dreamed of, you went along with the crowd or let somebody else, maybe your spouse, parents, friends, or employers, tell you what you should like, want, or do.

The list of sellouts can be endless, ranging from life's most important decisions—such as accepting the promotion you just got that you don't want (not only do you hate the new job, but it will force you to move to some isolated spot that you know you will hate, and your wife is pressuring you to do it because her sister lives there)—to what you wear each day or who you hang out with or even the money you spend to keep up appearances to please others. Peer pressure, unfortunately, is not an adolescent-only phenomenon. Adults behave to a peer/group/mob mentality every day, often because they are afraid to say "no" to the crowd or society and do what they truly think, feel, and believe. The dangerous thing about a fear-based mind-set is that it paralyzes you and puts you in a "comfort zone" or rut that's safe and predictable but causes you to waste precious time in your life, again working for what you *don't* want instead of what you *do* want.

It's like seeing a big, beautiful new cruise liner that just sits in the harbor, never heading out to the sea where it belongs. It may stay a little cleaner and shinier than those ships that get out there and are tossed and battered by the ocean's storms, but what is the point of its existence? It wasn't built to sit in a harbor—just as you weren't born to live the best years of your life for somebody else instead of yourself. You probably know the people I'm talking about; they have lots of opinions about how you should live, but at the end of the day they go home to *their* house. When the wheels come off of this phony existence and it all comes tumbling down, where do you suppose they will be then? I guarantee that you won't be able to find those big mouths with both hands.

I'm not saying you're the only one living this way. You're not. In my opinion probably 80 percent of all decisions can be fear-based. That's why I chose this topic as one of the seven days. Think about it: we are a society of conformists—conformists programmed by a meddling generation that came before us and a marketing machine that tells us what we need to eat, own, wear, drive, and consume in order to be "okay." Maybe we should weigh all of this input, but ultimately your decisions must be made *by* you *for* you—otherwise, we are talking "sellout." I suppose I may be stepping all over your toes here, but the title of this book is *Real Life,* and that's why we have to keep these conversations real. I'm not advocating selfishness here; the world already has enough of that. What I am talking about is being true to you when it comes to choosing to live your life but not in a way that hurts or exploits others. As we move through this chapter, you will see that it is entirely possible to choose to live this way.

WHAT IS A FEAR-DOMINATED LIFE?

When you discover (or finally admit) that fear may be driving your decisions and interactions with others, you may find that it's due to a disconnect between who you think you're supposed to be and your "authentic self." The authentic self is the "you" that can be found at the core of your being—it is the composite of your unique gifts, skills, interests, talents, insights, wisdom, strengths, and values, all of which need expression. This is in direct contrast to what you may have been programmed by others to believe or do.

The authentic self is the "you" that flourished unself-consciously during those times in life when you felt happiest and most fulfilled. It is the you that existed before you heard the "cool kids" talking behind your back and excluding you at school or before you heard people making fun of you for being "fat." It is the you that existed before you were scarred by your parents' divorce or were abandoned by your spouse or your grown kids—before you tried and failed or reached out and were rebuffed. It is the you that existed before you realized that life is a full-contact sport, and that when you go for it, chances are you'll get slammed—and slammed hard. It is the you that rises up to demand of yourself that you be more than you are, that doesn't know what it is to settle or sell out. Somewhere inside you, your authentic self is waiting for you to find your way back—to reconnect and get on with the business of living your life honestly and fearlessly. Fearless living is passionate, not reckless; it is directional, not irresponsible.

It is the you that rises up to demand of yourself that you be more than you are, that doesn't know what it is to settle or sell out.

Signs of a Fear-Dominated "Authenticity" Breakdown

You may be able to remember a day when you were living your own life agenda—when you followed your heart in love, made a decision to go back to school, or ditched the nine-to-five job you hated to give your dream of acting or writing or starting that small business a real shot. You were probably filled with excitement about your future because you were engaged in pursuits and relationships that fulfilled you and made you feel alive. But somewhere along the way, you let it happen. For whatever reason, you may have allowed your own script to be traded for someone else's idea of who you should be. That is the point when the breakdown began to take place.

Maybe the first signs were small. In the areas of your life where you were out of alignment with your true nature, you began to experience internal discomfort. For example, you resented your boss's controlling ways but were unable to confront him about it, so it became a stress you learned to live with. Maybe your sense of betraying yourself by not being honest didn't go away—maybe it just morphed into a need to self-medicate with alcohol, overeating, massive denial, or other self-destructive habits that brought momentary relief.

Being a slave to the marketing machine and believing that being "okay" means wearing the right designer clothes, driving the right car, eating at the right places, and hanging out with the right people replaced genuine values. Maybe you decided that your worth and decisions had to be validated by someone else, and you began to live in fear of being found out or judged as being "less than." Denying your deepest desires, even in the small things, began to change you, to sabotage who you were underneath it all. It may have crept up because it got easier and easier to ignore your own voice, to trade the courage to be yourself for the path of least resistance in your relationships, at work, and even in the dreams you once had for your life. Little lies grew into life-size lies, until everything you did was about maintaining the image you created, and you became one big sellout.

Maybe you can't even remember a time when you knew you were living authentically. You may have lived this way so long you can't imagine taking a stand on anything—from your choice of spouse, job, group of friends, religion, dress, personality, hobbies, car, neighborhood, hairstyle, politics, values, morals, and behaviors to even the city you live in. Maybe you've grown up in a comfort zone, scared to death that you would be rejected, that you would fail, disappoint, hurt, or be too much trouble if you dared to say, "Wait a minute, *what about me*? What about what *I* want or need?"

Instead of the sense of pride and accomplishment you should be feeling at this point in life, there is a sick feeling in your gut that you may be barreling down the highway at 90 mph in the wrong direction with no exit ramp in sight. The problem is, you're burning daylight. Days have turned into weeks, weeks into months, months into years—if you don't do something *now,* before you know it you'll look back and it will be over.

The reason you feel so lost is that you've violated your personal truth—that is, what you *really* believe about yourself when no one else is looking or listening—and betrayed yourself at the deepest levels possible. Your life may feel hollow because each choice you've made through the years that was inconsistent with who you were and what you believed caused a little more of the *real* you to die inside. That's when the panic sets in. You look in the mirror one day and say, "I am blowing it, and I have nobody to blame but myself."

I can't begin to tell you the number of people who have expressed to me that the biggest fear they have in life is admitting that what they have is not what they want. The reason this is so scary to them is because admitting it can create a tremendous pressure to do something about it. But that brings up all the old fears that got them where they are in the first place, such as fear of failure and rejection, and throws new ones into the mix, such as fear of compounding earlier mistakes or fear that they waited too long to fix things and now it won't matter anyway. They're left with the reality that not only do they not want what they have, but they may be stuck with it. The stakes are higher, and with each passing day the possibility of failure grows even more paralyzing.

Fear can cripple you in any number of ways. If you've given in to fear-dominated decision making, you'll probably see yourself in some of the results that show up in two of the most common types of inauthentic living: "Fake It to Make it" and "What I Fear, I Create."

Fake It to Make It

In this first "phony baloney" way of living, you feel you are masquerading and are just one step from being found out. Your decisions aren't made in order to grow or explore life—they are all about a false sense of self-preservation and a false sense of security. You don't aim to win; your goal becomes simply to not lose. I saw a lot of the girls I grew up with marry some old boy because they wanted out of their parents' house: *I don't really care who he is—he ain't my dad. He sure isn't "Mr. Right" but he is "Mr. Right Now."* Other people choose the path of least resistance in their work: *I want out of this job so badly, I'll take anything that comes along. Do I have a plan? Not beyond getting out of here!* Their decision making is based on *avoidance* rather than *desire*. The problem is that this usually results in losing sight of the plans and dreams that once inspired them.

In my own life, I've had to make the same choices. As I was finishing a pretty tough run in the master's degree portion of graduate school, I approached my academic adviser, whom I had come to know quite well (more important, he had come to know me), and asked him point-blank if he thought I would make it all the way to getting the Ph.D. Despite the fact that I had a straight-A grade point average, he looked at me and—without even blinking—said, "I seriously doubt it. You won't make it." I was stunned! "Why not? Am I not smart enough? Do I not have what it takes?" He shook his head and said, "It's not that you're not smart enough. It's that you won't bow to the process that grad school requires. Frankly, you have too many options and will never put up with the crap that comes with the package." Hmmm? Definitely food for thought. Although he was saying I would fail, it would be for the right reasons of individuality. Or would it? I didn't know what to think.

I could have been run off that day by what other people might have seen as good advice—and believe me, looking back, it wasn't necessarily bad advice. A whole lot of people and things seemed to conspire against me to keep me from that Ph.D., and it would have been far easier to walk away from my dream than to choose to pay the price to make it happen. But I did go after it and ended up completing the journey because it was something I wanted badly. This was a time in my life when I did not cave. I got that degree, and I guess you could say the rest is history.

It didn't matter to me that it would be one of the hardest things I would ever do or that less than 1 percent of the population ever attains the level of Ph.D. It didn't matter that others who were going for the same degree might be selling their souls in the process. What mattered was that despite the days I woke up wondering if any prize was worth going through that much hassle, I *did* get it—staying true to *who* I was and *how* I wanted to do things without being broken by the system. The truth is, I took a lot of heat for being different, for being an individual, but I'll tell you that I did not find it hard to look myself in the mirror every morning.

Now, don't get me wrong. I'm not saying I haven't made my share of bad or fear-based decisions. There have been other times that I sold out big time, particularly with some situations with family members and my father. As I've often said, I stayed in private practice way longer than I wanted to be (and ever should have been) because I was doing it for all the wrong reasons—for my dad, for my family, for a society that smiles on young, successful doctors who have thriving practices. There I was, doing exactly what I vowed I wouldn't do—and had for a long time. That's when I began taking steps to close my practice and open a trial-consulting firm that (while very risky) turned out to be more fun than the law should allow!

I'm not saying it was easy, and I'm not saying it all happened overnight—after all, I had a wife and two kids to think about. But I began the process. First, I had to deal with my fears and ask myself some hard questions: *Do I believe in myself enough to try something new and think I can be as successful at it? Am I willing to gamble my income, home, lifestyle—everything I've worked for these last twelve years—for nothing more than a chance at happiness doing what I think I really want to do?* I decided the risk was worth taking. I was able to take my shot. I've never looked back.

I did it again almost fifteen years later, when I felt it was time to evolve into a new chapter. I didn't do it in isolation, and I didn't do it selfishly. I sat with my family and was blessed to learn they supported my desire to move to Hollywood and pursue my own television show. Seven years later, here we are. The second time I was maybe a bit wiser because I didn't waste any time moving toward a new passion.

An interesting thing about integrity and self-acceptance is that when you're comfortable in your own skin, other people sense it and usually end up respecting you a whole lot more than if you spent all your time trying to please them anyway.

As I said earlier, there have been times when I looked in my mirror and was okay with the guy looking back—and others, like those years in private practice—where I wasn't so happy with who I saw. The important thing is that I finally saw what was happening and decided to do something about it. And that's the point; it's that person in your mirror who knows if you are being true to him or her, and as long as you can look into those eyes without shame, it doesn't matter if others don't get who you are or what you're doing. An interesting thing about integrity and self-acceptance is that when you're comfortable in your own skin, other people sense it and usually end up respecting you a whole lot more than if you spent all your time trying to please them anyway.

Maybe you've been through a major decision like mine, not necessarily a career change but something important in another way. It may have been getting up the courage to move to a new town or make a change in an important relationship or declare a different belief system. And by the way, if it *was* or *is* major to you, then it counts, period. Regardless of how trivial or simple it may seem to others, if it matters to *you*, it matters.

You may have endured abuse from a negative mother or other emotionally draining people in your life because you thought they wouldn't love you if you didn't, and you may have decided it's better to put up with them than be alone. Maybe you've been the dutiful wife to your husband, moving to the right town, entertaining people you have nothing in common with, and joining a country club you can't stand—all to help him get ahead. Or maybe you've been the obedient employee or child, following the party line to keep the peace and believing that you are allowed to "stay" only so long as you don't require much (if anything at all) from those in your life. You know, things like their giving you a vote in what happens to *you*, treating you with dignity and respect, and being sensitive to what you want or need.

The problem is that in some way it must have worked for you: maybe it was worth living a lie to have that false sense of security in your marriage or job, or maybe you faked it for so long and so well that you began to believe the lie. And because lies betray your own trust and what you believe to be true about yourself, right or wrong, it's only a matter of time before it all catches up with you.

Up to now, at least on the surface, you may not have thought you were doing anything wrong—that you were just playing the game like everyone else does. But today, the act is up, you can no longer fake it and, as the old saying goes, "you can run, but you'll just die tired." Maybe your Lexus was repossessed because you couldn't handle the payments. Maybe you accidentally stumbled upon what your teen really thinks about your fake life on his blog rant. Or maybe you just can't do it anymore—not because someone else "found out" but because *you* woke up and got real. Whatever the catalyst, you are finally forced to be honest with yourself about being dishonest, and to stop betraying yourself with a life built on lies.

Jessica knew all about living a lie. Her husband, Ken, was a computer industry manager making about $60,000 a year, and she was a stay-at-home mother caring for their three children. She was the one who managed the family's money, although the word "managed" is a stretch. She spent hundreds of dollars a month on fancy clothes, getting her hair and nails done, throwing lavish parties for her kids' birthdays, and enjoying daily smoothies and muffins at the upscale juice bar around the corner. Her own credit cards were maxed out, and now she was secretly taking cash advances from her husband's credit cards. At least once a week, she'd take her kids to the mall and buy them whatever they wanted, then hide the receipts when she got home and caution the children not to tell Daddy what they'd bought. She decorated her house with thousands of dollars' worth of new furniture and pricey rugs and artwork. She never wondered about whether they could afford it all—to her, there was no question that they had to have it.

Even worse than spending borrowed money on a fancy neighborhood, three cars, a pool, and all the clothes and electronic toys they could want was the fact that—in the midst of it all—her family did not have health insurance. She had three young children, and none of them had been to the doctor for checkups in years! When her son had an accident at school and was rushed to the emergency room, Jessica's house of cards came down. It was just a broken arm, but she realized that had it been anything worse, her family didn't have the money they needed to cover it. Their fancy cars, furniture, and iPods wouldn't be able to save them, and neither could the facade of this perfect, wealthy lifestyle. She dreaded the thought of sharing the news of their financial situation with Ken, but he was insisting on looking at the books.

Jessica's "day of reckoning" had hit, and she realized that her priorities had betrayed her family's financial security. She had been afraid to come up short in the image department, to *not* have the designer clothes or status gadgets she felt she needed to fit in with her circle of friends. She finally tallied up the money they owed and was stunned to learn it was well over six figures. The money she spent each month was almost three times the amount of money her husband brought home!

Yet despite her finally admitting that she had been living a lie, she was even more afraid to give it up. It was the only world she knew, and her identity was completely wrapped up in it. Without the latest, trendiest clothes, manicured nails, perfectly dressed children, newest cars, and renovated kitchen, she felt naked and scared. Who was she without this lavish life? And now that she had come clean to her husband about it all, would they have anything left of their relationship since so much of it had been based on lies and deceit? The fear of not being enough had driven her self-destructive pattern, and now the fear of getting real was so overwhelming that Jessica felt like she couldn't breathe. Her life was literally crumbling around her.

What I Fear, I Create

The second most common type of a fear-dominated lifestyle, in my opinion, is when your fear becomes so powerful that you actually create the thing that you most fear and dread. You set it up by allowing the fear of it happening to actually alter who you are, what you think, and what you do. The fear and anxiety that you experience is so distracting that you, in fact, compromise yourself to the point that what you're afraid would happen actually comes to pass. That is the way your mind actually works: if you obsess about an end result, especially a negative one, you may become so sensitized to those cues and be preoccupied that the combination of focusing on the negative and being distracted makes it so that nothing but the negative is possible. This is why I want you to "turn your ear inward" and listen to what you are saying to yourself, how you are programming yourself. Just as a "black box" holds the answers to why a plane crashes, your running conversation with yourself holds the answers for why you will soar in life—or crash and burn.

The "What I Fear, I Create" scenario may sound a little like a philosophical bumper sticker, but it is so much more. I have seen it come true time and time again. If, for example, you fear being divorced or left by your spouse, I believe you *can* and *will* create that reality in your life by obsessing over that potential outcome. If you fear hurting yourself on the athletic field, you will begin to play tentatively, which breaks your rhythm and reflexes and makes you vulnerable. If you fear looking foolish in a public speaking situation, you will distract yourself with an anxiety-ridden internal dialogue that you will divide your intellect, resources, and efficiency *at least* in half and will, in fact, make a fool out of yourself. Think about it: if you have a 120 IQ and you spend half of it obsessing about what the audience is thinking about you, only the remaining half is focused on delivering the speech. You are so distracted by the screaming, self-defeating dialogue in your head that the audience is now listening to a 60-IQ speaker. Perhaps that's a bit oversimplified, but you get the point. You have created what you feared. It's simple science, really; as I have said earlier, for every thought you have there is a physiological reaction, and whatever cues you are sensitized to, you will see to exclusion of all else.

Tammy is a classic case of someone who created exactly what she feared in life. Dan, an investment banker, met her through a friend and immediately adored her flashing blue eyes and sharp wit. They got married shortly after, and she moved to New York with this amazing man to start a new life that she believed was beyond the "real" Tammy. She obsessed over the gaps in their education and social background—she only had a high school diploma while he held two master's degrees and had a wall filled with various achievements and awards in economic pursuits. She believed from day one that she had fooled her new husband and everyone in her new world into thinking she was something she was not. She was afraid of being discovered to be not nearly as smart, beautiful, funny, or poised as she pretended to be. From the day she was married she feared she would ultimately get dumped: it was just a matter of time, she thought, until her dream became a nightmare. Would it be a week? A month? Or maybe tomorrow that the masquerade would come to an end?

Tammy went into private panic over her inadequacies, feeling she had married way over her head. Her fears of being found out plunged her self-image through the floor, and she began to turn into someone completely different from the laughing, vibrant girl

Dan married. Instead of being excited about her wonderful life, Tammy's fears and anxiety were so distracting that they compromised who she was, and all she could think about was how dumb she must look to this man who was so intelligent. She became defensive and combative, adopting a "get them before they get you" attitude.

Once the life of the party and a vibrant and contributing life partner, Tammy seemed to lose her confidence in the simplest situations. She began to dread going to company functions. When they were out with his friends, she could never relax, always sure that she would say something stupid and embarrass herself or both of them. Her once bubbly personality dwindled down to nothing. Her appearance deteriorated, pulling her self-esteem even lower, until Dan finally couldn't take it anymore and he just gave up. Sure enough, Dan grew weary of her negative attitude and constant defensiveness. Exactly eleven months after she and Dan walked down the aisle, she climbed up the steps to the courthouse for her first divorce hearing. It took almost a year but she did it; she created the reality she feared the most.

WHAT TO EXPECT

You may hate yourself for getting so deep into a fear-dominated life that you feel you can't get out of: *Isn't it too late in the game for me to make a change? After all, I got here because of lack of guts and backbone, so how in the world can I expect myself to stand up for me now, right?* It can be like pulling a loose thread on a knitted sweater. Try to change this false, fear-based life even a little, and you may think it can all come unraveled. It pains you to think of living your false life for one more day or even one more second. Yet the idea of giving up your life as you know it has you shaking in your shoes. You may feel stuck—damned if you do and damned if you don't. The fear that you have served for so long is compounded by more fear of what's to come.

You may be experiencing a mix of emotions, being resentful

that you wasted time trying to be someone you're not, and angry at those who pressured you to live this way. You may feel trapped. What will you do now? You could struggle to find some other neat roles to fit into, but those probably aren't going to work either. How can they when you still don't know who you are? Or perhaps you go to the other extreme—become a hippie if you were conservative or take on a traditional role if you were a free spirit. You may search for the "new you" by experimenting with a different group of people, religion, or sexual orientation. Whatever the case, you have to decide who you are and what you're about, which can be the scariest thing in the world. Having learned to live with lies, just the thought of telling other people that your charade is up can be very traumatic.

You need to watch out, because once you have been "outed" from the safety of your false life, you may find yourself extra vulnerable to using behaviors and addictions to help soothe your feelings of being lost and alone. You probably think these things will dull your fears and pain. Trust me, they won't.

Fear Audit: Identifying Your Fears

One of the only ways to break out of a fear-dominated mind-set is to identify the behaviors and attitudes (linked to the fears) that may have been costing you the most in lost opportunities in life. Although there are many different fears, below are seven of the most common and destructive fears that influence the decision-making process. This exercise will help you determine which fears have been motivating your decisions the most and which group triggers the greatest amount of emotional intensity for you.

The idea behind identifying the fears that rule you is to become more aware of their influence so you can keep them from ruling your decisions and interactions. This exercise is brief, but I hope it will help you start thinking about why you do what you do and give you insights into the most fear-dominated areas of your life.

These behaviors and attitudes reflect the corresponding underlying fears that you may have and need to learn to resolve. Choose the frequency at which you find yourself experiencing them: Never, Occasionally, or Consistently.

1. **I become irritable and angry when people of authority correct me.**

   Never __ Occasionally __ Consistently __

2. **I am resistant to ideas of changing anything in my life.**

   Never __ Occasionally __ Consistently __

3. **I will rebelliously do things even when I am told not to because I hate being told no.**

   Never __ Occasionally __ Consistently __

4. **I hide my resentfulness from others because I am afraid to express my real feelings openly.**

   Never __ Occasionally __ Consistently __

Scoring

If you checked "Consistently" three times, or "Occasionally" four times, fear of *losing control* is likely ruling a large part of your life. If this fear drives many of your decisions, you may find yourself using destructive ways to attempt to stay in control to reduce your feelings of vulnerability. The trade-off, unfortunately, is that it also reduces the sense of peace and joy in your life.

5. **I withdraw quickly when I am confronted, even if I am completely innocent of any errors or misconduct.**

   Never __ Occasionally __ Consistently __

6. **I am dependent on others for direction and guidance.**

   Never __ Occasionally __ Consistently __

7. **I am obsessive about details in order to get approval.**

   Never __ Occasionally __ Consistently __

8. I avoid being conspicuous in public because I dislike looking foolish.

Never __ Occasionally __ Consistently __

Scoring

If you checked "Consistently" three times or "Occasionally" four times, fear of *humiliation* is likely ruling your attempts at developing self-direction and esteem. It doesn't matter how talented you are; if this fear is driving your decisions, you will probably not fight for anything in life—even if it's worth fighting for.

9. I avoid interaction with authority of any kind.

Never __ Occasionally __ Consistently __

10. I make no assertions about my thoughts or opinions of any kind in public.

Never __ Occasionally __ Consistently __

11. I will agree with anyone in order not to offend or confront anyone.

Never __ Occasionally __ Consistently __

12. If someone makes any effort to observe or supervise my performance or behavior, I become extremely nervous and fearful.

Never __ Occasionally __ Consistently __

Scoring

If you checked "Consistently" three times or "Occasionally" four times, fear of *pain and punishment* is likely keeping you from challenging yourself for better rewards in life.

13. I am obsessive about proper manners and attire.

Never __ Occasionally __ Consistently __

14. **I freely give away any power to make decisions or take responsibility for events that affect me to others.**

    Never __ Occasionally __ Consistently __

15. **I always try to please others and place my own pleasures last.**

    Never __ Occasionally __ Consistently __

16. **Whenever I am punished or criticized, I try to smile as a response.**

    Never __ Occasionally __ Consistently __

Scoring

If you checked "Consistently" three times or "Occasionally" four times, fear of *rejection* is likely keeping you from being more transparent with others or taking risks to enjoy the rewards of friendships and partnerships.

17. **I reject opportunities for gaining self-improvement or advantages in work.**

    Never __ Occasionally __ Consistently __

18. **I envy others' successes but enjoy the anonymity that comes from not competing.**

    Never __ Occasionally __ Consistently __

19. **I rarely accept credit for successes.**

    Never __ Occasionally __ Consistently __

20. **I want positive attention but try to avoid it if given.**

    Never __ Occasionally __ Consistently __

Scoring

If you checked "Consistently" three times or "Occasionally" four times, fear of *responsibility* is likely keeping you from taking a stand in situations or from accepting your part in finding achievement and joy in your life.

21. I have had many sexual partners in a search for relationships.

Never __ Occasionally __ Consistently __

22. I cannot express affection and love easily.

Never __ Occasionally __ Consistently __

23. I accept a strict male or female role given to me by others.

Never __ Occasionally __ Consistently __

24. I visit porn sites and view explicit sexual literature frequently.

Never __ Occasionally __ Consistently __

Scoring

If you checked "Consistently" three times or "Occasionally" four times, fear of *intimacy* is likely restricting you from enjoying the affection and joy of a relationship.

25. I see myself as a victim.

Never __ Occasionally __ Consistently __

26. I purposely show my weaknesses.

Never __ Occasionally __ Consistently __

27. I avoid being compared to anyone else, even positively.

Never __ Occasionally __ Consistently __

28. I regret past attempts at performance competition.

Never __ Occasionally __ Consistently __

Scoring

If you checked "Consistently" three times or "Occasionally" four times, fear of *failure* is likely impeding you from seeking the real values and passions you want to explore.

Let's look at the first one together. All the behaviors in the first group are related to a fear of loss of control. For example, if you have this fear and you are married, it may show up in your marriage in different ways. In the financial area, it might cause you to open a secret bank account even though you and your partner both agreed to share finances and draw from one account. The problem is not that you want to have your own money but that your fear of losing control causes you to handle the situation in a less than honest way. The fact is, you're probably secretive in more areas of your life than just finances. Your chances of having intimacy issues are high, since your need to control things most likely keeps you from fully engaging with your partner emotionally, and maybe even physically. At work, fear of losing control might show up in the way you relate to your boss—maybe you always end up getting your work done, but only after a lot of resistance or debate over how to do it. The tension that comes out of this constant battle (which can take a passive-aggressive tone if you know better than to be too overt in your lack of cooperation) can possibly lead to things like less energy, less trust between you and your boss, and a reputation as a poor team player. Do you understand how far-reaching the consequences of fear in your life can be?

As I said before, this audit represents seven of the most common fears that drive your decisions. You may find you have one or several. But as you reflect on what you learn (or confirm) about yourself and your personal struggle with fear, you'll probably become more aware of your responses to people and situations and find that dealing with your fears in one area will help you with all your fears. Keep in mind that since you may have spent much of your life out of touch with your true feelings or might not be objective about your behavior, it would probably be a good idea to get feedback from others on any part that you are not completely sure about.

GETTING BACK TO BETTER DAYS

Now that you have identified your greatest fears, the following action steps may help you dig deep to expose the incongruencies between the life you've been living and the one you were born to live. Before you begin, give yourself permission to be brutally honest so that you can really drill down to the areas that are causing the deepest disconnects for you.

Before you read on, I can tell you that the eight action steps that follow are all based on one underlying building block: you must decide that it is your turn and that you fear continuing on the path you're on *more* than you fear changing. That means deciding you are worth it and you are *not* going to play the game of life with sweaty palms anymore. Will asserting your will go smoothly? Probably not, but that's okay because the "other" life wasn't so smooth either. At least, this way you are working for what you *do* want instead of what you *don't* want, and trust me, that is not something to be scared about. Again, let me say, being true to yourself and your needs is *not* being selfish. You cannot give away what you do not have. If you cheat yourself, you are not whole, and you cheat everyone in your life.

Action Steps

- **Find "True North" for your life (decide what you really care about)**
  This is where you think about what you really want and care about in life. For example, in a perfect world—where you would

have nothing and no one else to think about—what would your life look like? For right now, keep it simple. Don't qualify it. Don't give reasons or excuses for why your life doesn't look like that. Just paint in broad strokes in your mind and pull together those elements that best represent your ideal life. Write them down, starting with the most important—considering everything from your relationships, career, clothes, car, location, and pastimes to personality or character traits. Keep in mind that these need to be what you really value and desire, not what you believe others think you should want, do, or feel. Then write a second list—one that represents what you have and where you are right now in your life concerning each of these same areas.

- **Examine where you are now (how far off course are you?)**
  If comparing the lists of what you truly desire and what your life looks like right now makes you feel as if you have bailed out on yourself, the next step is to do an audit and see how wide the gap is from where you are to where you want to be.

  Ask yourself the hard questions: *Did I take this job because I didn't have confidence that I could get a better one? Did I settle on my spouse—he wasn't "Mr. Right," but he was "Mr. Right Now"? Did I choose my friends because I really like and enjoy them or because they are part of an image I was trying to present? Have I been a good friend to myself in taking care of my mental, emotional, physical, spiritual, and intellectual health? Do I find general satisfaction in my daily routine and really like the things I spend my time doing?*

- **Make a life decision**
  A life decision is your psychological and behavioral bedrock, the fundamental values that you've incorporated into the core of your soul. It is more than a passing fancy or casual commitment. It is a decision that is made from the heart with a powerful emotional commitment. It is beyond thought; it is a conviction that you live by not some of the time but all of the time. It is totally about you. Typically, you don't consciously

spend a lot of time thinking about them; they are engrained. Haven't you made a life decision that you will not steal? Refusing to be a person who steals is a life decision that you have incorporated into the core of your soul. You don't need to revisit this issue on a day-to-day basis, nor do you maintain an active, open debate about it. It has already been determined. If you are short of cash on your way to the movies, you don't think, "Gee, do I stop by an ATM or do I rob this 7-Eleven?" Some things are not open for discussion; you've made a life decision. It is part of who you are. Maybe this day and the crushing reality of acknowledging that you have been living a fear-dominated life is just what you need in order to make a life decision to leave what is unreal yet familiar. Maybe, just maybe, it's time to take action and insist on very different results.

- **Be true to yourself**

  As you work to resolve the conflict of what you *don't* want versus what you *do* want, be realistic about the things that really deserve to be on your list. Sometimes things happen that can't be undone or redone simply because goals change or time marches on. There might be relationship issues that aren't so easily untangled, especially with people who have moved on. For example, you should not define your ideal life as including a spouse who divorced you and has already remarried and had another child. That's just not realistic, no matter how much you long for it.

  There's a difference between not being fear-dominated and being reckless. If you've always wanted to be a Rockette dancer, but you're five feet, two inches and have a severe case of asthma and arthritic knees not to mention a husband and two kids at home, I'm not suggesting that you head to New York with nothing but a plane ticket and a dream. I want you to focus instead on the areas that you have always felt do not truly represent who you are and that you are able to change responsibly.

  Once you identify the areas that are in conflict with your authentic self and personal truth—that is, who you are and what you deeply desire to have in your life—you've got to make a resolve, that says, "I'm willing to take whatever risk is necessary to assert my own values and beliefs to make peace with myself. I'm not going to guilt-induce myself or allow myself to be guilt-induced by others because I assert my wants, needs, will, beliefs, values, and morals." And remember, it is not really Radio City Music Hall that you yearn for; it is instead the *feeling* that you believe the experience will give you. Trust me, there are many ways to create that feeling. Maybe teaching dance to children in the local theater group would come close. You never know until you try.

- **Make it happen (Make yourself accountable with a plan)**
  The difference between dreams and goals is a timeline and an action plan. Whether you chart your progress on a weekly, monthly, or quarterly schedule, the point is that you need a way to stop the days from turning into weeks and the weeks into months and years. Set up a workable plan that supports you and moves you closer to your ideal life, and (if you can) consider having someone close to you keep you accountable to those goals.

  If you and your husband have dreamed of leaving your cold Minnesota winters behind and heading to South Carolina to set up a cozy little bed and breakfast, what are you doing to make it happen? Are you online in your spare time, learning about the best areas for a B&B, looking for a good real estate agent to help you find that perfect place, and maybe checking out some grants you might qualify for? Are you reworking your financial situation and making changes so that 98 percent of your $60K salary will no longer be absorbed by your current lifestyle?

  If your goal every year for the past ten years has been to lose weight and develop a healthier lifestyle, my question to you is "What does your life look like right now?" You tell me you've got three kids, that you're working seventy hours a week, and when you're not working, you're at home watching TV, doing laundry, or on the phone with your mom while making french fries and mac and cheese for the kids. I say, "Okay, but what are you doing in that time to meet the goals that you set? Are you doing one single thing to move yourself in the direction of the life you say you really want?" Maybe the answer is no. If you haven't been to the gym in two years (if you haven't even put fifteen minutes a week toward exercise of any kind), and if you made a two-day attempt six months ago at making healthier meals but gave up and decided it was easier to just go back to what everyone was used to, then you are burning daylight and wasting time you can't afford to waste. If any or all of that is true or analogous to what you do regarding your goals, it looks to me as though you're working awful hard for what you don't want.

Recognize that there are risks involved, but they're risks that must be taken to complete the resolution of the conflict.

Remember, the idea is to close the gap between your current reality and your desired reality. It may take some financial and/or emotional sacrifices to bring your life into alignment with what you really want. And it probably won't happen overnight. But you can begin making new choices now that will, at some point, lead you there. And don't make the mistake of thinking change is necessarily external. You might not change *where* you are or *who* you're with; instead, you might change *how* you're where you are and *how* you're who you're with. If you are in a bad marriage, I'm not telling you to look at this as an automatic ticket out. This is not a time to run away from problems but to take the opportunity to look at them with new eyes.

Of course, if you're living with a controlling and emotionally unavailable husband and you've had enough of being torn down emotionally and mentally, then this is a good time to deal with it. Or if you have a wife who just won't stop running around on you and refuses to change, it's a good time to decide that you don't deserve that treatment. But it's also possible that if you take the time to identify where the pain is really coming from, you just might find that it is unhappiness with yourself that kept you from being really happy with anything or anyone else. So be sure you reflect and start with any changes needed on the inside before you start moving everything around on the outside.

Recognize that there are risks involved, but they're risks that must be taken to complete the resolution of the conflict. Be willing to endure losses in order to have what's on the other side; and always remember the high price you've already paid for being inauthentic.

- **Acknowledge your fears**
  As you go forward, it's helpful to understand how to deal with fear itself so that you do not find yourself dominated by it again. The following may help keep you from falling back into the same patterns that sold you out in the past and created the false life you are leaving behind.

  As I say frequently you have to acknowledge something before you can do anything about it. So now that you have identified your personal "fear demons," it may be easier to spot them in your decision making. Don't be too hard on yourself—you may remain unaware of some of their influence at first because you've been living with them so long. The point is to become more aware of your behaviors and attitudes and go deeper to find the fears that may have been driving them.

Challenge your irrational fears

We all have beliefs about ourselves, other people, and our lives. They reflect our understanding of our place in this world, and because these ideas have been repeated over and over, we see them as fact. We don't challenge them and we're unwilling to change them because we find it almost impossible to believe otherwise. Irrational fears are a category under irrational beliefs. Here is my list of the top irrational fears that I have seen people accept as their personal truths but are not true:

Irrational Fears about myself

I am afraid I do not deserve positive attention from others.

I am afraid to burden others with my problems or fears.

I am afraid that if I require even small concessions in my relationships that I will not be allowed to stay.

I am afraid that I am uncreative, nonproductive, ineffective, and untalented.

I am afraid that I am worthless.

I am afraid that I am powerless to solve my problems.

I am afraid that I have so many problems that everyone, including myself, might as well give up right now.

I am afraid I am so dumb about things, I can never solve anything as complex as this.

I am afraid of admitting to a mistake or to failure because it is a sign of weakness.

I am afraid that I am the ugliest, most unattractive, unappealing slob in the world.

I am afraid I am just one step ahead of being found out to be a fraud.

Irrational Fears about others

I am afraid that no one really cares about anyone else.

I am afraid of all men (or women) and they are never to be trusted.

I am afraid of relationships, and I believe I have no control over how they turn out.

I am afraid of other people's judgments about my worthiness.

I am afraid of the pain in a relationship; it makes no difference how I try to change it.

It's important to realize that these thoughts can impact every choice you make. Some of these beliefs created the fear that you've been living with, and they won't budge unless you challenge them. If you feel you struggle with these and decide to consult an expert, there are two ways that most professionals handle irrational fears: desensitization, wherein you learn not to be so reactive, and cognitive psychotherapy, which teaches you to control your innermost self-talk.

If you want to learn more about these two approaches, you will find more information in Appendix A.

- **Set yourself up for success (maintain your newfound freedom)**
As you walk through the above process, it's important to realize that this is only the starting point for you to begin to turn things around. Years of flawed thinking that got you where you didn't want to be must be replaced with new thoughts designed to get you where you're trying to go.

There are a lot of resources out there to help you, starting with informal options such as a trusted friend or loving partner who can assist you in identifying your most impacting fears and helping you stay on top of your resolutions and decisions. Or you can go to the next level with counseling, psychotherapy approaches, or pastoral counseling. Sometimes, just getting away from it all at a spa that uses massages, facials, music, and relaxation classes may be all you need to support your new life.

- **Know that you're not alone**
We live in a society that uses fear to manage our behavior. The media uses it to get us to tune in, society uses it to sell us things, and politicians paint the world bleak to get your vote. Fear can be used to control anyone. It can control a mob, a nation, and little kids. Some parents, religions, and teachers threaten you with talk of the bogeyman, Hell, and damnation and demons to get you to behave. As we get older, fears of the bogeyman can turn into fears of failing in school, getting sick,

looking foolish, losing a job, being intimate . . . the list goes on and on. These fears all work toward disconnecting people from who they really are over time as they lose the confidence to make decisions fearlessly. The good thing is that if you're still breathing, there is time to turn it all around.

You can find strength within you and ways to better use the energy spent on being afraid. By acknowledging your vulnerabilities and learning coping behaviors, you can begin to release a tremendous amount of the baggage that you've been lugging around for years, baggage that's been limiting your life. The amount of emotional energy that resides in your fears is tremendous. However, just imagine that same amount of energy redirected into those things that will bring you pleasure rather than distress.

FINAL THOUGHT

You need to understand that living inauthentically is a no-win situation. Even if you don't realize that you are being untrue to yourself, your subconscious is fully aware of it and won't let you get away with living a lie. Either you will live a life filled with self-sabotaging behaviors (if you choose not to deal with the real issues) or you can allow the crisis to bring you to a place where you reconcile the differences and make peace with yourself at last. In this new place, you may not have all the answers—but at least now you know which questions to ask.

6

Adaptability Breakdown

The Day You Realize You Are in Way over Your Head

Adapt or perish, now as ever, is nature's inexorable imperative.

—H. G. WELLS

What I call an "adaptability breakdown" is what happens if and when you wake up one day and suddenly feel completely overwhelmed and panic-stricken because you finally realize that you are in way over your head. Life is coming at you fast, way too fast, and you feel as if you are rolling backward down a hill, wildly out of control. You probably aren't even sure when or how it happened—all you know is that you are drowning in life's demands, real or imagined, and going under fast. You may have lost your confidence and ability to deal with the simplest problems. Maybe you're overcome by the sheer number of problems you are dealing with, or maybe it's the complexity of the challenges, but either way you feel completely powerless. You've gotten yourself in so deep, and you may feel so overcommitted, that you just can't hold things together anymore, and you know it. For a long time now, you may have been coming across as a confident and competent person—you might even have thought you were doing okay despite some struggles here and there.

But somehow the "rules" have changed. You might find your spiritual connection breaks down, and you feel betrayed, or even like a chump, for investing so much energy into a system that seems to let you down. Your moral compass seems to have stopped working, and everything you believed about being rewarded for playing by the rules has turned out to be a lie. This is the day that it all fell apart, and you wonder where the heck you'll get the money, the time, the energy, the brains, or the strength to get through it. You may be thinking, "*Who am I kidding? I don't have the answers. I've been trying to keep everything going, but I just can't do it anymore.*" In the thirty-plus years that I've been working with people, you'd be surprised how much of this I see. This can be an especially tough day for people who are living in the fast lane and used to having all the answers when the piper comes calling. They don't have answers for their kids; they don't have money to pay their bills. Even worse, they don't have a strategy for overcoming all of this. Today you may feel the same way when you realize that your life is a total train wreck, and you don't even want to try anymore.

Adapt-Ability

Your ability to cope in this world is called your adaptability. It has to do with your mental and physical capability to handle all aspects of your life, and when you are doing this well, you're efficient and productive. You're confident about who and what you are. I'm not saying that everything's perfect, but for the most part it at least goes in the direction you desire. You have the ability to handle the demands of your life without falling apart, even in the face of problems large or small, expected or unexpected.

As a human being, you are part of one of the most fascinating mysteries in the world, which is how mankind has survived throughout history despite the fact that we are among the physically weakest and most defenseless of all God's mammals. Think about it—we aren't exactly the most impressive physical species. We're nowhere near the strongest, we can't run very fast, swim very well, or fly at all. Our senses are inferior to most animals' (a hawk can spot a rabbit in the grass up to a mile away, dolphins can hear up to fifteen miles away, and bloodhounds have noses up to a million times more sensitive than ours), we have no natural armor—horns, fangs, claws, poison sacs—or camouflage capability to protect us from predators and other safety threats—yet here we are, long after many other more spectacular species have come and gone. I know what you're probably thinking: "We have intelligence!" True, but there are many different kinds of intelligence, and the most important may well be what is referred to as "adaptive" intelligence. That's how we've escaped extinction. That's how we're still here despite our many limitations.

The secret of our survival lies in our ability to use our intellect to adapt—to find ways to cope in hostile environments and flourish in less than ideal conditions. We've used brainpower to redefine ourselves over the centuries, and increasingly powerful technology allows us to do things faster and more effectively than ever before.

So let's focus this conversation on where you and I live, in today's fast-paced world. The fact is that survival is about your ability to adapt—not just to your environment but, more importantly, your ability to adapt to change. Your ability to thrive in hostile conditions and to respond to changing circumstances is really what this chapter is all about.

How Stable Is Your Foundation?

One of the most important aspects of your being is your need to feel competent and capable as you move through the ups and downs of life. Being able to take on the daily challenges and situations that you encounter is something that builds your foundation from very early on as you *observe* yourself "mastering" challenge after challenge in life. Whether or not you realize it, you observe yourself the same way you do others. Think about someone in your life whom you have come to admire and respect. You formed opinions about them by observing them do whatever it is they do well. You learn and form opinions about yourself in the same way—from the day you started school as a small child carrying your own lunch money to your teenage years when you were trying to prove to your dad that you were old enough to learn to drive to your big job interview where you shot for the moon—and got it. Based on your observations of yourself, you come to believe that you are wired for success (whatever that looks like to you), and you are most happy when you are working at a capacity that challenges you (within reason) and keeps you learning and growing and feeling productive in your life and relationships.

Being able to take on the daily challenges and situations that you encounter is something that builds your foundation from very early on as you *observe* yourself "mastering" challenge after challenge in life.

Your belief systems, or the basic "rules of life" by which you live and operate from day to day, are the key to how you will respond to the various crises that will come your way. We also have a belief system based on what we learn from our family traditions and models, as well as from the books we read, the television we watch, and the music we listen to. All of these influences connect us to a larger group and help us determine what we expect from the world. Probably the systems that we are most aware of are the spiritual strengths we gain from knowing that we are connected to something greater than ourselves. This gives us a powerful foundation for knowing that what we are doing is important. As we learn the ethics of survival and the moral compasses that we use to guide our actions, there are expectations that our deeds will go rewarded. Our self-confidence grows as the rules we learn for our life continue to work and serve our needs.

WHAT IS AN ADAPTABILITY BREAKDOWN?

This day comes to pass when your "grip" seems to slip and for some reason your beliefs don't meet your challenges. Maybe your life began to fall apart slowly, or maybe it came crashing down on you without warning. If that is the way it happened for you, then you may have been living with your head in the sand, because your life wasn't under control one day and then a train wreck the next. Either way, when your ability to keep up and adapt crashes, you may feel devastated and out of control, you may just want to crawl into a fetal position behind the potted plant in your bedroom. Maybe you began to feel that the education and skills that you saw as the ticket to a good future haven't gotten you anywhere you would want to go. On this day you may feel like you don't know a thing about life or anything else.

So many different things can push you over the line. Maybe this breakdown happens when you wake up to the fact that your finances are a total disaster. Maybe you were trying to give your kids everything that you never had or were trying to keep up appearances so you could fit in with your friends. Or maybe this day is marred by the reality that you're on the brink of bankruptcy and are close to losing your home and car. You may feel that you are just one paycheck away from being homeless, and maybe you're right. If so, caller ID might be your new best friend because it lets you screen out the collection agencies that are hunting you down. You may be living from paycheck to paycheck trying to make ends meet, get the kids' school shoes bought, keep a roof over their head and food in their bellies, and have some sort of discretionary income left over—but maybe you just can't keep up the pace anymore.

Because we are beaten over the head with nonstop images of the ultimate lifestyle, complete with the latest "must-have" products and beautiful people enjoying life and having it all, you have probably grown up with the idea that money is all it takes to fix your problems. But your problems have nothing to do with how much you have in the bank—they have everything to do with your ability (or lack of it) to adapt to whatever your current reality may be.

Maybe your whole life savings is gone thanks to some investment fiasco you weren't responsible for, and you have to face the fact that you will have to work for the rest of your life. Or you get caught on the wrong side in the office politics. Bye-bye, retirement, and hello, slide to the bottom, where your ex-assistant is now your boss. Financial bombshells are especially rough when you are well down the road of life, because you've lost your buffers of health and time—how can you recover so late in the game?

Tony's heart began to pound and he reached out to steady himself as he stood at the ATM, staring at the receipt. He could barely hold the paper, yet he kept staring as though the numbers would turn back to the right ones if he only waited long enough. It all made sense now. The vacant look as he kissed her before leaving for his trip. The home phone ringing continuously without an answer. The unreturned messages. Her disconnected cell phone. He had been irritated at first, thinking Maria's bad habit of forgetting to pay the bill had resulted in her service being shut off again. She had been acting strangely for months, but nothing had prepared Tony for his accounts to be empty. He felt so stupid. *How does someone not see something like this coming?* He had loved her. Trusted her. And here he was, twenty years later and thirty thousand dollars lighter. Just like that. His wife had betrayed him, left him with nothing, and now he felt completely alone.

Like Tony, you may have thought everything in your relationship was set yesterday, but today you find yourself desperately looking up "couples counseling" in the phone book. You have serious doubts about your ability to keep doing what you're doing. You've been passed over for that promotion or new job that you thought was in the bag. Or the big project that made you seem like a hero at work was just killed—permanently. You're no longer the big man or woman on campus, and everyone knows it.

For many people, this is where it ends. Without a clue as to how to survive or the motivation to find a way of climbing back on the horse, they (you, if you are in this state) give up. In lay terms it may be referred to as "falling apart" or "losing it," ramping up into a full-blown loss of control of life, because giving up and losing confidence in the ability to survive can be devastating. Your demons that, in the past, have been controlled with good coping skills can now seem as though they might take you over. This is one of the most vulnerable times in your life. (And by the way, it is often at this point that people become susceptible to turning their lives totally over to someone or something that they believe is stronger and can save them. It is in this mind-set that some people even join cults or fringe groups to try to "find themselves," escape a life gone "down the tubes," or feel connected in some way. But giving up on one belief system for another, fully formed one, isn't the answer. You have to work through this, and you have to do it on your own terms.)

WHAT TO EXPECT

I won't sugarcoat how you're going to feel on this day. Fear, paralysis, guilt, and shame may overwhelm you. You may feel sick to your stomach—literally—and find yourself hiding in your house, even in a dark room or anywhere else you can. The fear of being seen by anyone—even yourself—at this point may turn you into what people would call a complete "basket case." It is important to recognize what is happening on this day, whether it's your life or that of a loved one.

Initially, denial is also a common reaction on this day because you can't grasp the magnitude of change that has just struck your life. You might fight to hold on to the feeling that everything is normal and will be just fine with enough time. Many people who've lost their jobs still get dressed up in the morning because they don't want to admit that they have no place to go. Broken and lost, they simply can't imagine life without their identity as a manager, salesperson, or engineer—and sometimes, having been insulated from life by a single job that went down the tubes, they feel alone and hopeless.

Your relationships often do change when a crisis occurs, certainly during a crisis like this day, when your adaptability breaks down and you feel so overwhelmed. You may no longer have the money you once did to do things with friends or family, and you feel guilty and ashamed. Whether it's actually true or not, you may think they resent you for this. You'll probably feel embarrassed about your status change—so ashamed that you may not even tell your loved ones what's going on. You may not tell your best friend that you're having relationship problems or that you feel out of control. A role reversal may take place where the people who once looked up to you are now feeling sorry for you. This pity, which is the worst feeling in the world for many people—especially men—can make you angrier and more defensive. You don't want to admit your failure, so you try to hide it.

Denial may allow you to stall for a while, but it is especially dangerous when you choose doing so over making the hard decisions that you should be making so that you can start turning the boat around.

When your life turns upside down, you may feel victimized and blame others (rather than focusing on how to change yourself). You may become angry. You may feel that the world has treated you badly, and you don't have the motivation to increase your adaptability. You may feel like your wife lost the life lottery because she had the misfortune of marrying you, and your kids lost the genetic lottery because they came out of your gene pool, and you are the ultimate loser. Not surprisingly, your sense of self-worth is likely to plummet because you think nobody wants you. It may just be that at the moment, someone doesn't value your skills or that your relationship partner rejected you because their feelings changed, but you personalize things and make it all about you. You can see that you've gotten yourself into a deep hole, and you may be so overwhelmed by it that you don't know how to look for a way out. When you personalize the problem, it can feel as if the whole world is looking down on you, but odds are that's not really the case. As embarrassed, ashamed, or guilty as you feel, you are not the only person who has ever made a mistake like this, and you won't be the last. Don't talk yourself into believing that the problem is worse than it is, because that just makes it harder to do the work to get yourself out of it.

Strangely enough, many people report feeling a sense of freedom even as their world was crashing around them like this. Sounds strange, I know. It's not easy to feel positive when your world disintegrates around you. But there is often a sense of relief when you let everything go. No more pretending. No more living in fear. As bad as the situation is, at least everything is out in the open, You may find yourself thinking *It's over! I don't have to do it anymore! It's over!*

How Cognitively Flexible Are You?

One of the reasons that many people experience an adaptability breakdown is that they become rigid in their perceptions of who they are and consequently their skills in dealing with the world in which they live. (In psychological circles this is called "cognitive inflexibility.") When something happens to shake their world, they can't see beyond its narrow confines to find a solution. If this is you, you may feel stuck. Or maybe you have not hit this day yet but recognize the warning signs I'm talking about in your own life—such as resisting change or struggling with being able to adapt to the ever-changing world. For example, years ago, when computers were just catching on, I remember many people telling me that they didn't need to learn about computers or that they knew enough about them to get by. But with technology changing by the hour, these people were drowning and their skills were fast becoming obsolete. Either they needed to hop on the bandwagon and adapt, or they'd get washed out. I know a number of people who experienced the latter. They felt victimized by the computer, when in fact they were just victimizing themselves. Their thinking was about as flexible as a metal pipe, so they were left behind as the world marched on.

The more flexibility you have in your thinking, the better chance you have to adapt and be happier in general. But in the middle of a breakdown, you likely won't be in that place. Without cognitive flexibility, you may not see how your skills or talents that no longer work in one arena might instead be used in other jobs or situations.

Cognitive Flexibility Audit

Before we move into the next section, let's assess where you are with the following audit.

For each question, answer with as many single-word descriptions as possible.

1. Describe yourself in as many ways as you can.
2. Describe how many skills you have that might relate to a job requirement. Think back to the classes you excelled in at school or abilities that you were praised for most often by your teachers.
3. Describe your interpersonal relationships in as many words as you can.
4. Describe the dynamics in your marriage or intimate relationships.
5. Describe the jobs you think you could excel in, and what characteristics you have that qualify you.

Answer Key

Question 1: If you can't think of more than four different words to describe yourself personally, you may have restrictions in your abilities to think flexibly about yourself. If you are limited in your flexibility about your personal traits, you may be trapped into a self-concept that needs investigating, especially of your positive traits. *So* many individuals have perceived themselves being in the boxes others have created for them, such as "You are dumb, lazy, ugly, etc." We tend to take their word for it, especially the descriptions coming from those in authority, such as parents or older siblings. But you must remember that there is no better expert on you than you.

I have found it very helpful for people in this circumstance to go to a psychologist or counselor to take one of those personality trait questionnaires that measure traits and compare you to the general population. You might be very surprised about how you really are assessed in comparison to other people. A lot of people have a new vision of themselves with some objective feedback.

It is also a good idea to gather some close friends who know your good qualities and get feedback from them. They may be able to recognize the best you have to offer.

Question 2: If you can't think of more than five skills that might be strengths for jobs, you could have restricted cognitive flexibility in your assessment of yourself.

If you have a restricted assessment of your skills, run, don't walk, to your nearest counseling center. They have similar tests that can give you an objective comparison of your skill levels in various fields.

It may also be helpful to experiment with activities, such as drawing, writing, singing, cooking, or any other interest you might enjoy pursuing.

Question 3: If you cannot think of more than five ways to characterize your relationships with your friends, you are likely to be restrictive in your cognitive flexibility in your community relations and resources.

Relationships are often stereotyped very early in life by the attitudes in your family, which can be very unfortunate sometimes. You may need to examine every notion and belief you have had about relationships, including racial, gender, economic class, geographic origin, speech patterns, etc. There are many hidden stereotypes and biases residing in us, and the more we can eliminate prejudgment and prejudice the better we can be in our interpersonal relationships.

Question 4: If you cannot conceive of more than four ways in which you relate to your significant other, you likely have diminished cognitive flexibility in your intimate relationships.

Intimacy is a very blurred issue in our society, with all of our media sensationalizing sexual exploits. We become confused about what real intimacy is and may need some professional help in finding the skills to learn how to achieve true intimacy with another person.

Question 5: If you cannot find more than seven words that describe various aspects of jobs in which you might find some satisfaction, you may be limited in your cognitive flexibility in perceiving the job market.

If any of these areas suggest that you're limited in your thinking, it's time to expand your view of yourself and the world around you. You don't want to continue being rigid or (as my coaches used to say) "hardheaded." Because on this day, you will likely be going into what is often referred to as "cognitive paralysis"; you will probably start to question even the things you *know* you know for sure—who you are, what you believe, and everything anchoring your life. You can't think, you're seeing everything with tunnel vision, you're missing cues and opportunities, and your brain is overwhelmed. It's as if your computer froze, and you can't access the information that you know is in there somewhere.

Universal Steps for Cognitive Flexibility

To help you improve your ability to think outside the box, try this process. It is used universally by inventors, scientists, and other visionary thinkers.

Study Phase

This is a period when you collect all the information that you can on the subject at hand. If you're struggling with your marriage, you may want to get books about relationships, consult experts, go to lectures, and talk with your pastor, friends, or a therapist to get their ideas. The goal here is to gather all the information possible, even information that at this point you may not believe in.

If you have been fired, this is the time to find out everything you can about the job market—such as what the best-paying jobs are and which jobs are the most plentiful. You could go to the library and look in the Dictionary of Occupational Titles, which lists more than 12,000 job titles and everything you'd want to know about them. You can also get information from job fairs, career counselors, and friends or acquaintances working in the area you're considering. Naturally, you can find a lot of this on the Internet, so this is the time to surf the Web.

If you're struggling with your kids, immerse yourself in their world. Get all the information on what's going on in their lives from the iPod to MySpace so you can get into their heads. Talk to people their age, watch their favorite TV shows, and find out what music they're listening to.

Brewing Phase

At this point, you stop your information gathering and allow your brain to do what it does best: process and organize. This may sound a little esoteric, but you need to let your brain think and not get in its way. To help with this, you may want to consider meditation or try special breathing patterns where you count your breaths. You could listen to certain music such as classical or drum rhythms or take up dance. Even dreaming can help if you put a notebook by the side of your bed so you can jot down your dreams when you wake up. (You'd be amazed that sometimes your best information comes through while you sleep.)

Another option is fasting—not so much with food but by taking a break from all sorts of stimulation such as the radio, TV, and computer, for at least a week. You may need to change your environment. Get out of town, go to a church or temple, or take a long drive (by yourself and without the radio on). This may get boring, but that's kind of the point. You need to get away from your thinking, put everything else into neutral, and just let your brain process what you've learned in the study phase. This is not the time to act but the time to consider.

Brainstorming Phase

Here's where you review whatever ideas bubbled up during the brewing phase. Write them all down—even those that seem a little outlandish—and consider all the possibilities.

Next discuss these ideas with a few supportive people who know you and encourage you. Make sure you trust and feel comfortable opening up to the people you choose. It may not be your spouse or parents—and that's okay. It may be someone you pay, such as a marriage counselor or other adviser. The goal is simply to noodle on these ideas in a safe environment and get some feedback.

Weighing Your Options Phase

After all the thinking and considering, this is where practicality comes in. In other words, if you recognize that you're in this state then also recognize that it's time to evaluate your ideas with an objective eye. For example, what would it really be like if you were a chef? Would taking up golf actually improve your relationship with your husband?

Or maybe you need to take one idea that's not practical and rework it so that it is. For example, you may dream of teaching children, but your current reality doesn't allow you the opportunity to do so full time. So instead, maybe you can volunteer in the children's ward of a hospital.

In the next section, I'm going to talk to you about doing a "situational autopsy" about how you got into this situation—to determine what led up to your crisis. You may feel that you've been terribly mismatched in a relationship or life situation. Maybe you married someone with four kids and you're just not ready for an instant family. Or maybe you're in a job that you just aren't equipped to do, but you got stuck there anyway. Maybe you just made one wrong decision after another and compounded a problem to the point where you can no longer put up with one more day of lies and poor choices. You need to take an honest look at your life no matter how hard it may be to do so.

GETTING BACK TO BETTER DAYS

If you *want* different, you have to *do* different—and that includes your thinking. You may be in a mess, but you're going to have to *think, feel,* and *behave* your way out of it. The good news is that you can if you're willing to be straight with yourself.

When your adaptability breaks down, it's easy to fall into the trap of thinking in terms of black and white—*everything* is terrible, your *whole* world has *collapsed.* But has it, really? Though you may feel overwhelmed right now and everything in your life *looks* like a hopeless mess, your crisis is probably more severe in some areas and less in others. Actually, if you really think through each area of life, you can probably find something good somewhere that will help you begin to regain some perspective. You have to avoid talking yourself into thinking the situation is worse than it is. If you have problems, *real* problems, I promise that they will be enough of a challenge without convincing yourself that the situation is worse than it is.

The first thing you should do is to stop the avalanche of negative, self-defeating thoughts that will try to overtake you. Part of solving any problem is saying "Okay, what do I have to work with? What are my resources? What do I have in my life that is working? What can I build on? Who are my healthy supporters? Who am I? What do I know? What am I good at?"

Let's get a grip on what is positive about you and your life. One way to do that is to get some distance from it and focus on the basics—what you know for sure. Do you know that at a minimum you know how to do your job? You know you love your family. You know you're a good person. You know you have bounced back from problems before. You know you have made it this far. You need to write those things down, along with any other positive things about yourself that you know, and look at them every hour if you have to. You need to discuss them with someone who loves you and won't judge you. You are down in a hole and you can't see out, but by writing down some simple, basic truths you may find that the hole isn't nearly as deep as you thought it was. I don't mean to trivialize the problems in any way, and I am not suggesting that you deny them by focusing only on the positives. But the truth is that balance is a real key to success, and in a time of crisis you need to give some "airtime" to the good side of the ledger.

Action Steps

- **Do a "Situation Autopsy"**

  If you're going to dig yourself out from this wreckage, you have to figure out what went wrong in the first place. First of all, you have to take responsibility for what's happening. Chances are there are many reasons why you are where you are today, and some of them may relate to other people and their contributions to the situation. It is true that "stuff happens." But it doesn't really help a lot to spend much time focusing on what part others have played in your crisis (other than maybe to decide whom you consider to be toxic and therefore candidates to eliminate from your life)—as I say, with any major situation or challenge, you have to focus on *you* because you're the only one you can control. You can't control your partner, boss, or friends. You can't control the job market or stock market. You're the only one that you can influence (not to mention the only one reading this book right now). So if you're going to get out of this crisis and emerge from this place better than you were before, it is going to be because of what *you* do.

  To get there, let's go back to what happened and figure out what you did to get the results that you didn't want. What part did you contribute to this crisis? What have you been doing—or not doing—in the past that led up to this breakdown? I ask this because I believe the best predictor of future behavior is relevant past behavior. Take an especially honest dose of harsh reality here for a minute. If you are telling yourself that you are a "lazy, worthless slug who never does anything productive," that is *not* going to make you feel good about yourself. I would want you to change that language. *However*—and this is a big however—if you know that you really *are* lazy and you *do* lie around like a slug and you *don't* undertake anything productive, then you need to change more than your internal dialogue.

I want to remind you that taking responsibility for your less than perfect traits does not mean you have to beat yourself up. It is never good to have a negative internal dialogue, and I'm not trying to make you feel more guilty or worse than you already do. But at the same time, you have to step up if you want to change the situation you're in. You need to get off the couch and away from the television. Hang up the telephone and stop gossiping with your friends. Put down the video game controller and get busy! If your problem is that you don't have a job and you're now broke, get up and find a job! If you had one, you would spend at least eight or nine hours a day working at it, so spend at least that much time looking for one! The only way to get yourself out of this situation is by taking action and by actually breaking out of the bad habits and patterns that got you here in the first place. So yes, change your dialogue. But also stay in *close* touch with reality. Figuring all of this out may help you see how you could have acted differently and also how to change your thinking and thus will help you learn from this experience. And if you learn from your past and present, at least it can be counted as tuition in the education of your life.

- **Confront Your Myths**

Your "situational autopsy" can get you into high gear fast if you are willing to examine and confront your beliefs about yourself and the world around you. Although many of our beliefs are irrational, they've been in our heads so long that they may have become fact to us. Irrational beliefs, as we talked about earlier in the book, are those that are inflexible, illogical, and/or inconsistent with reality. They tend to interfere with your psychological well-being and get in the way of you pursuing meaningful goals. On this day, when your world feels like it's falling apart, you're going to believe the bad ones even more. You have to challenge these myths rather than accept them as fact. Here are some that you may have (and then use the sidebar on page 139 to evaluate the rationality of your own beliefs.):

1. I am too old to begin a new career or job.
2. The world has made me the way I am, and that's the only way I know.
3. I am not smart or talented enough to do anything else with my life.
4. I have a certain set of abilities that God gave me, and this is the best I can do.
5. I do not deserve a second chance to change my life for the better.
6. I am junk, and this is probably as good as it gets.
7. The world has passed me by, and I am powerless to do anything about it now.
8. I have made my choices, and now I have to live with them.
9. I have invested too much in my family and community to change.
10. No one would like me if I did what I really wanted to do.
11. I can't afford to go back and start over again.
12. I have too much responsibility to change my life.

Rational Beliefs

Rational beliefs represent reasonable, objective, flexible, and constructive conclusions or inferences about reality that support survival, happiness, and healthy results. They:

1. *Promote productivity and creativity*
2. *Support positive relationships*
3. *Prompt accountability without unnecessary blame and condemnation*
4. *Encourage acceptance and tolerance*
5. *Strengthen persistence and self-discipline*
6. *Serve as a platform for conditions that propel personal growth*
7. *Correlate with healthy risk-taking initiatives*
8. *Link to a sense of emotional well-being and positive mental health*
9. *Lead to a realistic sense of perspective*
10. *Further the empowerment of others*
11. *Stimulate an openness to experience and an experimental outlook*
12. *Direct our efforts along ethical pathways* *

* Bill Knauss, *Smart Recovery: A Sensible Primer* (W. Knauss, 1997).

- **Conquer the Present**

  The psychologist Abraham Maslow developed a model known as the "hierarchy of needs," in which human needs are met progressively, beginning at the bottom with the basic physiological needs of oxygen, food, and water, then moving up to safety, then love, affection, and belongingness, then to the need for self-esteem, then to the summit of his needs pyramid or ladder: self-actualization, or fulfilling your intellectual, spiritual, and emotional potential as a person. According to Maslow, the needs of a lower level must be met before moving up to the next.

The reason I bring this up here is that in order to get out of this hole you're in today, you need to see where you are on this ladder. This helps not only to acknowledge your needs but also to plan the steps that you need to take in order to move forward.

The real crunch comes when you're trying to meet one need at the expense of another. For example, if you are fired from your job as a corporate vice president, you may be upset that the only job opportunity is for a clerk or low-level manager. Despite the fact that you think these jobs are beneath you and you want to meet a higher need, you still need to feed your family. Yet because you're skipping ahead to meet need number four—satisfying your self-esteem—you turn down the job, and your family suffers. In other words, you'd rather starve than live with what you think of as shame—having to take a job a lot less prestigious than the one you used to have.

Now, you may be thinking, "Dr. Phil, what do you know about working as a clerk or low-level manager, you've got it made!" But the truth is, if all of a sudden I were in the position of needing to feed my family, I'd take *any* job to do what had to be done. I know I can do it, because I have seen myself do it before.

It's kind of like the theoretical question, "How do you eat an elephant?" Instead of being overwhelmed by the size of the task, you just grab an ear and start chewing. I'm all for goal setting, but when you're drowning in a river of guilt, pain, and confusion, it's likely that focusing on the future is just going to overwhelm you even more. So I actually want you to do the opposite and focus only on right now. You have to start small and go from there. The goal is to think about what really matters *right now* and not do anything else but focus on that. Start working your way out of it one step at a time. You don't try to eat the whole elephant at once. Instead, break it down into manageable little pieces and go from there. You're not Superman; you don't leap tall buildings in a single bound, you get to the top of that building one step at a time.

- **Redefine Success**

When your adaptability breaks down and you feel like you don't have the money, brains, resources, or energy to get your life together, pick something you *can* do and do it. We talked about dealing with the here and now first. When you do get to the point of setting a forward-looking goal, you need to make sure that (a) it is short term (b) it is something over which you do have control, and (c) it is at the top of your priority list. For example, is your priority to make sure you've got a roof over your children's head *tonight*? Then that's what you work on *today*. You identify your immediate resources *today*. As we have discussed, you need to redefine success in the *short* term. You need to focus on getting through the next few minutes. What do you need to do at 1:15 p.m. to get through to 1:30 p.m.? And then 1:45? And so on and so forth. It's the same thing that I tell people who are struggling with losing weight or dealing with alcoholism or drug addiction. It's scary for them to think that they'll never eat another bag of chips or will have to stay away from alcohol for the rest of their life. It can be so scary that it sends them right for that bag of chips or drink. But I tell them, "You don't have to stay sober for the rest of your life. You just have to stay sober right now. You just have to get through the next hour, and if that's overwhelming, then you get through the next fifteen minutes." Keep moving forward by putting one foot in front of the other. Think about the immediate steps you can take for success, which may be as simple as paying one bill, doing one errand, or making contact with one person who can help you.

If at any time you find yourself focusing on something other than the number one item on your list, stop what you're doing and go back and start working again on number one. Tell yourself, "I don't have to do it all, and I don't have to do it forever. I have to pick what really matters and do it well, and I have to do it right *now*." If you get enough of a handle on this, you can actually make a plan for the future, but right now you just have to get through, well, *today*! As I said earlier, the best predictor of future behavior is relevant past behavior. By creating a new history of small but positive events, you can begin to predict a new future.

If at any time you find yourself focusing on something other than the number one item on your list, stop what you're doing and go back and start working again on number one.

While you're at it, make sure to keep track of your progress. After you have achieved immediate success with your first step, review what you did. What positive things did you do to achieve that success? What should you have done differently? Understand the process that you went through and celebrate it so that you can do it again. Once you do this for a while and have some history of success, you may begin to feel less overwhelmed and may even have some new confidence in yourself. You'll have proven to yourself that you can get through it and survive. Then—and only then—can you start thinking about the future.

- **Don't Try to Solve Money Problems with Money**

You don't get into money problems because you can't add and subtract. You get into money problems because of wrong-headed thinking, making emotional decisions about financial matters, or getting waylaid by an unforeseen illness or other life crisis.

As I mentioned earlier, I grew up poor and we didn't have credit—good credit or bad credit. So I learned real fast that if you don't work, you don't eat. And if you do eat, you eat at the level at which you work. If you are in a tough financial spot, then you may have to make "survival" decisions. If it comes down to paying your credit card bill or your electric bill, that should be a no-brainer. It may not be fair to the credit card company, but you must protect your family.

When it comes to being financially healthy, it's math. It's not magic, it's not emotion, and your creditors don't care why you aren't paying. You can't make financial decisions based on what you want, or what you think you deserve. That has nothing to do with math. If you have $1,000 a month of after-tax income to live on, it doesn't matter what you think you need or deserve. That's what you have. If you go to the store and buy things because it makes you feel good at the time or because you're tired of doing without, that doesn't change how much money you have. If you lived on a cash-only basis, you would learn to live on $1,000. Why? Because you would have no choice.

Unfortunately there are also many people who got into financial trouble not from being irresponsible, but from unexpected illness or other uncontrollable events. In this case, there is no point in feeling victimized for too long, because the challenges are the same. Changes in lifestyle have to be made. It's not fair, it just is.

To me, it's just not a matter of having to make more money or having some financial counselor come in and whip up some fancy budget and plan. Sometimes it's just looking in a mirror and saying—*grow up!* Deal with the reality that you have what you have and you need to learn to live on that. You can't use finances to enhance your self-esteem or self-worth. You may get a high from going shopping, but think about it, that's about three minutes of exhilaration followed by five years of payments.

- **Find Positive Influences**

Surround yourself with people who have answers and distance yourself from those who are part of the problem. You may want to reach out to friends, family, or support groups. This is no time to try to do everything on your own, especially if your view of yourself is ill defined or where you want to go requires additional resources. I'm not saying it's easy to do, and you may not want to admit that you're in trouble. But trust me, it's likely to really help. For example, if your immediate goal and first *step* is to create a family budget, you may need to find the best financial coach you can afford or purchase budgeting software or get help from an online financial support group.

FINAL THOUGHT

One thing I know for sure is that most people who live through these days often look back and say that what seemed like the worst event in their life at the time led to some of the best changes that could have happened to them. Whether it's being fired from a job you hate but would never leave because you were afraid of change or having a relationship explode that was never right for you in the first place, you will probably see everything completely differently when you're a little farther down the road. Although it is never comfortable to go through a shake-up of everything familiar and stable in your life, these times of purging that wipe out the old lies and unhealthy parts of your life can open up new ways of thinking about your world. It may not seem that way now—but I am telling you that you can discover great things in yourself at a time like this. As I mentioned in "Attitude of Approach," you already have the answers and wisdom inside you; you just need to learn how to work with and adapt to the changes so they can take you to a better place than where you started.

But it is a choice. I'm sure you've heard stories of drowning people who inadvertently drag others under with them—so don't let panic get the upper hand. If you are drowning and certain you are going down for good, just stop thrashing and swinging—and instead lean back, take a deep breath . . . and float. It may seem impossible to do. It won't solve all of your problems. But it can give you the time you need to let the confusion settle so you can start making decisions that may ultimately move you forward.

As in every one of the other crises, you can get through this. In fact, what you learn from going through an adaptability breakdown may actually bring you much closer to a life you'll love, a life where you really *do* "get it all together," because you are forced to get back to basics and hopefully can keep it there. There is great freedom in living within your means, within your reality. I can promise you that the feeling of coping successfully with life—mentally, emotionally, financially, careerwise, physically, and in any combination of them all—is a place of peace you will come to treasure.

7

Health

The Day the Body Breaks Down

The first wealth is health.
—RALPH WALDO EMERSON

We all dread *that* phone call. We pray it doesn't happen. We try not to think about it. But if you're like most people, you know that *it* can come at any time. It's the call from the doctor where he or she pauses before speaking. Everything comes to a stop as you hear words that your mind rejects, words that suddenly split your world down the middle: your life before this news and your life now, which is changed forever—in ways you don't even know yet. It's like a whirling twister moving toward you, gathering speed and looming like a huge dark mass directly in front of you, ready to take you out. "The test results are positive." "It's cancer." "You've had a stroke." "Your wife has multiple sclerosis." Or, "There's been an accident."

In the blink of an eye, your life changes. You are a wreck as you imagine the worst-case scenarios. Your husband will be returned to you paralyzed, missing limbs, or even dead. He won't be around to help you raise your young children or grow old by your side. You have breast cancer just like your mom and her mother—and you see yourself going down the same painful road of chemotherapy as your mom did before she passed away at a skeletal 92 pounds four years ago. Or your dad's bothersome prostate problem has turned deadly, and you wonder if he'll be around for another Christmas. Whatever the news, you or your father, husband, daughter, or best friend will never be the same person, and things will change for everyone involved. I say "everyone" because a health crisis (whether it's a major illness, trauma, or disease) is not something that happens to just one person—the disruption and pain affect everyone connected to him or her. If Mom gets cancer, it's almost like the whole family "gets" cancer—you can't isolate her experience and have the rest of the family go on with business as usual.

I know all the above is pretty unpleasant stuff. Illness and accidents are things that most of us would rather not think about. Remember how just a decade or two ago people didn't even talk about things like cancer? Sure, they whispered about it in private, but no one liked to admit they had it or knew anyone who did, because sufferers were generally viewed with a sense of pity and then written off with little hope for recovery. Fortunately, things are now changing at a pretty rapid pace. We've begun to make great progress on many health issues in this country, and research on some of them is making serious headway. And that's great news. But still, it doesn't mean that you or someone you care about won't get sick or hurt. And if it's you who gets that call, it doesn't really matter that the number of people suffering from the same thing has gone down 70 percent in the last ten years—you're in the wrong part of that statistic. Furthermore, you may be in the 30 percent group, but you are having to deal with it 100 percent, so you need answers *now.*

It's going to take preparation in each of these areas to get through this day with hope for a better tomorrow.

This most challenging day usually starts a new chapter in your life, and from all indications, you won't like the story that lies ahead. Yesterday, your biggest problems were getting your kids to do their homework, juggling your to-do list, or finding a better job. Now you just *wish* that those were your biggest worries. You've gone from the ranks of the able-bodied and healthy to someone who is sick or injured and could become dependent on others. Or, in the case of a loved one, you're about to trade a carefree life for that of a responsible caregiver. The future couldn't be more uncertain, and no one can answer the questions of *how*, *why*, and *what* is to come. All you may be thinking is that things most likely will never be the same—especially if you have been caught unawares.

It doesn't matter how much money, success, or status you have, none of these things can guarantee a healthy or tragedy-free life. Hopefully, after reading this chapter, you will have gained an understanding of the power of prevention, which can improve your odds and help you take ownership of your health in many ways. But even doing all the right things—such as exercising, eating right, and taking care of yourself—may not stop this day from coming, and probably more than once. This isn't a "maybe it will happen" kind of deal. Life is finite. Health is finite. The question is not *if* it will happen but *when*; the question you should be asking yourself now is whether you will be able to meet this crisis head-on. Will you be ready to survive—not just physically but mentally and emotionally? It's going to take preparation in each of these areas to get through this day with hope for a better tomorrow.

WHAT DOES A HEALTH CRISIS INVOLVE?

It can show up as meningitis-based seizures and hearing loss in your three-year-old child or as a genetic heart condition that catches up with you in your early fifties. It might start as vague aches and pains in the morning that eventually turn into a full-blown case of disfiguring arthritis. Or it might just be the steady age-related decline of your faculties, which all seem to be going at the same time. Whatever way it enters your life, this is one crisis that all of us will have to deal with at some point—for ourselves or our loved ones. Like it or not, our bodies have built-in expiration dates, and some of us spoil sooner rather than later. Having to come face-to-face with the realities of your body's limitations can be frightening if you have not given it much thought ahead of time.

If there's ever a time when your self-confidence takes a hit, it can certainly be when your body lets you down. The old saying "When you have your health, you have everything" becomes more than just a saying when kidney failure has you at the dialysis center four times a week or an auto accident has left you paralyzed from the waist down. What's worse, physical breakdowns are frequently accompanied by depression and emotional suffering,[1] and they can all add up to a crisis on many levels. The truth is, whether we like it or not, our body image and self-image are inextricably intertwined. If your body image is compromised by disease or injury, your self-image is likely to take a serious hit. The problem is that the time when your body (or that of a loved one) is under attack is the time that you most desperately need positive self-talk, positive internal dialogue, and positive imagery. Does it always make the disease or injury go away? No. Can it improve or enhance your likelihood of returning to a stable and productive state of health? Without a doubt.

A health crisis is especially difficult if you've taken a lot of pride in your body and its abilities. In the past, you may have looked down on people who were not as agile and healthy as you were. It's hard to admit, but you may even have seen people in wheelchairs or with other physical handicaps and secretly thought of them as being unlucky, unworthy, or somehow forgotten by God. Maybe you automatically judged all obese people as being lazy or self-indulgent—even going so far as to think that they deserved their poor health.

For as long as you can remember, you may have been a productive multitasker who could do everything yourself. Now everything has been cruelly turned around and you're laid up in a hospital bed, depending on others for the most basic bodily functions, such as feeding yourself and going to the bathroom. I know lots of people who say that it's not only humbling but mortifying. Don't be surprised if you suddenly have a sense that you're less than whole or have a distorted image of yourself because you've lost some capacity.

Celine couldn't stop touching the empty place where a mastectomy had taken her left breast. Despite her head telling her that the operation had saved her life, she couldn't help feeling her femininity had been deeply violated. Every time she touched the area where her breast used to be, she felt deformed, mutilated, and sexless. The bedroom became a place of agony, where—no matter how much her husband assured her of his continued love and desire for her—she rejected any signs of intimacy. She shut down completely, never regaining her playful sexuality. She felt that she would never be whole again. As I stated earlier, the tie between body image and self-image is deep and should never be underestimated when dealing with a physical change of this magnitude.[2]

As a behavioral medicine practitioner, or medical psychologist, my practice frequently had me involved with men who had suffered back injuries. I usually got involved with them postsurgically to help manage the pain and begin the rehabilitation process. Many of these men were blue-collar workers who were strong, powerful, and pretty macho in their self-image. They measured their worth by their strength and their ability to do hard and demanding physical tasks.

As a young and admittedly naive practitioner in my early years, I could not understand why, when I visited these patients in their hospital rooms postsurgically, they were very shut down and only reluctantly engaged in conversation. I didn't think it could be anything I was doing—I felt I had a pretty good bedside manner and, in most circumstances, was well received. I was sharing my frustrations about this with a neurosurgeon who was a good friend of mine. He asked me if I was standing next to their bed while talking to them. I replied that of course I was, that's what I always did. He got a big smile on his face and seemed to be relishing the opportunity to tell "Shrink Boy" something about psychology. He said (and I quote), "Look, dummy, you're six foot four and athletic. You are a strong and macho guy, and here you are, talking to men who have just had those characteristics taken away from them. These men feel compromised and inferior when you tower over them. I predict that if you will pull up a chair and sit down and talk to them at eye level, you will get a very different response."

He could not have been more right. Seeing the complete change in their response to me was real-world proof that body image and self-image are closely tied together and need to be understood in relation to each other.

As a lifelong student of relationships and human behavior, I also want to emphasize again the importance of the relationship between the loss of health and "chain reaction" type of consequences that can follow. For example, a study was done[3] on the effects of stress upon caregivers for Alzheimer's patients who were given flu shots. It was found that while 66 percent of noncaregivers responded to the vaccine (with a fourfold increase in antibody response), only 38 percent of the caregivers responded. The long-term care they provided for family members and loved ones was taking a toll on their own health as well.

There are many cases where one person's physical breakdown has impacted others. One of the most striking response patterns that emerged from the survey I talked about in earlier chapters* was the report about the link between a major change in health status and suicidal tendencies. I found the respondents' answers regarding the impact of a family member's crisis especially interesting—the odds of struggling with suicidal thoughts and actions were reported at near double levels when it was someone close to them rather than their own health breakdown. While those numbers may apply only to those specific survey respondents, I'm sure you would agree that, even if you think you are not likely to struggle in this area, it can only benefit you to stay alert to any changes in your own mental or emotional state, or that of a loved one, during any kind of health event, particularly when it involves a family member or someone close to you.

The reason I am pointing this out is not to *scare* you, but to *prepare* you to recognize the many areas a health crisis or event can affect you or your loved ones. This simple survey yielded results consistent with many occurrences that I and a host of others in the health care delivery system have observed over the years.

* This survey is referenced in chapters 1 and 3.

Not to mention what your mom knew all along. I'm sure you probably heard her say it a thousand times—"Get some rest! You're so run down you're bound to catch a cold, or the flu, or whatever is going around." Your mother was right. The stress that accompanies crisis can set you up for a breakdown on a large scale. If you are aware of the possibility that these things may statistically be working together against you, then you may already be ahead of the game. You can avoid some of the emotional and mental land mines that you might not otherwise be aware of during a health crisis, the hidden parts that often bring us down after we think we've gotten through the actual event. And you know what they say about an "ounce of prevention." In this case, it's worth more than a "pound of cure" —it may even save a life.

WHAT TO EXPECT

When big changes take place in your own health status or in that of someone close to you, expect life to feel off course or out of control. Initially, you may simply refuse to take on your new role. Perhaps you feel sorry for yourself or opt for the "ignore it and maybe it will go away" approach. Unfortunately, no matter how difficult the circumstances, burying your head in the sand won't help. In fact, it will make matters worse. So will self-pity, which can immobilize you and suck the life right out of you. It is understandable and definitely human, but this is not a time to shut down or punch out.

Your self-worth may be shaken and your feelings hurt because you may think of yourself as handicapped, and handicapped is something that describes *other* people—not *you*. It feels awful and strange to be this vulnerable, and the last thing you want is for others to feel sorry for you, so you may actually find yourself denying your condition. You may keep your diagnosis to yourself or tell people that you didn't have a heart attack—even though there you are, sitting in a hospital bed with wires connected to your chest. Part of your identity is gone, and you may not want to face the reality that you're not the same person you used to be. Your relationships can suffer tremendously as everyone tries to adjust to the changes.

Kyle could not abide his family treating him differently after his stroke, so he simply stopped talking afterward rather than allow his slurred speech to betray his frustration with his new physical reality. He was embarrassed and angry about his inability to communicate well and afraid they would no longer respect him, especially since he himself had never had much compassion for anyone in life who was handicapped or slow. He couldn't see the damage his pride was doing to his relationship with his family as his three kids began to lose touch with their father. Although he loved them, he couldn't adjust to the changes his stroke had caused, so he just shut down. After a while, they stopped coming around as they grew more uncomfortable with his silences, and he spent the last years of his life pretty much alone. Sadly, he had driven away the very support system that could have helped him get to where he could accept life's changes and move on.

Asking Why

Why me? What did I do to deserve this? Why is my body turning against me? These are just some of the questions that may race through your mind. If you're religious, you may wonder what you did to make God mad at you. Interestingly, the word pain comes from the Latin word "poena" for a penalty or punishment, and that's exactly what you may be thinking: *Why is God punishing me?* You've been good and faithful—so what's happening here? After all, we're often told that if you want to have the health or wealth you desire, you need to "get right" with God. So maybe the opposite seems true here—since you're not healthy, what did you do wrong?

Even if your spiritual beliefs don't include God, there is a universal understanding that having a healthy, strong body is a blessing. So when your body is sick and weak, it can be easy to feel as if you've been cursed. This feeling can be magnified and even more puzzling if you're one of those people who has led an active, healthy life, getting your fill of fruits and vegetables, shunning bad habits, and breaking a sweat regularly. You've obeyed all the rules, so where is the justice in the situation?

In addition, illness, accidents, or life-changing health breakdowns bring us all face-to-face with our mortality. You may not have thought about it much until now, but you should anticipate that it may be on your mind on this day. It suddenly begins to sink in that you just may not live forever. You are not invincible, and it's not just other people who get sick or injured or even die.

Worse yet, you realize that life may not always follow the natural order of things. You may have to bury your child—something no parent ever wants to do or imagine. There is no grief that is comparable to having to watch a part of you that came to life be taken back, before enough time had been spent together or enough memories had been made. Expect that these days may test your faith like never before.

Losing Your Balance

When you come face-to-face with a physical illness—your own or someone else's—it isn't unusual to go to extremes in how you respond. On the one hand, you may become overly sensitive to every little ripple or change in your body or situation. These fears can begin to rule your life. I know people who have had heart attacks who avoid the tiniest bit of stress or excitement and almost stop living life in the process because they're so afraid of having another one. A small muscle cramp in your chest or shoulder can send you into a panic, even though your checkups have been perfect. You may become hypervigilant about the smallest things. Those recovering from cancer may start worrying about *every* detail of *every* day, afraid that anything they do may trigger a relapse. I'm not talking about being cautious or wise about your lifestyle choices—it's smart to use crisis as an opportunity to get a shaky life on track. What I'm talking about is living in fear, where it's all-consuming, and worries about your illness or injury are on your mind 24/7 to the point of ruining the quality of life for yourself and your loved ones.

At the other end of the spectrum are those people who think, *I'm going to die anyway, so why bother trying to take care of myself?* They go "hog wild," doing everything they're not supposed to, such as drinking, smoking, or eating the greasiest fat-filled food they can get their hands on. They may take risks they would never have dreamed of prior to their disease or illness, and instead of living in fear, they scare everyone around them with their recklessness or apathy.

Then again, you may avoid both extremes and instead spend your days on a mission, seeking out anything and everything to remedy this health breakdown. That can mean spending hours online doing research or consulting any and all experts that others recommend. Gathering information and being proactive is great. So is getting a second or third opinion and connecting with people who've dealt with a similar crisis. Just be careful to check things out thoroughly. When you're desperate for advice and information is when you can also be most vulnerable to every snake oil salesman who says they have a cure for what ails you.

During this difficult day and all of the challenging days that follow when the problem is chronic, there may be a major role reversal that takes place with some of the people in your life. For example, say that you're the one who is having a health crisis but who also typically runs the household or is the breadwinner. Well, you may not be able to work or be the primary caretaker of your children anymore. Facing that can be overwhelming. You may no longer be in charge. You may no longer have the responsibilities that made you feel valuable to others and good about yourself. Without that identity, you may wonder, *Who am I?* If you've been the caretaker, you may suddenly struggle with control and pride issues and resist having other people cater to you. You may not want to ask for help, even with something that's tough to do, when you're used to running the show.

For Melanie, it was just the opposite. Her husband, John, had always taken care of everything. He had made the money, paid the bills, ran the kids to soccer and the mall, and generally enjoyed keeping things humming along while Melanie spent most of her time working on a law degree. But everything changed when John was hit by a drunk who sideswiped his SUV and sent him to the hospital with spinal injuries. He was in traction and therapy for many months, and Melanie was frozen with fear when she realized that she would now have to juggle both their loads with no clue where to start. It didn't help that John felt useless and therefore was always in a bad mood when she took the kids to visit. By the time he was back on his feet, a lot had changed and the two of them had a whole new set of challenges to work through.

I Don't Remember Signing Up for This . . .

If you're in a situation where a loved one is bedridden or suffering from a debilitating disease, you may have to take over duties that you never had before—and perhaps never wanted. Maybe you have to get a job when you've been happy to stay home and raise your kids. Or maybe you have to step away from a fulfilling and interesting career so you can hold down the fort at home. Or you have to balance the family's finances when you flunked math, or figure out how the car pool runs when you still have trouble remembering where you left your keys. In all these scenarios, and many I didn't mention, you are stepping out of the role that you have grown comfortable in and into one that you didn't originally sign up for. Change is hard, and you may find yourself feeling resentment about the fact that things are so different from the way they were before. You don't want to be a full-time patient, but you may have no choice. You don't want to become the sole provider and caretaker, but again, you didn't get a vote.

Having a sick or hurt child can bring you to your knees faster than almost anything. As a parent myself, I know this is one of the biggest fears you can have. I have often said that as a parent you are only as happy as your saddest child. But if the unthinkable happens and your child is diagnosed with a severe disease or suffers a major trauma, we suffer doubly—for them as well as ourselves. I can't count how many times I've heard parents of sick children say, "How I wish it were I who had this disease and not my precious and innocent child." It hurts us terribly to see our little ones hurting. We want our kids to enjoy the fun, carefree time before the responsibilities and pressures of life hit. But instead, your child may have to deal with physical therapy, medication with difficult side effects, and, worst of all, debilitating pain. They don't understand why they have to be different from other kids, and it's not unusual for them to experience depression along with whatever physical challenge they're up against.

Managed, Not Cured

If you are familiar with my set of Life Laws, you know that my position is that life is managed, not cured. This goes for most health issues as well, and the reason it is important to understand this is because you are the manager. Your lifestyle choices, from getting enough sleep and having good nutrition and exercise habits to avoiding stressors, dealing with environmental toxins—from lead and mercury to pesticides—and seeking professional help when needed, can make all the difference in the world. If you look at the treatments for the top six preventable causes of death—heart disease, cancer, stroke, chronic obstructive pulmonary disease (COPD), accidents, and diabetes—you'll find that most of them are lifestyle-based. There may be a medicinal element, but we need to have a strong foundation to support everything else. This is especially important when genetic factors are involved.

From the research on DNA and other genetic potentials in our system, it should not be a surprise that you might be headed for some problems if, say, your parents are alcoholics,[4] your mother has diabetes,[5] or your father has a history of heart trouble.[6] Don't ignore the signs of trouble ahead and hope that these issues will pass you by. These conditions are only potentials, but they will always be present as your vulnerabilities. And that's the good thing—if you are aware of these predisposed problem areas, there are lifestyle choices that can give you a definite edge.

My father struggled with heart disease, so I know that is an area I need to keep an eye on, which I do. I've taken ownership of my diet and the kind of exercise I do, and I search the journals and medical literature regularly to stay on top of the latest information and recommendations related to heart disease. I may not be able to control every part of my world, but the parts that I can, you can bet I do. And if you are faced with any kind of health challenges, chances are you can find others who are successfully dealing with the same thing just by watching the news or going

When you adopt a healthy lifestyle it begins to add up in a powerfully positive way.

online and doing some research. You won't be a perfect health manager—I know I certainly am not—but when you adopt a healthy lifestyle it begins to add up in a powerfully positive way. And the sooner you get started, the better off you will be.

I've heard of many remarkable healing stories, and other people who have traveled the same paths. The point is that these days, you have many more resources and options than others who have gone before you, so be sure to take advantage of them.

GETTING BACK TO BETTER DAYS

You have the ability to influence when—if not how—many of these health events will occur by choosing to be part of the solution rather than the problem. Stress and anxiety are the antithesis of healing, and you need to be on guard for them, as they can throw you into a state that will work against your recovery. Patients with negative imagery never do as well as those with positive imagery, so keep in mind that a diagnosis or event is not your cue to panic but instead a cue to cope in a new, self-empowered way.[7]

Action Steps

- **Identify Your Health Perception**
  One of the first pioneers in the development of health attribution assessment is my good friend and colleague Dr. Frank Lawlis. He has worked with these dimensions for more than thirty-five years, and his insights into the consequences of various health attitudes are particularly helpful on this day.[8]

  Your health perception (what you attribute your level of health to) is a mind-set that has to do with your expectations and beliefs about what creates, controls, and influences your health. I will be referring to this as your "locus of control" as well. Locus, which means "location" or "place," designates the source of your belief or expectation. For example, you may expect that your personal lifestyle of vegetarianism and exercising three times a week might prevent you from getting certain diseases or that your job as a hospital worker might subject you to many people's germs, which could influence your vulnerability to those diseases. On the other hand, you may believe that nothing really has any influence on your health and that people get diseases randomly.

  Identifying what weight you give these various sources, or how you perceive them, gives some indication of your health expectations and the actions you're willing to take to get yourself or someone you love back to optimum health. It can help you devise a plan for getting through this health crisis and help you halt behaviors you perceive as being destructive.

  The best way to avoid feeling like a victim when this day hits is to be ready for it. Know what you believe in so you can go into action with a plan already in place. You are in charge of your body. It's the only one you're given, and as the "health manager" of your private "facility" you need to take an inventory of what you have and have a decent idea of how it all works. What do you believe? Do you need to change your bad habits—stop drinking alcohol or smoking—even though they may provide you with temporary relief or pleasure? Are you living in a way that promotes your health according to what you say you believe? If not, why not? You've probably heard or read that just about any kind of medicine or therapy works better if you believe in it. For example, I have seen pain medicine and even powerful drugs such as chemotherapy work much more efficiently when a person believes they can help. I have also seen people get well eating chicken soup because they believed in it. Choose your weapons and then get on with winning the battle.

As you work through the health perception questions, think of this as a time to find your most powerful medicine and your arsenal of healing practices. How much control you believe you have over your health is probably the single best indicator of how much you actually do have.

Understanding Your Health Perception

For each of the following, circle the number that indicates how much confidence or trust you'd place in each of the resources mentioned below. This is on a scale from 1 (no confidence) to 10 (full confidence). Remember to be honest in your answers (I always say this, but just as a reminder, the answers are obviously for your eyes only).

1. My willingness to follow a good nutritional program in order to maximize my body's healing abilities.

1	2	3	4	5	6	7	8	9	10
No confidence		Moderate confidence		Half-hearted		Much confidence		Maximum confidence	

2. My willingness to exercise my body in order to reach maximum recovery.

1	2	3	4	5	6	7	8	9	10
No confidence		Moderate confidence		Half-hearted		Much confidence		Maximum confidence	

3. My belief in my ability to use focusing techniques to accomplish my goals in health.

1 2 3 4 5 6 7 8 9 10

No confidence	Moderate confidence	Half-hearted	Much confidence	Maximum confidence

4. My belief in my ability to calm my stress issues and use that energy to succeed in my physical healing.

1 2 3 4 5 6 7 8 9 10

No confidence	Moderate confidence	Half-hearted	Much confidence	Maximum confidence

5. My belief in my inner strength to heal my body.

1 2 3 4 5 6 7 8 9 10

No confidence	Moderate confidence	Half-hearted	Much confidence	Maximum confidence

6. My belief that my doctor(s) will heal me.

1 2 3 4 5 6 7 8 9 10

No confidence	Moderate confidence	Half-hearted	Much confidence	Maximum confidence

7. My belief in medicines to heal my body and mind.

1 2 3 4 5 6 7 8 9 10

No confidence	Moderate confidence	Half-hearted	Much confidence	Maximum confidence

8. **My belief that if I follow all the instructions given to me by my health care professional, I will be healed.**

1	2	3	4	5	6	7	8	9	10

No confidence | Moderate confidence | Half-hearted | Much confidence | Maximum confidence

9. **My belief in the concept that if I have faith in my religious symbols or teaching, I will be healed by the spiritual power.**

1	2	3	4	5	6	7	8	9	10

No confidence | Moderate confidence | Half-hearted | Much confidence | Maximum confidence

10. **My belief in the healing power of my friends and family as crucial to healing my body and mind.**

1	2	3	4	5	6	7	8	9	10

No confidence | Moderate confidence | Half-hearted | Much confidence | Maximum confidence

11. **My belief that health and healing are a matter of fate and nothing changes that result.**

1	2	3	4	5	6	7	8	9	10

No confidence | Moderate confidence | Half-hearted | Much confidence | Maximum confidence

12. **My belief that when I get sick or be disabled, it is a purely random event over which I have no control.**

1	2	3	4	5	6	7	8	9	10

No confidence | Moderate confidence | Half-hearted | Much confidence | Maximum confidence

13. My belief that regardless of what I do, I cannot affect when I will die or how sick I will get.

1	2	3	4	5	6	7	8	9	10

No confidence	Moderate confidence	Half-hearted	Much confidence	Maximum confidence

14. My belief that one's genetic makeup determines one's future, regardless of what else may happen.

1	2	3	4	5	6	7	8	9	10

No confidence	Moderate confidence	Half-hearted	Much confidence	Maximum confidence

15. My belief that we have little control over whether or not we get a disease or die.

1	2	3	4	5	6	7	8	9	10

No confidence	Moderate confidence	Half-hearted	Much confidence	Maximum confidence

Scoring

Add up your ratings for items 1–5 and compare to the following:

5–30	Low confidence in self-direction
31–40	Average confidence in self-direction
41–45	High confidence in self-direction
46–50	Very high confidence in self-direction

Add up your ratings for items 6–10 and compare to the following:

5–20	Low confidence in others as healing agents
21–30	Average confidence in others as healing agents

31–40	High confidence in others as healing agents
41–50	Very high confidence in others as healing agents

Add up your ratings for items 11–15 and compare to the following:

5–25	Low confidence in random health actions
26–37	Average confidence in random health actions
38–42	High confidence in random health actions
43–50	Very high confidence in random health actions

Internal Health Perception

If you scored high or very high on health self-confidence (items 1–5), you may believe that you can make a difference in your health by your own choices and behaviors. That means you think that whatever happens—good or bad—is the direct result of your own efforts. Whether that's by eating your broccoli and carrots, exercising, taking your medicine, or following any other specific regimen, your faith in yourself and what you do or don't do has a big impact. That's a good thing because research has shown high health self-confidence is a positive predictor of how much you will improve.[9]

In my experience, it is a common belief among many who treat chronic diseases and injuries that patients with positive and upbeat attitudes tend to respond better to treatment over time than those with a more negative and pessimistic attitude. A great example is Lance Armstrong, who had testicular cancer. He had huge odds against him. But he not only beat his cancer, he went on to win seven Tour de France bike races—an athletic event that many would argue is one of the toughest out there. He likely has high health self-confidence, which helped contribute mightily to his dramatic recovery and continued success. Lance's lifestyle and mind-set supported his belief that he could influence and manage his health situation to a great degree, and to this day he is reaping the benefits of his chosen belief system.

If you're in this high-self-confidence group, it is very likely that you take responsibility for your health condition. Although that's generally a good thing, one downside, to thinking that your health is *too* internally controlled, is that it may keep you from reaching out to other people—who can potentially provide a wealth of critical information and support. Also, you may be so internally oriented that you blame yourself for events that are in actuality out of your control. For example, you may have been born blind or with a heart defect, and despite the congenital nature of the disorder, you may fault yourself unrealistically. This goes beyond the more reasonable position of just actively managing an inherited disorder.

Let me be very clear on this issue: blaming yourself for conditions over which you had or have no control, or for an inherited history you cannot change, has no place in the constructive management of any disease or health event. Even if there could be a strong correlation between a disease and a previous behavior, such as alcoholism and liver disease or smoking and lung disease, it is far better to focus on what you can do now rather than beating yourself up for what you did in the past. Yes, you are accountable for what you do now, and high-risk behaviors need to be eliminated as you go forward, but the guilt and self-condemnation for what is already done need to be eliminated, too. You need to make peace with yourself so that you can have the best shot possible at getting well. Bottom line, I'm saying that the more *mentally* healthy you are, the better the chance that you can maintain or return to optimal *physical* health. You may not be able to "think your way to health," but positive thoughts clearly have an effect, just as do negative thoughts.

External Health Perception

A high or average score here (items 6–10) means that you may be highly dependent on other people or influences in your life to get you out of a health crisis. You may believe that any positive results come from someone or something outside yourself. For example, you believe that you're going to fully recover from an accident because your doctor is the greatest doctor in the world. Or you're going to beat your disease because you believe that the medicine you're taking surpasses all others and are totally convinced it *will* work.

The upside of having an external locus of health perception is that you are willing to reach out to trusted others for help and you'll gain from their knowledge and expertise. The key for you, then, is to bet on the winning horse. In other words, if you believe in a doctor's ability to help you heal, make sure you're working with the best doctor possible. If you believe that medicine can cure you, do your homework and figure out what and where the best medicine is. The individuals who have this high level are usually excellent in compliance with medical regimens and considered a physician's model patient.

Tips for Finding a Good Doctor

- *Identify the best hospitals in your area, and check with the staff there.*
- *Check with trusted references, such as friends and family, for recommendations.*
- *Most importantly, make sure the doctor you are looking into is board certified. This determines whether or not they have had proper training in their field of specialty.*

One downside of the higher scores is the absence of a healthy dose of intelligent skepticism about any big promises of an easy cure by a highly confident doctor. It is very easy to become passive and be an inactive member of your own treatment team—when in fact you should probably be the captain! No matter what your style of perception of causation, you will always be a powerful force in the outcome of your own quality and longevity of life. You have to take ownership of this crisis in order to increase the chances for success. You can't blame others, and you can't just rely blindly on them to get you out of your predicament. You have to take control—and responsibility. That may mean admitting that your heart attack might have come from unhealthy eating, lack of exercise, and a stress-filled life. Or, if you were genetically predisposed to it, that you have an even higher duty to live the kind of lifestyle that minimizes your already high risks. If you got into a car accident you need to acknowledge that you may have contributed to the outcome because you were speeding down the highway at 1 a.m., distracted, and too tired to be properly vigilant. Be accountable for your own actions and choices. You do have the power to change, and you can actively influence your life and your health.

The upside to the lower scores on the External Locus of Control would be the Missouri attitude that "I can do it myself." As I just said, rebellion against authority is not always a bad thing, because you may have an intuition that pays off. For example, I have seen dozens of patients who rejected the medicine we practice in the United States and adopted those of Asia or Europe and had tremendous benefit. It is a consistent finding that even though the American citizen pays twice as much for medical care, we are usually rated at the bottom of most surveys of medical care in civilized countries,[10] so maybe a healthy dose of doubt has some value.

The downside of a low score is that you may not believe in anyone's approach and usually take no action because you might not be convinced of the chances for success on any plan.

Chance Health Perception

If you scored high here (items 11–15), you tend to believe in fate and may feel that your health or that of a loved one is just a roll of the dice. You probably have little or no belief in yourself or anything else. You may not see a link between smoking a pack of cigarettes a day and your cancer or a link between your obesity and heart disease. In your mind, there's no course of action, control of, or impact on your health that comes from you or anyone else.

Let me just say that this is risky thinking. Because if you don't see any point in changing your diet or lifestyle, taking medication or actively complying with your physician's plan, or even learning more about your condition, you probably won't get any better. Your thinking may be, *why do it when my behavior has nothing to do with how I got into this health crisis?* You don't believe in yourself, doctors, medicine, God, etc. For example, if your mother, grandmother, and sister all died of lung cancer and you believe that it's inevitable that you'll suffer the same fate, too, and you can't do anything about it, your outcome probably won't be very good. There may be a feeling of powerlessness, and a sense that you've been dealt a bad hand. This can be deadly because you're missing important chances to take control.

Elena was a 42-year old diabetic. Although her roommate was alarmed by Elena's swollen, red foot and pressed her to get treatment, Elena insisted it was a family problem and there wasn't much she could do about it. Because her feet were numb, it was easy to ignore them, until ultimately she had to have one of them amputated due to an infection. Tragically, it didn't end there. She went into a fast decline after surgery and died two years into her recovery, which she did not know was typical (once a leg or foot is amputated, up to about 70 percent of diabetics die within five years, according to data published by the National Institutes of Health[11]). Although most people's stories aren't as drastic as Elena's, the truly terrible part is that *she could have avoided the amputation*. Recent research shows that 50 to 85 percent of diabetic foot amputations,[12] once viewed to be inevitable for most diabetic foot wounds, are now preventable with early detection and treatment. If Elena had had confidence in her own ability—or even her roommate's—to get the help she needed, her story could have ended far differently.

There is no real upside to a high score on chance because these scores are consistently correlated to bad outcomes regardless of the disease; however, there is a positive to the low scores. The lower the score, the more you are probably saying to yourself that there must be a health formula for you personally, and your job is to find it. In some ways the journey toward success can be as valuable as the cure. I have never met a cancer survivor who didn't feel empowered and blessed in the process of becoming healed. Most survivors find new friends, develop new skills, and learn the true depth and value of who they are.

- **Make a Plan**

  Although a health crisis can rock you to the core of your being, it's not the end, and you need to get a grip on how you perceive, talk about, and act on the situation so you don't run the risk of contributing to the problem instead of the solution. Remember that for every thought you have, there is a corresponding physiological response—in other words, you can "think yourself sicker" if you don't work toward accepting yourself and your new reality. This is not an end, it is a new beginning, and you can even use the momentum of change to address many other areas in your life that you've been wanting to work on for some time now.

  Now that you have more insight into what you believe in (or what you don't), you need to use that information to make a plan. The power of the mind is huge. For example, if you have a lot of self-confidence in your ability to exercise, talk to your doctor and get moving because working out can be one of the best things for both your mental and physical well-being. If you believe in healthy eating, clean up your diet. Toss out the fatty, sugary, highly processed foods and focus instead on vegetables, fruits, and lean meats (or find out the specific diet that can help your condition). If you don't know much about nutrition, go online and do some research or consult with an expert such as a nutritionist or weight loss coach.

  If you trust in the ability to be healed by your faith and spiritual beliefs, practice what you preach. Start going to your place of worship. Start praying as part of your plan to recover. There's plenty of well-known research showing that this helps both physically and mentally;[13] however, be careful that you don't become one dimensional because you want to avail yourself of all the legitimate modalities that could facilitate you or your loved one's return to health. If you believe that medicine is your number one weapon in your quest for health and healing, then see your doctor, find out what medicine you can take to assist your efforts, and make sure you stick to the plan.

The critical point here is again to practice what you believe. Now, if you don't believe in *anything*, you'll need to do some serious study to change that, and fast. Not having faith in anything may negatively affect your health. For example, if you don't think that your medicine is going to work, then you probably won't take it anyway.

If a loved one is sick, find out what they believe in and embrace it. Not only may it help that person get well, it may put you both on the same wavelength so you don't get irritated with each other. This may be tough, especially if you don't agree, but that's not what matters. You can try to influence thinking, but the point is not to convince your loved one what *you* believe; it's to "buddy up" to support whatever belief system your loved one feels can help them the most.

- **Create a Health Team**

Managing this challenging day of your life isn't something you should try to do on your own, and I'm betting you need the support of others to get you through and win this health battle. The key is to assemble a winning team, and that means making sure all the players are supportive, positive, and helpful. You need people you can trust and people who can energize and inspire you because there is strength and power in support. You'll come closer to reaching your health goals if you have friends, family members, coworkers, spiritual leaders, and doctors, among others, who lift you up. This is not a time to expend energy trying to convince negative friends to be positive—you need to break away from those who tend to sabotage you. People in your life will either contaminate or contribute to your health goals, and you need to first identify both types, then focus on partnering with the contributors.

This is important, because your relationships have a huge influence on your health—both your lifestyle choices and how you go forward in dealing with this health crisis. To get through it, those around you have to help lead you down the right road, not the wrong one. Avoid people who will sabotage you, whether they do it intentionally or not. Some of these people may not mean to do you harm; they may actually love and care about you. But unfortunately, that doesn't mean that what they do is in your best interest. Saboteurs can be anyone, from the friends who bring over a dozen donuts when you're supposed to be slimming down, to those who declare you're "no fun" when you no longer drink alcohol on girls' night out when you are trying to stay sober.

Some people may not want you to get better or change your habits because it affects their life. Maybe they like the fact that you rely on them while you're laid up in your hospital bed, or they're in a similar health crisis but aren't motivated to get out of it. As a result, they want to pull you down, too. There are also those who won't encourage you to change because, whether they realize it or not, they want you to keep the status quo—something that feels safer to them. For example, your spouse who is usually your couch potato partner in crime may resent the fact that you're spending time walking after dinner rather than downing his-and-her pints of ice cream while watching *Grey's Anatomy*.

After you kick the wrong people off your team, you need to recruit those who will help move you toward your goals. Here are four team members who I believe are indispensable, and if you take a look at the people already in your life, chances are good that you will find your team members among them. (If not, think outside of your immediate nucleus. Reach out to your spiritual network or look online for existing support groups in your area. If you cannot find one that suits your needs, why not start your own?)

First, there's the **Coach**—someone who has some professional expertise or training, such as your doctor, a nutritionist, physical therapist, psychologist, etc. These people give you practical help and information. They also have some positive power over you because they've got status as an authority figure. A coach can help you manage an illness or recover from an accident. He or she can give you information to help your sick loved one, too.

Next there's the **Teammate**—someone whose goals or issues are similar to yours. Maybe this is another wife whom you meet at the rehab center where your husband is recovering or a friend who is also trying to slim down. Having a companion who is focused on the same goal can help you stick with it. It's a lot easier to go to the gym when you know you'll have a friend to talk to while you walk on the treadmill or to go to support group meetings when you know you'll see a friendly face. You and your teammate can share ideas, compare notes, and monitor each other's behavior. Not only is this a natural motivator, but also it's nice to have someone who is in the same boat you are. You may be energized and inspired, and have someone to push you along on the tough days.

You also want to have a **Cheerleader** on your team—someone who encourages you and helps lift you up when you're down without being judgmental or critical. This person offers honest encouragement—he or she isn't telling you you're doing a great job even when you skip your medication or eat foods that are bad for you—but specializes in providing the inspiration and unconditional support that you need to believe in yourself.

Last, there's the **Umpire,** the person who will give you constructive criticism. They don't do it to be mean or harsh, they do it because they care and want you to reach your goals. The Umpire should be a good listener so you can share your true feelings and a good observer so you feel confident you're getting the right feedback. Usually, an Umpire excels at calling the shots as they are, and you need to respect this person's judgment enough to accept helpful criticism willingly. The point is that even if the Umpire is a bit tough, you don't need to get your warm and fuzzy support here—that comes from your **Cheerleader.**

The bottom line: be honest with yourself when it comes to people in your life. I admit it's not easy to cross some negative friends and family off your list, but in some cases it's crucial for your success. Remember: you come first, and you need a strong team to win.

- **Get Your Thinking Right**

  As I've said earlier, what you believe about yourself guides and directs your actions. So if you believe that you can't stick to a healthy diet to help ward off another heart attack, you're probably right. Then again, if you do truly believe that you can successfully do everything your doctor has advised, it's likely that you will succeed. If you tell yourself that you'll never recover from this accident or illness and that your life will never be the same, your thoughts may very well make it so. Why? Because what you tell yourself is directly related to your emotions, so you're likely to feel stressed, anxious, worried, or depressed. Unless you eliminate wrong thinking, it can gain momentum and take over. Think about it: after working so hard to make sure there are no saboteurs on your team, you don't want to discover that you're the weak link in your own plan.

  But if you change your thinking and beliefs, you may greatly improve your probability of overcoming your illness or disease. You can cope with a sick spouse or child. Know that your choices, attitudes, thoughts, and behaviors together can lead you to either a positive result or a negative one. This means that the answers to some of your health problems may well lie *within you,* and that's a good thing because it means you can control them.

- **Start Taking Better Care of Yourself Now**

  If you are in a crisis now, use this as a time to begin to focus on the aspects of your health that you can control. There *are* consequences to smoking, drinking, not exercising, and other such behaviors. That's the reality. Nobody gets out of this world alive, but there are things you can do to stay as healthy as possible while you're here.

If others are depending on you, it's even more critical to make sure you'll be there for them. Take this as a wake-up call to get your health act together and consider starting with one area first—exercise or nutrition. There are terrific programs everywhere to help you get into the habit of caring for yourself on a daily basis, and even if you can't put together a full team to support your efforts, you can always get help online. There you'll discover a whole host of free resources from daily calorie counting to logging your walking or jogging goals to articles that can help you fine-tune your efforts.

- **Focus on the Positive**

Though your life may be in turmoil, you have to find one positive thing in this health crisis. You may be rolling your eyes right now, but it's just too easy to say, "Poor me" or "How can this happen to me?"—an attitude that is certainly not going to improve your health. As bad as it is, let this experience be tuition in the education of your life. Maybe your legs don't work, but you appreciate how strong your mind is. Maybe your husband's sick, but this rough patch has brought you closer together.

One of the most positive things you can focus on is the day you happen to be living in. We are making such giant strides in medical technology that I tell anyone diagnosed with a disease to just *stay alive one more day*. Stay alive one more week, one more month. Something could happen in the medical labs that could change your prognosis in a major way. Stay alive today—something could happen tomorrow.

I recently went to an event with twenty-five community leaders at Cedars-Sinai Medical Center in Los Angeles, and I saw some "Star Wars technology" there that was unbelievable. I was stunned by what I saw. If they had had what they have today back when my father was dying in 1994, he would easily have had at least another ten years of life. It wouldn't have even been a close call—it would have been routine with the technology they have today. They didn't have it then, so he's gone.

But you're still here.

So I encourage you to simply stay alive another day. You do it a step at a time. By focusing on the good things—and there are *always* good things—you will set up a strong foundation to build on no matter what circumstances you find yourself in.

FINAL THOUGHT

No doubt, a health crisis makes your world a different place. But it's your response that will, for the most part, determine if it will simply sidetrack your life for a bit or throw it off course completely. And I'm certainly not saying that's fun. It's tough, it drains you, and it can be downright scary. So your best bet is to use this situation as a time to rethink some of the things you're doing and as permission to take a new direction. Learn from it, and take away whatever good you can—but the one thing you *shouldn't* do is let sickness or a physical breakdown become your life. Don't let a health crisis rob you of your identity and turn you or a loved one into a "patient" instead of a wife, mother, father, or friend.

Remember, crises don't make heroes, but they do cause people to be more of who they are. What is this crisis revealing about you? Your choices are important and empowering in a world that can feel out of control, so take ownership of your attitudes about your health and decide how you can best support your own long-term emotional and physical health plan.

8

Mental Health

The Day the Mind Breaks Down

The statistics on sanity are that one out of every four Americans is suffering from some form of mental illness. Think of your three best friends. If they're okay, then it's you.

—RITA MAE BROWN

Janette's parents, Paul and Ruby, had been married for forty-five years and were as much in love as newlyweds. When Ruby was diagnosed with cancer, she suffered a long and painful decline and Paul was with her through it all—the surgeries, the chemo, the hair loss, and misery. When she died, Paul lost his interest in life. After a year of intense grief, it looked as if he were moving forward—he went back to his work as an insurance salesman part-time, began spending more time with his friends at church, and even picked up his bowling ball again. He had always been a welcome addition to any gathering, someone you could depend on to make people laugh. But since Ruby died, he had not been acting like himself.

When Janette took her father to her cousin's wedding, she quickly regretted it. It was the first time she had been at a public event with her father since her mom had passed away. Throughout the reception, he seemed to be agitated and preoccupied with things she couldn't see. He would stop talking in midsentence, as if listening to something else. His eyes would squint, and he would nod and even laugh. He sought Janette out to ask with an intent look, "Can you hear the music, can you hear the songs?" As he wandered away, he grabbed a few grapes off a stranger's plate, ignoring the guest's startled response. Later, when he emerged from the restroom, he did not notice that his fly was unzipped or that his shirt was partially outside his pants. Janette was beyond embarrassed. She tried to pull him back toward the hallway, but he jerked his arm away and looked at her as if he didn't know her.

As the situation at the wedding worsened, Janette grew afraid. Paul's breathing began to quicken, and it was clear he was anxious and losing control. Suddenly, he grasped Janette's arm and started pulling her toward the door. "Let's get out of this place. There's no one here who gives a damn anyway." Driving home, Janette's mind was racing with thoughts as her dad rode beside her in silence. She got him home and made sure he had changed clothes and was safely in bed asleep before she left for her house. She cried the whole way home as she tried to make sense of what she had seen earlier, wondering what was happening to her father and what (if anything) she could do to help him. That night, Janette couldn't sleep as she finally accepted the possibility that her father, the person she relied on for guidance, was a changed man, maybe forever. She was filled with questions about what that meant and what might come next. *Was it a tumor? Was it Alzheimer's? Had he finally just snapped under the burden of grief from losing the love of his life?* Janette felt as lost as her father had seemed earlier in the day.

Down the Rabbit Hole

Situations like this occur every day in people's lives, and the greatest anguish often comes from the fear of the unknown. Or maybe instead of a loved one's world, it's *your* world that has just come tumbling down. You may feel as if someone has pulled the rug out from under you and there is no safe place to stand. Maybe it's hit you like a ton of bricks out of nowhere, or maybe you've been in denial for a while, but either way, you have finally come face-to-face with the realization that you or a loved one is in serious mental and emotional distress. If it is you, you may be filled with feelings of confusion, shame, guilt, and weakness, and I'm betting that you're asking yourself a million questions without having any answers: *What is going on here? Am I crazy? Am I having a nervous breakdown? Why can't anyone understand me? Why does everyone walk around me as if I didn't exist or act as though they're afraid of me? Am I weak for losing control? Is it curable? If I don't get better, will my family commit me to a mental institution? Or will I embarrass them by admitting I'm in trouble? Will I have to make that decision for a family member? Will people know I'm seeing a shrink? Will I lose my job? How will I ever face the people I know? Will they judge me and turn away from me? How bad can this get?*

I plan to answer these questions and more, but before we go any further, I want to address the way you and I need to think and talk about mental illness as we deal with this challenging day.

This chapter is not intended to be a comprehensive discussion on the broad and complex subject of mental illness as a whole, (about which volumes have been written on each of the scores of disorders). My goal instead, is to focus on certain examples of specific disorders that seem to traumatize and shut down people's lives with a significant and growing degree of frequency. The mental illnesses I have chosen to include are often marred by stigma and complicated by fear, confusion, and misinformation. There are, of course, many disorders that I am not addressing, such as sudden dementia, personality disorders, and other disruptive and life-altering mental illnesses. I certainly do not mean to ignore or trivialize those disorders, because all challenges you might face regarding mental health are important. However, the goal here is not to prepare you to be a psychologist or psychiatrist but instead to sensitize you to the challenges you may well face if this day comes into your life. Many of the points made regarding what to expect and the information on getting back to better days are relevant to most, if not all, challenges you may face in this area of life and can potentially be helpful in understanding and dealing with a long list of mental illnesses.

I want to demystify these examples of mental illnesses and maladjustments by discussing them in plain language rather than professional lingo, which can often be intimidating and misunderstood. I am *not* attempting to empower you to self-diagnose or to diagnose your loved ones. In the same way that you wouldn't operate on yourself if you thought you had a tumor, you shouldn't try to treat yourself for mental illness. Proper diagnosis is a complex process that needs to be done by skilled professionals. However, with some clear and understandable information and a degree of sensitivity, as opposed to denial, you may be able to recognize (hopefully early on) when a level of mental and emotional functioning has reached a point that calls for change and perhaps professional help.

The Scarlet Letter

In the last chapter, we looked at what happens when the body breaks down. As difficult or painful as a physical challenge can be, at least, for the most part, it can be identified and treated. But what do you do when your own mind seems to turn against you? I know the term "mental illness" is scary because it has always been associated with the other "C" word (crazy), but I want to strip away all the drama and ignorance right now so we can get to the truth about what it means to suffer from a mental disorder.

If you have a mental disorder—if you are depressed, anxious, confused, obsessive in your thinking, or compulsive in your behavior, or have difficulty differentiating reality from fantasy, you are not "crazy." You are not a second-class citizen. You do not have some inadequacy or spiritual deficiency that should cause you to be ashamed or to cower from dealing with or talking about this problem. Stop judging yourself and/or others with ideas and standards that have been proven false or are outdated or just plain ridiculous. The only way you're going to get yourself—or someone you love—through this challenge is first to get rid of the emotional baggage that clutters up the situation and paralyzes you at a time when you need to be dealing with the simple facts.

You are not a second-class citizen. You do not have some inadequacy or spiritual deficiency that should cause you to be ashamed or cower from dealing with or talking about this problem.

Although mental issues have been around as long as people have had brains to malfunction, it was only in the mid-1800s that mental illness finally began to be treated more humanely instead of as a mystical or evil state caused by witchcraft, demons, or the like. And believe me, if you fear judgment in today's "enlightened" society, be glad you weren't born a few generations ago, because you might have found that a trip to the mental institution actually meant being left to rot away and in some cases tortured. Thankfully, the work of early psychological reformers such as Dorothea Dix and Clifford Beers helped to raise awareness of the terrible plight of the mentally ill and establish regulations and facilities that resulted in more humane treatment.

The social stain and stigma attached to mental illness often causes *real* "desperate housewives" to secretly pop pills or have several happy hours a day, refusing to admit they are depressed or struggling. If you don't believe me, just think about the last time someone at a cocktail party or barbecue casually mentioned they were recently hospitalized for a bout with schizophrenia. Can't think of any? I didn't think so. On the other hand, they'll surely tell you about their sore back, gallstones, arthritis, and an endless list of other physical complaints. Clearly there is a huge difference in the stigma we place on mental versus physical diagnoses. To make matters worse, more and more people are trying to avoid having to deal with mental and emotional issues by putting on chemical straitjackets. The problem is that tranquilizers and antidepressants—although valuable tools in some cases—sometimes do little more than mask the problem and allow us to keep running away from it. Here's a story that still amazes me: The famous composer George Gershwin saw a psychiatrist for years because of his depression before he died of a brain tumor.

Doctors had dismissed any biological cause of his depression because he spent so much time talking about his childhood and his mother. After he died, it was clear that the brain tumor was the cause—something no amount of psychotherapy could have remedied on its own.

Let me be very clear here: I'm not putting down appropriately prescribed medications, particularly when they are utilized in conjunction with appropriate individual, couples, family, or group therapy. I'm also not putting down psychiatrists, because they are among the most highly qualified, compassionate, and caring professionals I have had the honor of knowing and working with. What I *am* criticizing are pill pushers who take the easy way out rather than really digging into and getting involved in helping a patient learn to overcome or deal with mental illness. What I am doing here is calling for careful, thorough assessment and good judgment in determining which therapeutic modalities should be utilized. Mental problems are complex, and answers are rarely simple. You deserve nothing less for yourself or your loved one and should not settle for anything short of such care.

In some cases, when an expert can diagnose *appropriately*, medication might be the only way to impact the brain in the needed fashion. Those who adhere to the medical model of mental illness would agree that all the talking therapies in the world will never get any traction until brain balance is restored. The treatment team may be a multidisciplinary one, including medical as well as psychological and other professionals working together to stabilize any biological factors, create psychological control, and begin the process of clarifying the stressors, whether they are thinking errors, social pressures, or other issues. Failure to acknowledge and treat the important physiological issues can mean you are building a house on sand with talking therapies. You want to do everything you can to ensure that your thoughts, feelings, and behaviors are voluntary and not an involuntary reaction to biological imbalances.

So this just may be the day when you're faced with the uneasy truth that it's not everyone else who has changed but you. It's *your* mind that has stopped doing its job and—whatever the specifics—you realize there's something seriously wrong. Lately, you may have felt that you have been "off" in your thinking and in your ability to navigate the twists and turns of a typical day. You may be overly anxious or seem to be experiencing a disconnect in your mental processing somewhere. You may find yourself thinking strange thoughts and are unsure of where they're coming from. You might not know exactly what the problem is, but you *do* know you're losing your grip and you need to do something to stop this "emotional hemorrhage" and turn it around before it begins to destroy areas of your life. It may have already started to affect your relationships or job, or you might be on the verge of coming unhinged. Or maybe it's not you—it's your favorite aunt who has started the heartbreaking mental decline that comes with Alzheimer's disease—and you feel helpless watching her leave you, piece by piece.

It's time to talk about ways to deal with the day you realize that mental illness has found its way into your life or the life of someone close to you and the biggest question on your mind is, *What is this thing I am dealing with?*

Whether it is physical or mental, one of the greatest reliefs I have seen with patients undergoing this type of life struggle is when they get an answer—when they hear a diagnosis or at least a treatable scenario, there can be a beginning of hope. Although I don't believe in labels being thrown around irresponsibly, giving your problems a name can give you power over them in several ways. It takes away the unknown, which is almost always scary in its ambiguity. Of course we want to be told that everything is going to be okay. But even if the news is anything except what you wanted to hear, once the truth is known you can begin formulating a strategy to deal with it. Being in the dark and/or hanging in limbo is seldom, if ever, preferable to the truth. "Knowing" in some way conveys a sense that it can be dealt with. It also gives the assurance that this is not totally unique and that other people have gone before you toward safety and wellness. There is almost always comfort in knowing that powerful others, such as doctors and therapists, spiritual leaders and advisers have dealt with your dilemma before and that you are not alone and not a freak.

In this chapter, I want to speak to you in plain terms about this important subject that has historically been locked up in thousand-page diagnostic manuals so complicated that you need the Rosetta Stone to interpret them. Let's move this discussion to a practical level and continue to break the silence and the shame once and for all.

WHAT IS A MENTAL HEALTH BREAKDOWN?

Although there are no simple answers and certainly no single causes of the many and varied forms of mental illness, most experts agree that triggers for mental instability include biological factors such as hormonal imbalances; fatigue and/or lack of sleep; exposure to toxic environments, genetic dispositions that we inherit, and the numerous social and psychological stressors that we are forced to react to throughout our lives.[1] These are only the minimum number of considerations when evaluating a case, as there are always variations—sometimes in very complex combinations. An imbalance or disruption in any of these areas—such as a stressful life event, emotional upheaval, or even a change of medication—can result in far-reaching consequences. For some people, tendencies toward mental illness have already come packed in your family's DNA baggage. Just as certain people are genetically predisposed to being overweight or to being an alcoholic, others are predisposed to mental illness. In fact, my own family has struggled with mental disorders on both sides.

But in order to deal with mental dysfunction, you have to identify it or at least understand it enough to talk to yourself about it. I have received so many letters over the years from people asking whether or not some pattern of conduct or behavior is "normal." I read these letters pretty much thinking that whoever's writing them has decided that the conduct in question is *not* normal or they wouldn't be asking. Nonetheless, I almost always give the same answer, and it's this: if a pattern of conduct or behavior is disrupting your flow of life or keeping you from healthy goals, I consider it to be abnormal. If a pattern of conduct or behavior is "quirky" or in some way atypical but it does not interfere with your life or pursuit of healthy goals and objectives, then, by definition, I would consider it normal regardless of how idiosyncratic or even eccentric it might appear to others. I say this with the qualification that the person is not dangerous to themselves or others. On the other hand, narcissistic personalities, sociopaths, and mental, physical, or emotional abusers are not what I'd call "quirky" or eccentric. Because, while they may believe that their lives are "working" just fine, and may appear to be quite happy, their impact on others is *not* okay. If they are sick and damaging to themselves and others, it is appropriate to call for help.

The psychiatrist William Glasser's basic model for good mental health is this:

> You are mentally healthy if you enjoy being with most of the people you know, especially with the important people in your life such as family, sexual partners, and friends. Generally you are happy and are more than willing to help an unhappy family member, friend, or colleague to feel better. You lead a mostly tension-free life, laugh a lot, and rarely suffer from the aches and pains that so many people accept as an unavoidable part of life. You enjoy life and have no trouble accepting other people who think and act differently from you. It rarely occurs to you to criticize or try to change anyone. If you have differences with someone else you will try to work out the problem; if you can't, you will walk away before you argue and increase the difficulty. You are creative in what you attempt and may enjoy more of your potential then you ever thought possible. Finally, even in very difficult situations when you are unhappy (no one can be happy all the time), you will know why you are unhappy and attempt

to do something about it. You may even be physically handicapped and still fit the criteria above.[2]

The gist is that no matter what gets thrown at you in the short or long haul, you're able to deal with it and move on at some point. The problems I'm addressing here come when—for whatever reason—you *can't* or *aren't* dealing with it.

When "Speeding up" Results in Breaking Down

As I said in chapter three, no one would deny that life has become more complex in recent times, especially in terms of our all-access pass to information and technology. The metrics of life have changed dramatically in the last few decades, and we have become a generation addicted to stimulation.

But it all comes at a price. The faster pace of life creates a higher demand on you and me, which can mean that we become susceptible to breaking down under the load. It's not much different from the classic scene from the old *I Love Lucy* show where Lucy and Ethel got jobs wrapping chocolates in a factory. Everything was going along fine until the conveyor belt began speeding up, and the two panicked as they tried to keep up with the candies that were suddenly rolling by at an all-too-rapid pace. Since they wouldn't get paid if they dropped any, the chocolates that didn't make it into the wrappers ended up in their pockets, hats, and mouths—and ultimately on the floor in a big candy mess. This may have made for great TV, but in real life, it's not so funny. Some people thrive on frenzy, but for most of us, we can get overloaded.

Blowing Up the Myths

Despite the increasing numbers of people suffering from some kind of mental disorder,[3] the truth is that you will face some judgments if you happen to be one of them. There's just not enough public awareness of the facts surrounding mental illness for people to be comfortable with the subject. A recent survey reported by the National Mental Health Association (NMHA)* revealed that most people still hold outdated and incorrect beliefs about mental illness. This would explain why, for the most part, sufferers hide their personal struggles and are afraid to confide in others for fear of alienation or other consequences.

Of those surveyed:[4]

- 71 percent believed mental illness is caused by emotional weakness.
- 65 percent believed mental illness is caused by bad parenting.
- 35 percent believed mental illness is caused by sinful or immoral behavior.
- 43 percent believed mental illness is brought on in some way by the individual.

Five Myths about Mental Illness[5]

Myth 1: People who are mentally ill are dangerous or violent.

Reality: Although there are extreme cases where sufferers have reported being guided by voices to hurt themselves or others, the vast majority are nonviolent. In fact, those suffering from mental illness are two and a half times more likely to be the victims of crime, rather than the perpetrators.[6]

Myth 2: People who have a mental disorder are less intelligent than those who don't.

Reality: Mental illness affects people regardless of intelligence, social status, education, or income, and frequently afflicts those of average or above average intelligence. Some of America's greatest

* NMHA has since changed its name to Mental Health America (MHA.)

writers, scientists, musicians, and politicians suffered from mental illness even as they were making extraordinary contributions to our history and culture.

Myth 3: Most mentally ill people end up poor and on the streets because they can't hold a job.

Reality: Every day, people manage mental dysfunction. Most hold jobs, raise kids, have relationships, and involve themselves in their communities and churches.

Myth 4: People with a mental illness have some kind of character deficiency or moral weakness.

Reality: Mental disorders have nothing to do with character, weakness, or lack of willpower—it simply may be a sign that coping abilities have broken down that need to be addressed and brought back into full working order. This can result from external stress and social pressures or a biological dysfunction (organic/internal source) that needs to be balanced and restored.

Myth 5: Mental illness is a life sentence.

Reality: Many mental disorders can be treated effectively through programs, support plans and, if necessary, medication. The most important step is to acknowledge that there is a problem so that you can get the help needed.

So that's what mental illness *isn't*. Unfortunately, it's not quite as simple to nail down what it *is*.

WHAT TO EXPECT

An initial clue for you that something may be mentally off course is inappropriate behavior in social settings. As things start to snowball, differences often become more pronounced and "inconvenience" can turn into "disruption." People around the "mentally ill" person may start to pull away in fear and begin to judge them with labels.

If you believe that you or someone you love is "falling apart," having a "breakdown," or simply "going off the deep end," there are hundreds of diagnoses that can be assigned to you. Such labels may help by identifying the specific challenges to be expected, but the same labels may also have a negative "pigeonholing" effect (in no small part for insurance purposes), which can sometimes result in failing to recognize individual differences and needs. Having said all of that, basically the problems that you or a loved one are experiencing are likely to fall under one of the three major categories of mood disturbances, anxiety disorders, or more severe disorders that are generally classified as psychoses. I say this based on the preponderances of occurrences reported by the National Institute of Mental Health[7] and the categories of symptoms defined by the American Psychiatric Association in the *Diagnostic and Statistical Manual of Mental Disorders*, Fourth Edition (DSM-IV).[8]

Mood Disturbances

The psychological term for exaggerated emotional states that interfere with our mental well-being and ability to function is "mood disturbances." If you are experiencing a mood disturbance, your emotions may seem out of your control and magnified to the point that they overwhelm your abilities to cope with usual life demands. If you are hitting emotional walls, such as feeling deep, aching sadness, loss of self-esteem, and chronic emptiness, the clinical term for the extenuating low state you may be experiencing is called "depression." On the other end, an extremely high emotional period, marked by unmanageable excitement and/or irritation, is referred to as a "manic episode." If you fluctuate between the two extreme emotions, your diagnosis might be termed "bipolar."

Of these two extreme emotional disturbances, depression is by far the most dominant and common complaint. In fact, according to the World Health Organization, depression is one of the leading causes of disability in the United States and worldwide. I'm telling you all this because I want you or the person you are concerned about to understand that you are not even *almost* alone.

"Normal" versus Clinical Depression

In my years of experience, I have often dealt with people who didn't even realize they were depressed until they *weren't*. Think about it: if the only car you'd ever driven was a tiny '58 Volkswagen with a broken heater and no suspension, one ride behind the wheel of a new, smooth-driving luxury Buick with a GPS and heated seats would wake you up in a hurry to what you'd been missing.

I have often dealt with people who didn't even realize they were depressed until they *weren't*.

So how do you know if you are clinically depressed?

Here's the deal. It is not unusual to have a "down day" here and there or even a week where you experience unexplained sadness or "the blues" due to any combination of factors, especially if stress is in the picture. Most people would agree that life isn't always a bed of roses, and many things can happen to frustrate or frighten us, causing us to have to adapt to new demands and/or change. Everyone handles crises and stressful life events differently, making it difficult to tell where your own threshold is until you've crossed it.

So where is the line between your garden-variety blues and more serious forms of depression?

"Down days" may become "depression" when they begin to *chronically* interfere with your life—impacting you in a really negative way, and/or keep you from accomplishing what you want to accomplish. Normal periods of sadness are generally time-limited and usually have a cause. But if your mental, emotional, and physical energy has dropped down to first gear and stayed that way for an extended period of time, such as weeks or even months, then chances are that you're depressed and need to do something about it. You're the best barometer. Let common sense be your guide. If it's really grinding you down, then you might need to seek help.

What Causes Depression?

Stress has consistently been linked to depression (with some studies showing that as many as 50 percent of people being diagnosed with depression have experienced severe stress beforehand.)[9] It is unclear which came first, the chicken or the egg. Does stress cause depression, or is depression a stressor that generates stress reactions within the body? I suspect there is some truth to each alternative since each situation is different. What matters is that they often occur together, which is important in planning an effective intervention. Clearly, as I have already discussed, it is very important to be attentive to the stressors in your life and to realize how you may be vulnerable to allowing stress to convert to depression and vice versa. For example, certain medical conditions can trigger depression. Research has shown that physical changes in the body can be accompanied by mental changes as well and might be linked to some biological reasons for depression.[10] For example, up to 20 to 25 percent of individuals with diabetes, myocardial infarction, carcinoma, and stroke will develop severe depression during the course of the condition. Heart attacks, Parkinson's disease, and hormonal disorders can also cause depression, making the sick person apathetic and the recovery process longer.[11]

Some depression is strictly biological (or endogenous), meaning that it comes from the inside out rather than being reactive to something in your life or environment. For example, hormonal changes can cause postpartum depression in new moms or depression in postmenopausal women, as can a thyroid problem or chemical imbalance for some people. And if any of your chemicals are out of balance, you can bet you'll be feeling that way too.

Some confusion often occurs with how this term differs from exogenous depression. Just for clarification, exogenous depression is an inappropriate mood state that you would expect as the result of a life event, such as an exaggeration of sadness from the death of someone you care about or an unhealthy and perhaps prolonged reaction to a career setback.

How It Feels: Life, Interrupted

There's a reason it's called the "pit" of depression—in severe cases you may feel as if you've tumbled down into a blackness so thick you can feel it and you're bumping off the sides, reaching out into nothing, sure you'll never see the sun again. You may feel like screaming because of how alone and cut off from life you feel. You also may be thinking a stream of thoughts that you don't want anyone else to hear: *Why can't I stop crying? I hate myself—I hate my life, and I don't even know why I hurt so bad. On the outside things are better than they've ever been—I've got a great job, a new house, my spouse is terrific with the kids, and I know they love me . . . but somehow, on the inside, I can't feel any of it. I snap at my children and I don't feel like being romantic with my spouse. I feel so guilty for feeling so negligent and so hopeless. I don't know what to do—I don't want to go to some doctor who will charge me $200 to diagnose me with something I don't want—or worse, tell me that I'm totally fine, so what in the world is my problem? I know I need help, but I have no clue where to start.*

One of the confounding aspects of depression that may keep you from reaching out for help is just plain apathy. People usually think the opposite of passion is sadness and avoidance, but in truth it is more like apathy. This depression marked by apathy is full of feeling empty, disengaged, and disconnected. When you have withdrawn your feelings to the point of being apathetic about your life and everything and everyone in it, you don't cry, you don't laugh—you are just numb. This may be one of the most difficult parts of depression because it makes itself worse. The more apathetic you are, the less you try, the less things you try means your chance of creating any needed "currency" is diminished. With less reward, you can sink deeper and deeper into depression and the apathy that often comes with it.

If it's a loved one who is depressed, you may see them withdraw and seem to be lost in their own world. They may be sad, lethargic, and unable to find any relief from their pain, making you feel even more separated and helpless.

Watching others struggle can be hard to understand, especially if you've never experienced serious depression yourself and you're wondering why they can't just "get over it." On paper, your friend, husband, or daughter's world seems fine—yet they're still overwhelmed with sadness. Your best friend never leaves her home anymore and no longer calls you "just to say hi." Your husband is uninterested in playing ball with the kids, going out to dinner, or having sex. Your daughter stopped hanging out with her friends, sleeps whenever she can get a chance, and doesn't want to go on any family outings. You can't seem to connect with them and feel that you are outside their reality, unable to get in.

Since their mental struggles are affecting your life, it's not surprising that you may alternate between feeling angry and resentful rather than compassionate and caring. Although you are concerned, it can get really annoying that your husband just lies in bed all weekend rather than helping with the yard work or paying bills. Not only do you feel bad that he's so down, but also that he leaves you having to carry much more of the load around the house and with the family. And then, of course, the addition of self-guilt complicates everything, because how can you be mad at someone who is so sad? It's hard to know what to expect if you don't understand depression or how much is too much.

Warning Signs of Suicide

Although women are almost twice as likely as men to suffer from depression,[12] *men are two to four times more likely to commit depression-based suicide.*[13] *Even so, there is no "typical" suicide victim. It happens to young and old, sick and well, rich and poor, and some people certainly take their own lives without overtly displaying typical warning signs while others may display the signs and not ever act on them. Fortunately, according to the National Suicide Prevention Lifeline, there are some common "red flags" that may help alert you to the fact that you or someone you love is at risk.*

These include:

- *Threatening to hurt or kill oneself or talking about wanting to hurt or kill oneself*
- *Looking for ways to kill oneself by seeking access to firearms, available pills, or other means*
- *Talking or writing about death, dying, or suicide when these actions are out of the ordinary for the person*
- *Feeling hopeless*
- *Feeling rage or uncontrolled anger or seeking revenge*
- *Acting reckless or engaging in risky activities, seemingly without thinking*
- *Feeling trapped, like there's no way out*
- *Increasing alcohol or drug use*
- *Withdrawing from friends, family, and society*
- *Feeling anxious, agitated, or unable to sleep, or sleeping all the time*
- *Experiencing dramatic mood changes*
- *Seeing no reason for living or having no sense of purpose in life**

To be clear. I am not suggesting that just one or two of these signs means that you are at risk. The risk factor goes back to the original meaning of what I consider "abnormal." Are any of these examples detrimental to a person's ability to function in life and achieve his or her life goals? The more specific the problem is, the easier it is to resolve it. However, it is usually an accumulation of factors that keeps you stuck in a quagmire of confusion that only professional guidance can get through to the basic problems.

**National Suicide Prevention Lifeline. What Are the Warning Signs for Suicide? http://www.suicidepreventionlifeline.org/helo/warning_signs.aspx (accessed June 27, 2008).*

The Other Side of Depression

As I mentioned above, the term for mood swings that include both depression and mania is referred to as "bipolar disorder," which is just the way it sounds: "bi" meaning "two" and "polar" referring to the extreme poles of mood. During mania you might experience a period of intense, "euphoric" highs where you feel indestructible, talk faster than usual, have an overinflated self-esteem, racing thoughts, and/or have more energy than usual but need less sleep. Sometimes mania can be dangerous, putting you out of touch with reality and producing agitated thoughts and behaviors that can lead to impulsive spending or gambling, rash decisions, and risky substance use and/or sexual behavior.

If you experience similar symptoms that are less severe, this would be called "hypomania." Hypomanias are milder forms of mania that may not last as long. They usually do not require hospitalization, and people experiencing hypomania do not go to the dangerous extremes that a fully manic person would go to. This mood state is also characterized by agitated thoughts and behavior, but there is a lower degree of impact on functioning. You may have the greatest desire to act out, but you know the consequences. Nevertheless, you still have an intensity of mood elevation that can cause huge levels of frustration internally, especially if decisions are made based on impaired judgement or the over inflated sense of self confidence that a hypomanic episode can bring.

The range of moods in bipolar disorder is a very real problem that affects many people, but you have to be careful because this label has become somewhat overused in recent history and is sometimes inappropriately assigned. For example, the broad mood swings that typically occur in adolescence can sometimes be mistaken for this diagnosis, as can mood shifts in women that often occur in association with hormonal changes.

Leah's Story

Leah woke up in a sweat as the sound of banging on her apartment door made its way into her brain. The phone started ringing, and at the beep of the answering machine she heard Kaelyn's voice, anxious and irritated. Her friend was calling on her cell from the other side of the door, wondering why she wasn't ready for their Saturday tennis match—for the third time this month. Leah squeezed her eyes shut—how had she forgotten it again? How had it gotten to be Saturday so soon? What had happened to Friday? *Why was she such a screw-up???* Things were getting harder to juggle—everything had crashed to a stop, and even the smallest tasks took so much energy. She hadn't touched the laundry in weeks, and her place was looking as if it had been hit by a tornado—her belongings were as scattered and twisted as the thoughts in her head.

It was starting again. She had been avoiding her mom's calls, and things at work were starting to get a little shaky, too. She had run out of sick days, and recently her coworkers had started acting strangely around her, as though they no longer saw her as a valued member of the team. As the knocking on the door continued, she felt bad about what she was doing and thought for a second about getting up, but instead she pulled the covers over her head. She couldn't do it—just couldn't talk herself into getting up despite her deep shame over hiding from her friend. Finally the noise outside stopped. She only wished she could stop the noise *inside* her head as easily. But ignoring it was only making everything worse.

What's more, it wasn't always like this—Leah cycled in and out of these extremes, and when things were good, for a while they were *really* good. When she was "on the rise," she was the darling of her company, working lots of overtime and churning out amazing amounts of work—*quality* work. She was a star, leading discussions and offering insights that marked her as someone who really understood the marketing business. She felt brilliant, filled with enormous energy and intelligence, and able to play and party just as hard as she worked. Every day would bring more excitement, and Leah felt like she had it all.

And then everything would speed up into a jumble of broken thoughts and frenzied activities. Something would snap, and she would continue to spiral upward, as if some regulator on her mind were broken, sending her veering dangerously out of control. Her speech would get faster and more fragmented. She would have to repeat things and explain them until they didn't even make sense to *her.* And then, inevitably, it would shift again. Like Cinderella at the ball, a clock would strike and Leah's world would collapse. Her glorious achievements would all deflate, and everything would unravel. Her crashes would leave her unable to get out of bed for days at a time, while she let missed calls pile up like the dishes in her sink.

After years of denial and suffering from the judgment of others who thought she was "not living up to her potential," Leah finally decided to take charge of her own recovery, doing some research and working with her doctor to come up with a plan that was right for her. In addition to medication, she began an exercise program, made better food choices, and became more careful about how much sleep she was getting. The bipolar mood swings that had once left her in an exhausted heap evened out to a manageable lifestyle. She went on to share her success with others through a play she wrote on mental health challenges that has helped many people face their own issues and get help. Looking back, she believes that God allowed her darkest hour to be turned into one of her greatest strengths, which is offering hope to others that they, too, can take back control of their lives.

You will find more information about some of the types of mood disorders in Appendix B and more information about some common warning signs of depression in Appendix C.

Anxiety Disorders

In psychological language, anxiety is a broad category of emotions that covers incapacities due to extreme apprehension, fearfulness, terror, and intense dread. Some anxiety is a natural part of life—all of us experience "the jitters" or a "case of the nerves" now and then, especially before major steps in our lives like getting married, the first day at a new job, having a baby, or watching the kids go off to college. The difference is that if you are an individual with an anxiety *disorder* you feel this way a vast amount of the time. You might even be afraid of everyday activities such as leaving the house to go to work or the grocery store. It's not a passing phase. You can spend so much energy on your anxiety that you lose many opportunities to experience peace and joy.

Can you imagine what kind of stress and associated drain that kind of ongoing arousal puts on your body—to be in "fight-or-flight" mode all the time? As I discussed in the stress chapter, this can result in a very unhealthy physical reality. If you are one of the 40 million Americans whom the National Institute of Mental Health[14] reports to be suffering from an anxiety disorder, that could be exactly what is happening to your body and therefore your defenses. Your adrenal system (which underlies your arousal) is probably burning itself up, because your body is continually fighting enemies that may not even exist in a war that isn't really going on, except in your own mind. To spend time and energy worrying over things that never come to pass, or to experience a disproportionate level of fear in the absence of any clear and present danger, is worse than nonproductive—it is downright destructive. Because anxiety is such an ongoing, continuous, and gnawing distress with little in the way of true threats or facts to support it, people in this state often wind up spending precious and needed resources with no gain. The worst part is that the actual dreaded consequence never has to happen to cause damage because your internal reaction to the anticipation is enough to leave a life of physical and emotional ruin in its wake.

Anxiety versus Fear

I do want to state the obvious here in saying that fear is not always a bad thing if it is rational. As we discussed earlier, there are differences between rational and irrational fears. Rational fears are those based on a reality that may cause us real harm. We need to have a certain level of awareness and vigilance to keep ourselves protected in day-to-day situations.

For example, every time you get behind the wheel of a car, especially on a crowded highway, a healthy dose of arousal and increased awareness can serve you quite well. There is sometimes good reason to listen to your instincts as a natural signal to pay attention and go into protection mode. Too many crimes have been committed because people did not heed their sense of intuitive, rational fear.

Anxiety is experienced by everyone at some point and is considered a natural aspect of mental functioning. As I have said earlier, mental arousal can have a beneficial impact and anxiety can be part of that process. In contrast, anxiety becomes a disorder when you become trapped at the higher arousal levels and your control mechanisms are overwhelmed. There are many categories of this trap, which will be dealt with. What I want you to understand is that the disorder starts when you fear something that, while not neccessarily totally imagined or based in fantasy, can't be easily identified or agreed upon by others as being at the perceived threat level. Many times the objects associated as a trigger to anxiety are objectively identified as fears of events that have a much lesser probability of happening and yet they still cause mental arousal, hypervigilance, or nervousness. For example, you might fear snakes crawling around in your bed (which is not so rare among children after they have seen a scary movie with snakes in people's beds). If you were spending the night in a jungle village somewhere, that might be more reasonable. But when such a fear exists with no stimuli, it may be an issue. For example, if you are lying in your bed in the middle of an American suburb and are still too frightened to go to sleep, you have an irrational fear that is likely of clinical significance. Many of our irrational fears become embedded in childhood with messages, either verbal or behavioral, intended or otherwise, from adult power figures or from uncomfortable situations that can play upon us because we are so vulnerable to irrational logic at that time in our young lives.

Some anxiety may be the result of a childhood incident or trauma such as sexual or physical abuse. As a child, you may not report what's going on or talk about it because the mind tries to protect you and verbalizing it is just too traumatic. If you're young enough you don't have the language to understand the meaning of what's happened.

Anxiety can be attached to *anything*, however illogical it may seem later. A child may have been insecure about a highly unstable family situation, but rather than acknowledge any of that she may have associated her fear with birds or dogs or doorknobs. However, twenty years later, when she is an adult entering into her own family situation, the painful memory of her insecurities may emerge in various ways to disrupt the peace of her new marriage and relationships.

Although they are frequently related, I want to make clear that neither anxiety nor depression are always connected with or a product of stress. However, high levels of stress can lead to either of the disorders. As I discussed in chapter three, stress is the body reacting to the pressures (or stressors) of life—which, for the most part, are quite real and verifiable—for example, typical changes in your marriage or job, caring for a sick child, dealing with financial troubles, etc. On the other hand, anxiety isn't necessarily connected to a verifiable threat, trigger, or stressor, and, more importantly, the irrational focus on the "threat" can often overwhelm you and make you feel as if you have no control over your emotions. With stress, other people besides you can see the problems. The difference with anxiety is that you may be the only one who sees the threat or at least the level of threat to which you are responding.

The Many Faces of Anxiety Disorder

Another form of anxiety is post-traumatic stress disorder (PTSD), when a traumatic event creates memories that invade your state of mental health with overriding anxiety. These memories take away your sense of joy and harmony. You often hear this happening with war veterans who experience horrific events. Months or years after they're removed from the situation, something happens to trigger that event and the anxiety comes roaring through. For example, a soldier in the Iraq War comes home from his tour of duty and seems to be fine. But then one day he's walking down the street and hears a car backfire. Suddenly he's back in Iraq with guns going off all around him. He falls down to the ground and panics, looking for the enemy who fired at him even though he's thousands of miles from any danger. If the soldier maintains this associated fear in his everyday reality, he might lose touch with the current reality and can become quite dangerous. There have been cases in which an individual has grabbed a gun and started shooting at people—like their friends and family—whom they have mistaken for the enemy.

Obsessive-compulsive disorder (OCD) is considered another form of anxiety disorder, characterized by recurrent, unwanted thoughts (obsessions) and/or repetitive behaviors (compulsions). Repetitive behaviors, such as handwashing, counting, checking, or cleaning are often performed with the hope of preventing obsessive thoughts or making them go away. Performing these so-called "rituals" provides only temporary relief, and not performing them markedly increases anxiety. The anxiety may be triggered by persistent, unwelcome thoughts or images, or even by the lack of opportunities or barriers to engage in specialized rituals that may have become so important in the attempt to cope with anxiety and fears. You may be filled with doubts and feel the need to check things repeatedly, such as whether or not you turned off the iron or stove when you left home.

Although most of us indulge in odd behaviors and don't think twice about it—whether it's knocking on wood, avoiding cracks in the sidewalk, or even hitting the elevator button twelve times when you know it only takes once to register, OCD sufferers differ in that these irrational behaviors take over and stop them from living a normal life. For example, if you were raised by a parent who made you feel stupid because you couldn't keep your bathroom clean, you may have translated that disapproval of your habits into a personal sense of being inadequate or unworthy. Whenever there is a trigger of that emotion in your adult life, you might engage in some obsessive-compulsive pattern of thought and behavior as a temporary relief of your anxiety. In this case, it might mean cleaning your bathroom seventy times a day or washing your hands until you bleed. By internalizing this critical voice of your parent, you may believe you're finding ways to resolve the overwhelming anxiety. Not finding long-term relief, the behavior itself becomes magnified. In other words, the more you clean the bathtub or wash your hands, the more anxious you become in the long run.

Phobias are anxiety disorders that affect approximately 36 million Americans* in one form or another. These persistent and irrational fears cause an emotional and physical response to perceived external threats, such as apprehensions about certain events or circumstances, that have no basis or logic. It's unclear how they start, and there's no rhyme or reason for why you feel this way. They often develop in adulthood. Sometimes phobias or OCD compulsions are small and don't impact your life much—like the actor Harrison Ford's need to color-code his socks or the soccer star David Beckham's habit of meticulously arranging the soda cans in his refrigerator. Rituals like these don't affect the overall quality or direction of life and may even come across as quirky and endearing.

Then there are people who will walk the stairs to their office on the thirty-seventh floor because there's not a chance in a million that they'll get into an elevator. The phobia can be so strong that trying to get them into an elevator would be like trying to

*This number is an aggregate of the numbers associated with three types of Phobias; Social Phobia, Agoraphobia (without a history of Panic Disorder), and Specific Phobia, as reported by the *Diagnostic and Statistical Manual of Mental Disorders* (DSM-IV).

put a cat in a bucket. It just isn't going to happen without a big fight! Or those whose careers require heavy travel, but rather than taking a plane, they drive from city to city. John Madden drives all over the country to cover a football game rather than set foot on an airplane. The game show host Howie Mandel has both OCD and mysophobia (a fear of germs) that he jokes about openly. Although it probably doesn't matter much that he doesn't shake hands with his show's contestants, it may be problematic at some point that he won't use any other bathroom but his own. In these cases, while not completely unmanageable, a phobia has begun to interfere—to varying degrees—with their quality of life.

You will find more information about some of the types of disorders related to anxiety in Appendix B and more information about some common warning signs of anxiety disorders in Appendix C.

Severe Mental Disorders

These disorders, often referred to as psychosis, include the range of problems involving both reality testing and thought disorders. This broad definition describes mental illnesses characterized by impairments in the perception of reality, most commonly observed as auditory hallucinations, paranoid or bizarre delusions, or disorganized speech and thinking interfering significantly with the social or occupational life of an individual. Often individuals with these disorders cannot judge reality with any objective means and react abnormally, such as using strange language and using other identifications for themselves. When observed, these symptoms often lead to misunderstandings about the person exhibiting the symptoms—who might be stigmatized as "dangerous" or "aggressive."

Probably the largest, the most feared, and the most misunderstood of these diagnoses is categorized within the broad term "schizophrenia." Despite the fact that the word schizophrenia translates roughly as "splitting of the mind," it is not the same as multiple personality disorder, referred to by clinicians as dissociative identity disorder.

Dissociative identity disorder is actually a rare condition that falls under an anxiety category known as dissociative disorders and involves several actual, distinct, and separate personalities within one person; whereas schizophrenia, or "split personality," is related to *disjointedness* in the personality (where you might be crying at the same time that you are telling a funny joke). Both of these terms have crept into common everyday language and are often confused and misused—leading to unhelpful reactions by oneself and others. Most people use these terms to describe behavior that is erratic or inconsistent or broad mood swings, but this is factually incorrect and most people don't know what they mean when they say it.

If you suffer in this category, you may be unable to separate reality from fantasy—for example, you might see imaginary bugs crawling onto your feet and/or hear voices telling you to harm yourself or someone else. Or you may believe that you can't trust people and that anyone who likes you must be up to no good. You also may have constant suspicions or mental torment that you can't explain or overcome—such as believing that someone is poisoning your food or that the government is spying on you (which actually may not be such a bizarre thought these days). These types of hallucinations can be very distressing, and it is not uncommon for people who are experiencing psychosis to physically injure themselves in attempts to escape the hallucinations or delusions that are plaguing them. In a *USA Today* interview,[15] actor Alan Alda discussed writing about his mother's lifelong struggle with psychosis, stating, "I got a much greater understanding of what she went through—especially the idea that her hallucinations took place in the same part of her brain that all of our nightmares take place. I have experienced what she went through, except I could wake up from it, and she never could."

What has often been intriguing and informative to me over the years is not just the presence of voices but, more specifically, the *messages* of thoses voices that helped to accurately diagnose this particular mental illness. You or your loved one are likely suffering from this if the voices are telling you to do things that are either self-destructive or distructive to others. Examples can be found in many high-profile crimes and stories, such as the mom who drowned her children because Satan was telling her to do so. But if the voices are telling you positive steps, they are considered, more often than not, to be from a higher power. After all, many of our religious leaders openly proclaim to have heard "the voice of God," and this has led to very positive results in their lives and in the lives of others and is in no way regarded as evidence of mental illness.

What Causes This Type of Mental Illness?

These symptoms have often been linked to a chemical imbalance of dopamine,[16] but there are other factors. In fact, under certain conditions, such as extreme fatigue and a highly stressed environment, it's likely that most people would get into this type of a psychotic state. One example was a patient who I will call "Kaye," who was referred to a colleague of mine with the diagnosis of schizophrenia. But when he interviewed her, it seemed more likely that her behavior was related to a high stress level that she had experienced in the last five years, when she had been living in a commune. During that time, she had been given unhealthy garbage to eat, had slept very little, and had been subjected to constant abuse. The goal of the commune's leaders was to get her to conform to their rules, and the daily abuse reaped them the results they wanted. She often had to spend time in solitary confinement without water, isolated from supportive, loving people. Fortunately, she eventually escaped and made her way to a mental health facility (though later she had no memory of how she had done this).

At the time when my colleague saw her, she had regained her sleep cycle and her hormones were back in balance. She was not on medication and appeared to be in control of her reality. After he worked with her for several sessions in which a great deal of effort was spent helping her to find her stability, all her schizophrenic symptoms disappeared. My point here is that mental illness can happen to any one of us, given extreme circumstances. Being sleep-deprived is a huge factor in experiencing temporary psychosis—just ask any new mom if sleepless nights are causing her to question her sanity!

The more we deal with mental health in an open and honest way, the less fear we will have of the subject. Depression, anxiety, and even temporary psychosis can be a part of many productive people's lives and generally need to be addressed only when they cross the line into "abnormal" territory, which again is when it is interfering with relationships, goals, responsibilities, or peace of mind and safety.

You will find more information about some of the types of severe mental disorders in Appendix B and more information about some common warning signs of schizophrenia/psychosis in Appendix C.

The more we deal with mental health in an open and honest way, the less fear we will have of the subject.

GETTING BACK TO BETTER DAYS

The goal for yourself or when seeking to help someone else on this day is to minimize the disruption and maximize the recovery.

Below are some basic do's and don'ts to better equip you in dealing with the challenges of this day.

Don'ts:

DON'T become a slave to a label. Remember that descriptions of feelings and emotional responses are merely descriptors of behavior and do not reflect on the quality of the individual.

DON'T take drugs from anyone except your doctor. Medications are intended to be specific to an individual's needs.

DON'T feel guilty. These days can happen for multiple reasons, but guilt implies intent, and that certainly doesn't fit here, because you or your loved one did not intend to lose your mental and/or emotional grip.

DON'T consider mental illness as a moral issue in which you or someone you love is suffering in life as the result of sins or religious transgressions. It is true that mental illness can cause doubts or create unusual spiritual expressions, such as actually thinking you're a deity or God.

DON'T shun a person with mental illness. As human beings they are deserving of all the love they can receive, and love can be very healing.

Do's:

DO seek psychotherapy and counseling. When your mental pressures begin to overwhelm you and enter into our definition of mental illness, you likely need professional help because you may well be in over your head. I mentioned psychotherapy and counseling before, and both can be highly effective ways of dealing with depression and anxiety. Psychotherapy can help you redirect your life rather than focusing on everything being bad and overwhelming.

What you'll also learn is that it's not necessarily the events in your life that affect you but your reaction to them that counts. I've been talking about this since the first chapter of this book, but it bears repeating. No, you can't change what's going to happen to you—you simply don't have that much control. However, you *can*, if you are neurochemically balanced, change how you will react. On the other hand, I think that one of the biggest issues that many people suffering from some form of mental illness may face is that they cannot or do not know they have a real choice in reacting to a stressful situation because of the chemical imbalances in their brain. This is expecially true of someone in a psychotic state.

If you are in a psychotic state, you are probably not reading this book. And if you are, then you are most likely capable of making choices. But if you love someone who is in a psychotic state, you need to recognize that that person may *not* be capable of making rational choices. You must realize this so that you do not further complicate the situation. Asking someone who is biochemically imbalanced to voluntarily control their behavior and make active choices would be like asking them to "get taller." They may want to, but it is just not a matter of choice because of the biological limitations. Similarly, failing to require them to function at their highest possible level would be a disservice as well. If someone is actively psychotic and/or has a brain imbalance, they need to be stabilized on appropriate medications before you can get them to sit down, look at you, talk to you, and make logical decisions.

For example, if a driver is in a car and the cylinders in the motor start misfiring, no amount of proficiency training or talent that the driver brings to the situation is going to help the car run better. In other words, there is very little that the driver can do on their own. Similarly, as I mentioned earlier, if the brain is chemically imbalanced—due to such things as fatigue, drugs, or poorly developed brain mechanisms, there is very little that one can do in "talk" therapy until the balance in their brain has been restored. Once the brain is stabilized—through medication and/or the individualized treatment program as prescribed by a good doctor or mental health facility—that person can then begin assuming an active role in making choices in response to the stressful events around them.

This ability to make reality-based choices often has to be developed through a training process after some psychological stability is regained and you can look internally into your thinking patterns. If you learn that you have choices in how you react to stressors, you can discover self-control and empowerment from within. The training process is based on learning what you can do instead of what you can't do. What you can do—in any situation—is choose how you're going to respond and how it's going to affect you. The events of your day-to-day life only have the meaning that you assign to them. Once again, it's the notion that there is no good news or bad news, there is just news. It is your *perception* that makes it good or bad, and you have the power to choose your perception. This is a really important thing to understand. Now, I'm not saying that you can choose whether some things are good or bad. For example, an injury or death of a child is bad any way you slice it. However, you have a choice whether or not you are going to let it swallow you up and leave you curled in a ball in your bed or try to move forward and handle it in a constructive and positive manner.

DO talk to your doctor about medication. Some depression, anxiety, and most psychoses have an organic cause, which means they can be helped, at least in part, biologically. Hormone levels need to be examined, and neurotransmitters should be measured. Even psychoses may be the result of a thyroid problem[17] or chemical imbalances in some people's brains. Even if the causes are primarily situational, or exogenous, such as extended grief or trauma, medication taken under a doctor's care can be what you need to get unstuck.

DO identify de-stressing activities that enhance self-care. The primary agent for help of a mental disorder is the person themselves, so it's extremely important to figure out ways to strengthen coping skills. If there are stressors present that can be eliminated, even for a short time, it is very helpful for the person to be relieved of those stressors for a time in order to rehearse more applicable coping skills.

DO support creative, constructive activities that enhance self-worth. The immediate result of being overwhelmed is the destruction of self-worth. Explore activities that bring new strength to self-esteem and shore up the persistent loss of confidence.

DO express interest in others. If you have a friend or loved one who is depressed or anxious, try to express interest in them. I know that talking about mental illness isn't easy and approaching another person about mental issues can be a touchy subject. It can seem intrusive, and they may very well resist you, but you may also be saving their life. Think of it as a first step to getting communication going. No matter how awkward you feel, give it a try. You'll see how serious their mental state is and maybe get a clue as to how you can help them get on the road to recovery. What to say? Start off with "You're obviously unhappy and having a tough time right now, and I'm concerned. I want to understand what you're going through so I can support you."

DO break a sweat. One of the big problems with mental illness is the feeling of being stuck. Exercise—especially rhythmic exercise—can be powerful therapy in battling this "stuckness." Physical exercise increases oxygen to the brain, improves the flow of feel-good brain chemicals called endorphins, and harmonizes your organs with your brain. In my opinion, I have found the results of exercise to be comparable to those of taking certain medications. (Though you should talk to your physician before making any changes to your treatment plan.)

DO explore or ask your therapist about media and art therapy. I believe that going to carefully selected movies or reading carefully selected books (in which characters exemplify desirable values and beliefs) can provide good stimulus in the form of modeling. There are countless books and movies about people overcoming huge problems and issues, and these demonstrate that positive endings do exist. By vicariously experiencing these things, you may be encouraged to overcome your own obstacles.

You also might want to try art and music therapy. Many people with mental-health issues seem to connect with and benefit from the creative process that is involved in artistic self-expression and in music. Art therapy uses the creative process to improve and enhance emotional, mental, and physical well-being and to treat anxiety, depression, and many other mental and emotional problems.[18] Music therapy uses music to address the physical, mental, emotional, and social needs of people of all ages. Among other things, music therapy can be tailored to promote wellness, improve communication, manage stress, alleviate pain, express feelings, and enhance memory.[19]

DO learn to breathe correctly. It's something we do hundreds of times a day; however most of us do it wrong. Yes, breathing. Typically, when we get anxious, we take light, shallow breaths, and this causes other physiological changes in the body that make us feel even more anxious. When we are depressed, we take slow, almost nonexistent breaths that slow down our brains' problem-solving capacity.[20] Learning to use correct breathing techniques helps us instruct the brain and the rest of the body to step up to better coping methods. It is like training your brain, as an athlete would a body, to be in better shape and be stronger to deal with challenges. One technique that's simple and quite effective is exhaling and inhaling for the same amount of time.

DO explore desensitization. As I mentioned briefly in the fear chapter, desensitization is a process that helps you separate an event from your fear of it. Rather than feeling overwhelming fear when you meet an event, you learn to associate it with relaxation. For example, if speaking in front of an audience makes you anxious, your therapist may start with the image of you preparing to talk in front of people all doing this relaxation exercise. Then, when the event actually takes place, you've gone through a mental dress rehearsal often enough that you can relax. Since you know what to expect, you're no longer anxious. Whenever stress starts to overwhelm you and beat you down into anxiety or depression, you can disconnect from that fear and climb back into the saddle.

You will find more information about the desensitization process in Appendix A.

DO change your internal dialogue. I mentioned this earlier in the book, the conversations that you have with yourself about the world around you. If you suffer from mental and emotional challenges, chances are your internal dialogue is saying negative things—things like "You're going to mess up," "You're going to get destroyed by this," or "No one likes you." All this does is increase your mental problems even more. That's where cognitive therapy is really helpful in challenging and ultimately changing those thoughts. You can learn to counter negative self-dialogue with positive self-dialogue. You can also learn affirmations that you use to replace every negative thought. It needs to be repeated over and over in order to erase those negative tapes, but it can happen. You can do it.

DO try journaling. One of the most successful ways to cope with anxiety or depression is to write something down in your journal every day. It doesn't have to pertain to one specific problem, and there is no right or wrong way to journal. It's more of a way to record your thoughts, and research has shown it to be one of the most successful approaches in learning how to adapt. One reason that journaling is effective may be that when you journal, your mind allows itself to adjust. If you record your dreams, which are your brain's way of symbolizing your conflicts in your journal, you may find unconscious ways of resolving them.

Crisis Do's for Helping Someone in a Psychotic State

If you're dealing with a friend or family member who is psychotic and behaving erratically and out of control, you urgently need to get them help and protection. You should call 911 or, if possible, take them to the nearest emergency room. When some psychotic patients become agitated, they can lapse into such a confused state that they may unknowingly hurt themselves or someone else (as discussed in the myth section on page 187, people who have mental illness are not typically violent people, but being disoriented can add danger to the mix).

There are, however, some important steps you need to take before the doctor enters the picture. Be aware that people suffering from severe mental illness can be prone to bizarre and detached behavior, which is often triggered by high stress, fear, and disorientation. Taking them somewhere like the E.R. may cause these emotions to increase and even spin out of control.

Here are a few suggestions to help minimize those reactions:

- ***When getting ready to take your loved one to get help, be specific and give concrete instructions.*** *This is especially important when dealing with a person who is displaying an inability to focus or remain oriented. They need structure and direction, so be as detailed as possible. For example, if you are taking them to the emergency room you might say, "Walk over to the closet and open the door. Take out your coat and put it on. Then stand by the door and wait for me to walk you out."*
- ***Be a compassionate supporter.*** *Try to be supportive without being condescending. Avoid confrontation if at all possible and maintain a calm, slow interaction. Verbal reassurance can be very helpful as can explaining things to the point of eliminating unknowns. Your goal is to make them feel comfortable and safe while striving to treat them with dignity and respect.*
- ***Encourage your loved one to remain compliant with any and all instructions from professional care givers.*** *For example, taking medications and maintaining sleep patterns, nutritional assignments, and behavioral-type things, such as exercise and relaxation techniques. You want to keep their environment as close to the typical structure that they are used to.*

- ***Make sure that your loved one has clear identification on them*** *that mentions their mental illness and includes emergency phone numbers to call in case they become disoriented and end up outside their normal surroundings. This is important so that they are not misunderstood by other people, such as the police, and so that they do not regress to a lesser level of functioning.*

FINAL THOUGHT

Mental illness is nothing new. But it has for too long been surrounded by mystery and stigma and has triggered a whole pathology of its own regarding fear and guilt about something that should have no more reactivity than having your appendix taken out or fixing a broken arm. So many people hide in fear from a mental diagnosis—and with good reason, considering the public response. Although we've come pretty far since the days of believing mental illness was a result of witchcraft or demonic attack, we are still learning how to separate the person from the condition and to treat sufferers with dignity and respect. Experts are also still learning why and how it occurs. Overall, the modern generation of medications, while in some cases lifesaving, have limited success and in some cases can even make matters worse.

But despite challenges like these, I'm optimistic. I believe that we can face mental illness and succeed in getting better. I remain hopeful that the dialogue on mental illness will continue to open up, causing less panic, shame, and guilt. And as we go forward, we'll find more answers that will help more and more people.

9

Addiction

The Day Addiction Takes Over

Addicts turn their pleasures into vengeful gods.

—MASON COOLEY

If this is the day when you have been hit square between the eyes with the reality that you have a genuine addiction—are a junkie, a dope fiend, or a drunk—then let me be very clear: your life is in danger. If you are functioning in this world, parenting children, driving a car, or performing other activities that can and do affect others, you may also be putting other people's lives in danger. I don't care how smart you are, how sophisticated you are, or how nice a house you live in—if you're a drug addict or an alcoholic, you are out of control and you'd better wake up *right now.* If the problem is not you but someone you love and care about, whether it be a child, spouse, family member, friend, or coworker, everything I just said is true for them as well. I included this as one of the seven days because I believe addiction is headed for epidemic proportions in America. You, me, our children—all of us—are potentially at risk.

Don't con yourself into thinking that the situation is different if you get the substance legally versus scoring it from some dealer in a dark alley. The fact that you or your loved one may have a prescription signed by a doctor folded up in your purse or pocket doesn't change the power and life-threatening nature of addiction. It also doesn't matter if you started taking the drugs for a legitimate reason. Maybe you had back surgery or knee surgery and had to have pain medication. If you are now "doctor hopping" or getting drugs off the Internet, you are no different from somebody who is buying from some dealer on the streets.

The face of substance dependence has changed drastically. It's easier than ever to get your hands on alcohol and drugs (both prescription and illegal). Drug pushers are no longer only in the inner cities or hiding in parks and alleys. Meth labs are popping up in suburban homes, and dealers are as close as your computer. Often they come looking for you in an e-mail, or you can log on to one of the many sites that sell prescription medications, answer a few questions, pay with a credit card, and in just days your pills will arrive in the mail in a plain brown wrapper.

Your kids are growing up in a world with new rules, where the boundaries between what's socially available (and even accepted in many circles) and what's not are more blurred than ever. The *San Francisco Chronicle*[1] reported a 200 percent increase in methamphetamine use alone in the upscale area of Lafayette between 2003 and 2005, averaging one arrest each week. Dr. Alex Stalcup, a nationally recognized expert on meth addiction who runs a clinic there, says that Lafayette is nowhere close to the worst area in the United States—he claims it's a national epidemic. "You name the demographic: CEO types, CFO types, people who make huge amounts of money, soccer moms, every segment of the population—from grandmas to kids."

If you or someone you love is suffering from an addiction, you are certainly and sadly not alone. The statistics are staggering: nearly 18 million Americans abuse alcohol or are alcoholics.[2] That's one in every thirteen adults! And 5 to 6 million have drug problems[3]—and that is with numbers being vastly underreported. No wonder addiction is now the nation's number one health problem,[4] damaging families, overloading our health care system and our penal system, and creating a public safety threat. Almost half of all traffic fatalities are alcohol-related.[5] Chemical dependency and substance abuse cause more deaths, illnesses, and disabilities than does any other preventable health condition. And believe me, the dangers are closer to home than you think.

These days, even legal, seemingly harmless products found around the house or office can be turned into deadly drugs. Twelve-year-old Nate never dreamed that "huffing" (inhaling) computer cleaner could really be that dangerous—it was only compressed air, right? He had heard about the computer cleaner from his middle school friends, who used it because they had limited access to "real" drugs. Unfortunately, they didn't know that the refrigerant in it was unpredictable. You could do it twenty times and get nothing but a buzz, or you could do it once—and die from having your lungs freeze up. A schoolmate found Nate in the corner of the gym locker room, doubled over with his eyes open and the can in his hand—no longer breathing. It had happened in seconds, with no advance warning. Nate's parents—and everyone else, for that matter—were shocked that something so common and easily obtained as canned "air" could literally stop a kid dead in his tracks.

Whatever the specifics of this day, the bad news is that either you are an addict or are in a relationship with an addict—a one-sided relationship in which everything and everyone else takes last place on the list of someone who is addicted.

If this is the day you have found the guts to step up and acknowledge the truth, good for you—that is step one.

Addiction is ugly, no matter the substance. You may have convinced yourself that there are recreational drugs or salved your conscience with the fact that alcohol is legal, but trust me—there are no recreational addicts and there are no "social" alcoholics. Even if you consider yourself to be "high functioning," if you are addicted to drugs or alcohol, you might as well be racing downhill in a car with no brakes for all the control you have. If this is the day you have found the guts to step up and acknowledge the truth, good for you—that is step one. But acknowledging the problem and doing something about it are two drastically different things.

In this chapter, I will tell you the truth whether you want to hear it or not, because it's just too important a subject to soft-pedal it. Whether the addict is you or your teenager, your spouse, your mother or father, or a friend or coworker, denial can be deadly. And let me just deal with something right up front. If you have found drugs, drug paraphernalia, or alcohol in your teenager's room, car, drawers or other personal space, just accept that it is theirs. They are not keeping it for somebody else; they knew it was there, and it's not just a coincidence. If it walks like a duck, looks like a duck and acts like a duck, then come on, Mom—it's a *duck*. Don't join the ranks of all those self-righteous and clueless parents who insist on thinking little Billy or Susie would never do that. And don't believe for one second that it's "just what kids do today." If your kid is doing drugs or alcohol and you don't do something about it, you are being foolish, and, what's worse, you could be held legally responsible. More important, you're *allowing* your child to be in harm's way.

Talking to a Child about Drugs and Alcohol

It can be difficult to find the words when talking to your child about drugs and alcohol. Here is an example of the kinds of things you might want to say to help get the conversation started: You're my daughter, and I love you. I want you to love me, but that's secondary to my job as your parent, which is to get you through these years without hurting yourself. Don't underestimate my resolve. If you think for a second that I'm willing to accept the idea that "everybody's doing it" and let you pursue this behavior, you're wrong. I want you to have fun, freedom, and the opportunity to find yourself, but I'm setting up narrow boundaries and tall fences to contain you until you prove—to me and to yourself—that you won't violate those privileges. You can like me or not—my job is to do for you what you're not doing for yourself. I will never accept these self-destructive behaviors, so let's make a plan we can both be excited about.

So there you have it—that's the truth as I see it. Pretty darned grim picture, wouldn't you say? But when it comes to addiction, either you get it or you don't. I want you to get it, so we need to talk about it. It only stays grim if you stick your head in the sand or decide that you are the exception to the rule and can handle this on your own. You cannot afford to make that mistake. I'll be honest with you here. Alcohol and drug addictions are very difficult to resolve because just like other diseases such as diabetes, asthma, or hypertension, they are complex, often resistant to treatment, and frequently subject to relapse, or recidivism. As dangerous as denying the presence of a true addiction can be, it is also dangerous to use addiction as an excuse for bad behavior or poor performance, so let's not go there!

Now here is the good news: as with those other diseases, the appropriate medical and/or psychological treatment can help, and with serious commitment you can work your way out of this state of dysfunction. Addiction is very treatable with the right guidance and programs. The progress that has been made in understanding and treating alcohol and drug dependency is a great reason for having hope. If you are addicted, your life is not over; you are not doomed to living that life forever more. But you must face the reality of the situation and get the progressive help that is now available to both inpatients and outpatients. For those who go to structured rehab programs for substance dependency or alcoholism, the rate of success varies depending on two things: the quality of the program and the patient's investment in the aftercare process.

Addiction is very treatable with the right guidance and programs.

WHAT IS ADDICTION?

Addiction is a term used to explain an attraction or pathological attachment to a substance, such as a drug (prescription or illegal) or alcohol. The National Council on Alcoholism and Drug Dependence (NCADD) says that scientific research defines alcoholism and drug dependence as a disease that has roots in both genetic susceptibility and personal behavior.[6] It is a serious, debilitating circumstance that is characterized by loss of control, preoccupation, narrowing of interests, dishonesty, guilt, and chronic relapse.[7] Observationally, you are very likely looking at addictive behavior when you see yourself or your loved one continue to use a substance despite significant negative consequences being caused by that use. Simply put, it is not working for you or them, but either one of you continues to do it anyway.

Before I get more into what a true addiction is and why your life (or someone else's) may depend on your being able to find your way through this terrible day, I want to talk a bit about what it is *not*. To me, this is a crucial point. I think that the word "addiction" has become an overused, wastebasket term in our society for people who have a strong preference for something or are undisciplined and self-indulgent and looking for an excuse for being less productive than they could or should be. Claiming addiction can be a great excuse for "punking out"—that is, making poor choices or exhibiting poor conduct or not being all you can be as an individual, mother, father, son, or daughter. It's like, "Hey, I'm sick: Addiction is a disease; I can't be blamed for not being in the game. I am a victim and you should feel sorry for me, support me, and clap for me when I straighten out for a few months. But please do not hold me accountable." Unfortunately, this kind of drivel protects the addict from any expectations that he or she must change with the help of competent treatment and at the same time trivializes the crippling and devastating nature of genuine addiction.

The term has even become part of our everyday language. For example, people say things like "I'm addicted to chocolate chip cookies." No, you are not addicted; you just like them a lot. Or they'll say "I'm addicted to *Desperate Housewives*." No, you are not. You just like to have something to do on Sunday nights. If you were forced to find something else to do or something else to satisfy your sweet tooth, you wouldn't have withdrawal symptoms such as seizures, vomiting, night sweats, or "the shakes" (delirium tremens)—which in some cases, can be fatal.

The greatest treatment success comes one life at a time and one day at a time.

When you're truly addicted to a toxic substance, you can lose control and become totally focused on your addictive substance or behavior, making you a slave to your addiction mentally, emotionally, behaviorally, and/or physically. Any plans you may once have had in life all bow to your new master. The biochemical changes caused by the substance use can be life-threatening, and the dependency can become so powerful that it actually does become impossible to stop the addictive behavior without professional help.[8] I'll get more into that later, but every situation is different. The greatest treatment success comes one life at a time and one day at a time.

Understanding Addiction

Although the list of addictions can cover a lot of ground—from pornography and gambling to a host of other secret, destructive vices—I'm focusing on *chemical* dependence, which means addiction to chemical substances. I want you to understand the ins and outs of addiction because knowledge is power, and whether it's you or a loved one who is involved, you are going to need all the "power" you can get. So, here we go. I use the word "dependence" because it is different from "abuse." Dependence is the formal term for addiction, while abuse describes the precursor stage just prior to becoming an addict. The list of substances includes alcohol and any other mind-altering drugs that one might become dependent upon (which can also include prescription drugs and common household products). If we are going to talk about this problem, we need to get our terms right.

As I stated earlier, one of the reasons it's so hard to successfully treat people who are dependent on drugs or alcohol is that addictions are complex. Genetic predispositions, physiological and psychological dependencies, and lifestyle and social components all factor into why one person is attracted to addictive substances or behaviors and someone else is not. Of all substances, crystal meth has the highest relapse rate at 92 percent,[9] due to the "double whammy" of the psychological and physiological aspects of the addiction, with cocaine coming in second. Although the cocaine itself is usually out of the body in about two to five days, the physiological damage from the substance may last for months, if not longer.[10] And there is a psychological hunger for that high that can hook even the strongest-willed people.

The psychological dependency can be even greater if you've used your addiction as a mechanism to escape, celebrate, or control your anxiety or as a social lubricant. Social elements are a big part of the picture, because often the people an addict hangs out with are doing the same thing and it is part of the culture they are in. All these factors play into any addiction, and you have to address them all in order to beat it.

Sometimes people are especially vulnerable to alcohol or drugs when they are living in the "fast lane." Derek and Miranda were the couple most likely to be invited to anything going on in their Silicon Valley circle. Derek was a software development executive who looked like Gary Cooper, and Miranda was his perfect blond match. She had been overweight as a kid, but these days there wasn't an ounce of fat on her tanned, fit frame, even after having their three boys. Everything was perfect—except for the dirty little secret that the Silicon Valley group shared. Derek and most of his friends—who also had to keep up with relentless seventy-hour workweeks and heavy demands on their time and energy—had learned early on that a little help from crystal meth made the impossible possible.

Many of the women were also addicted, although for a different reason. For them, it was the perfect weight loss plan; not only that, but it could help them keep up their social activities and clean a two-story home in less than two hours with plenty of energy left for the kids. What they didn't realize was the toll the drug was taking on their minds and bodies. After a couple of years, it started showing up first in the form of depression, then paranoia, and later even things from domestic abuse to the physical tell-tale signs of "meth mouth," with trips to the dentist to try to save their rotting teeth.

Miranda crashed first, with hallucinations and anxiety disorders leaving her a sleepless wreck. Even though her body was being destroyed and her marriage was falling apart, she still couldn't give up her little "helper," until one day she went into heavy convulsions and one of the kids called 911 in a panic. Later she broke down and faced the fact that she was killing herself and hurting her kids. She forced Derek to seek counseling with her to break the vicious cycle, but since their friends had not yet reached the same point, they decided to make a complete break and move to a small town in the Midwest. Derek traded his high-powered position for a less glamorous one and they had to learn to live on less, but it was a small price to pay to buy back their health, peace of mind, and freedom. They had never planned to get addicted, and they had never dreamed they would almost lose everything, although anyone watching this little drama unfold could have seen it coming a mile away. They had been certain they were "too smart" to get hooked; that only happened to other people who didn't "get it" the way they did. They were wrong.

Predisposed but Not Predestined

Now let's talk a bit about the genetic aspect of addiction. In most cases, genetics tell you who is *more likely* to experience a certain phenomenon rather than who will. When it comes to substance abuse or drug dependency, a family history means you need to be especially cautious, because you may be predisposed to this problem. For example, children of alcoholics are four times more likely than the general population to develop problems with alcohol[11] (you also grew up in an alcoholic environment, and that exposure has an impact, too). However, it doesn't mean that you are doomed. It just means that you shouldn't play with fire. My dad was a serious alcoholic, so I have no doubt that I am more susceptible than someone who doesn't have an alcoholic parent. But that doesn't mean I'm going to be an alcoholic. Early on, I made the life decision that I just wasn't going to drink. I remember looking around at some of my friends and family and seeing the dead-end situations that alcohol put them in, and deciding that it wasn't for me. Just like me, many children of alcoholics do not drink because they have experienced the devastating effects of the disease firsthand. But frequently *their* children (the alcoholic's grandchildren) missed the chaos but are still very susceptible to becoming addicted genetically, and therefore the disease frequently skips generations.[12] That makes it critically important to not hide a family "secret" but to instead discuss it openly at the right time to avoid an innocent grandchild being blindsided because he or she did not know about their susceptibility.

It's the same thing if you have obese parents. It doesn't mean that you're going to be obese; it just means that you may have a tougher battle than someone else. My point is that you can still make the choice. So yes, there is a genetic component to your addiction, and that part you can't do anything about. What *can* you do? You can change a lot of things—your environment, your internal dialogue, your friends, and what you are willing to accept. That is the part you have control over, so that is what I will be focusing on.

When you realize (or finally admit) that you have a crippling and life-threatening addiction and that you are in a fight for your life, you may have already turned a very important corner, which may mean that your most challenging day was yesterday, *before* you found the courage to get real with yourself. You may have heard me say that you cannot change what you do not acknowledge. If you have acknowledged your problem, this can be a day of hope—a day of new beginnings.

WHAT TO EXPECT

Whether you are addicted or you are in a relationship with someone who is addicted, you need to know what you can expect to be dealing with on this most challenging day.

If it is you, think about it: the day before you got real with yourself, you couldn't even look in the mirror because you would have had to admit that you were no longer in control of your own life. Because the moment before you admitted where you were, you had given your power over to drugs and alcohol. You had no resistance. Addiction was the monkey on your back whose grip around your neck only tightened as you went from one day to the next. When you are dependent on a substance, it can consume you 24/7, and all your energy goes toward how you're going to get that next high. It can become so powerful that you will choose your addiction over your friends, family, and even your children.

Somewhere in the back of your brain, you know that the decisions you may be making—such as abandoning your kids, selling your wedding ring, or not showing up for work three days in a row—are downright stupid. But you can get to a point where you just don't care as long as you can get your fix. You may even steal from your best friend, parents, employer, or even your children's college fund to pay for your addiction. At any price, you'll find a way to support it. You may get to where you crave it so desperately that even when you do get a hit, your first worry is that you won't get another one. And with a substance abuse or dependence on drugs like meth or cocaine, even your body conspires against you.

The first-time use of most drugs causes a "dopamine flood," where your brain releases hundreds of thousands of times the amount of your body's "pleasure" chemical for a onetime ecstasy that will never be repeated. But that just doesn't seem to stop an addict from trying to feel that high again. What's worse, messing with this part of your brain often causes long-term problems from brain damage to these delicate intrabrain communication systems, where the ability to "reset" the dopamine release is damaged, and depression can set in.[13] Paranoia and psychosis can also result from meth and cocaine use.[14] This brain damage is also what causes the cravings going forward—these neurotransmitter (brain chemical) systems (i.e., serotonin, dopamine, and GABA) are short-circuiting.[15] In a magazine article, the popular singer Fergie from Black Eyed Peas discussed her former addiction to crystal meth. Extreme paranoia accompanied her addiction, and she insisted that everyone—from the FBI to her closest friends—was against her. "I had about 20 different conspiracy theories," said the star, who dropped down to ninety pounds during her darkest days. "I painted the windows in my apartment black so 'they' couldn't see in." She talks about one incident when she had hit rock bottom: "One day, a guy comes up to me. I'm searching in the bushes for clues about whatever 'they're' after me for. I'm in a cowboy hat and red lips. He hands me a muffin. I'm thinking, *He's in on it. Is there a message inside?* So I tear it up. Looking back, I realize he assumed I was homeless."[16]

Life as an Addict

Today, expect to feel alone. Very alone. You've probably hurt and lied to so many friends and family members that very few want to have anything to do with you. After all, you don't really care about anyone but yourself. You may feel like a different person and may not even recognize or remember the old you. When you're halfway sober, you may feel guilty that you stole from your parents, cashed that check that someone sent to your daughter for her tenth birthday, or lied to a friend about why you needed to borrow that hundred bucks. You may have made horrible choices, and you know it. But unfortunately, this overwhelming guilt actually plays back into your addiction. You want to escape, so you reach for that drink or drug, hoping it will ease the pain.

Maybe you were found out by a friend or family member, and, if that's the case, expect an array of emotions such as anger and embarrasment. You may become defensive when they confront you. You may start spewing lies. Maybe you'll say that you can handle it, you're not hooked, or you just had a couple of drinks. You may be worried about how you're going to resolve this. You want to pull yourself away from this master, but you haven't got a clue how. All this panic only makes you want it more.

You may feel desperate and anxious—especially if being found out has somehow affected your ability to indulge in whatever you're addicted to. In other words, your wife took your credit cards so you can't buy alcohol or your parents took your car so you can't meet up with your dealer. Your mind may race with ideas about how you can get the money to support your habit: steal from a friend, sell your body, hold up a Starbucks. These things aren't legal, and you know it. But you may not really care. All you're thinking about is that you'll do whatever it takes to get whatever it is that will kill your pain. And if it's been a while since you last used, you could be feeling a lot of pain. If you are on the early side of withdrawal, you will probably be feeling extremely agitated, with vomiting, tremors, insomnia, or flulike symptoms. If you are deeper in, you could be going through anything from seizures and the DTs (delirium tremens) to hallucinations and cardiovascular and neurological disruptions.

An Addict in the Family

If your loved one is the addict, your most challenging day is when you realize that you have been lied to and betrayed by someone you thought you could trust. They don't respect or care about you. They will lie, steal, and cheat and take advantage of you in any way possible to feed the addiction. In fact, if you get between them and whatever they're addicted to, you may become the enemy. You found a bottle of vodka under the front seat of your spouse's car. The two of you have been struggling to make ends meet, yet a receipt shows that four other bottles were bought at the same time. You go to set the table for the holidays but you can't find the heirloom silverware that has been in your family for three generations. Later you learn that your adult daughter—a wife and mother of three—sold it for money to support her cocaine habit. You find a Ziploc bag of marijuana and rolling paper in the pocket of your son's jeans when doing laundry. Shocked, you search his room and find a box full of drug paraphernalia in the back of his closet. Words can't describe how painful it is to realize that a friend or family member has an addiction. If you didn't suspect it before, you may be mystified and thinking to yourself, *How did this happen? How did the spouse I thought I knew or the child I raised go down this path? What did I do to contribute to this?*

Expect that you may feel anger and resentment since you've been lied to and betrayed. You may feel as if you've failed in your relationship. If it's a spouse who is addicted, you're facing the high probability that your marriage may be over. It's also a strong possibility that you'll experience feelings of shame and embarrassment when you imagine what others will say when they find out. They'll think that you married or raised a loser—a bum who doesn't love you and cares more about a bottle of alcohol or a hit of heroin than he or she does about you. You may feel helpless and alone and you may feel as though you've been deserted.

Or maybe this is the day you realize that your loved one is dying from this terrible disease and you do not seem to have any control over preventing them from continuing to destroy themselves. You may also feel guilty or stupid for not knowing that something was up. Or angry at yourself that you didn't do anything about those little red flags that you *did* see. When it comes to a child being addicted, expect that you might feel that you have failed as their guardian and caretaker. You may even blame yourself. *Was it something I did or didn't do? Could I have prevented it?*

If you confront your loved one, they may lash out and verbally (or even physically) attack you. You may not even recognize them anymore; their drug of choice is controlling them and has changed them so drastically. You schould expect that every single thing they say is a bunch of lies. They may lie outright and tell you that the pot was not theirs or the credit card charges for those bar tabs "must be a mistake" and they'll call and straighten it out right away. And even if they do fess up, it may not be the whole truth.

Maybe they'll tell you this was the first time or that they have it under control and will never do it again. Don't believe a word they say. Don't be naive and in denial.

You may also experience other difficulties as a result of your loved one's addiction. For example, if an addiction is the reason they got fired from their job and they're the family's sole provider, your financial situation may be in jeopardy. Or if your spouse is the one who takes care of the kids while you work, you'll probably need to find a new child care situation. There may be legal problems to worry about if your loved one has done something like stealing or forging checks to support their habit. All this can make you feel out of control. Now you're forced into these awful circumstances, and you may feel like there's really nothing you can do about it. You may have no clue of where to even start.

Addiction Audit

The following audit will help you figure out if you or a loved one may have an addiction. For each description of specific feelings and attitudes about substances and activities, determine which of the four responses listed below is most appropriate.

Never: These thinking patterns have not been present or you have not been aware of them.

Occasionally: You have been aware of them, but they have not interfered with your relationships or restricted you from normal personal functioning with your work or employment.

Significantly: You have experienced these ideas and thinking every day and have been significantly restricted in your social relationships, personal life, or work in the last two weeks.

Severely: You have been severely restricted in your relationships, personal life, or work such that you are incapable of changing your habits or use of substances or engaging in these activities.

Note: "Substances" in this questionnaire means any substance you use for psychological needs, including any drug, such as marijuana and cocaine; lifestyle substances, such as nicotine and sugar; and prescription drugs. "Activities" in this questionnaire means any activity you engage in that is used for emotional needs, such as gambling and sex.

1. **I crave a substance because it makes me lose my self-doubt and gives me self-confidence.**

   Never __ Occasionally __ Significantly __ Severely __

2. **I have failed to fulfill promises to stop using this substance or participating in this activity.**

   Never __ Occasionally __ Significantly __ Severely __

3. **I have a physiological craving for a substance that erases pain and discomfort.**

   Never __ Occasionally __ Significantly __ Severely __

4. **I think about consuming a substance or participating in a behavior more than I think about anything else.**

   Never __ Occasionally __ Significantly __ Severely __

5. **I prefer to be alone and consume this substance rather than be seen and observed by others.**

   Never __ Occasionally __ Significantly __ Severely __

6. **Participating in the specific activity is my greatest need, over others.**

   Never __ Occasionally __ Significantly __ Severely __

7. **I find it hard to imagine life without this substance or activity.**

   Never __ Occasionally __ Significantly __ Severely __

8. **My life is centered around this substance or activity.**

   Never __ Occasionally __ Significantly __ Severely __

9. **When this substance or activity is not available to me, I become irritated and antisocial.**

   Never __ Occasionally __ Significantly __ Severely __

10. **I have no control over my need for this substance or activity.**

    Never __ Occasionally __ Significantly __ Severely __

Scoring

If you checked "Severely" at least once, you are most likely suffering from severe addiction and need some professional help.

If you checked "Significantly" at least twice, it is likely you are dealing with major addictions to substances listed at the beginning of this audit. Listen up and pay attention for some basic ways to start laying the foundation to deal with this problem and consult with a professional if necessary.

GETTING BACK TO BETTER DAYS

As I have said repeatedly in this chapter, addiction is a chronic disease and I feel very strongly that you can't break the cycle of addiction on your own. It isn't because you are weak or you don't have the willpower but because you're at a point where your decision-making abilities are no longer in play. Your use may have started in a way that you could control. Maybe you could have one beer after work to relieve the anxiety of the day or believed that smoking marijuana on weekends relaxed you and gave you a clear picture of reality. You may have believed that cocaine answered your prayers for your lack of passion and energy. You may have even felt that your focus and attention were better when you popped some prescription drugs.

But once you're hooked, you need help. Once you are a pickle, you are never a cucumber again. That's because, as I mentioned earlier, in the case of physiological addictions, the toxicity and chemicals have actually changed your brain. They've changed the very connections that affect your judgment. They may have also damaged your brain's chemistry so much so that you actually have a physiological craving when you are trying very hard to stop. Many times this level of toxicity and biochemistry can require at least a year of being clean and/or sober before you can have the judgment to make good choices.[17] (That's the reason why a person can do well in a thirty-day rehab program but fail if he or she does not invest in a long-term aftercare program. When that line is crossed, you are in the disease state. And you need help.)

Action Steps

If You're the Addict

- **Find Your Personal Truth**
  The problem with the alcohol or drug culture is that admission is free—seemingly. To be on a debate team, you have to be a good debater. To be on a basketball team, you have to have a good jump shot. To be in a choir, you have to have a good voice. To be accepted into the alcohol/drug culture, you just have to be willing to do alcohol or drugs. You don't have to be cute, smart, tall, short, fat, skinny, talented, skilled, funny—you just have to use and/or drink. The problem is that, as I've often said, for most people the number one fear in life is rejection and the number one need is acceptance. So if you have a negative personal truth—whatever it is that you, at the absolute, uncensored core of your being, have come to believe about you—the world of drugs or alcohol is a place you know you can get into. That makes it very easy to gravitate in that direction.

  Another reason you may turn to alcohol or drugs is to medicate yourself for things in your life that you don't like. Maybe you think, *I'm boring sober, but when I'm drunk I'm funny. I'm more interesting and people want to hang out with me.*

That may be true. It may be the easy way to get your personality out there. It may be the easy way to be comfortable around people. It may be the easy way to escape the doldrums. It is certainly an easy way to numb your pain. But the price you have to pay isn't worth any of those things, and there are alternative ways to get what you want—ways that don't have the downsides that drugs have. In the long run, nothing about being an addict is easy. The side effects are horrible. You're not boring or sad anymore; you're drunk or stoned. It's the easy way out as opposed to tackling the real issues, such as overcoming your depression, changing your life, developing your personality, establishing relationships, and honing your skills and abilities so that you earn acceptance into a community of peers rather than settling for the one thing you can get into free.

- **Consult with an Expert**

  It's a fact that certain substances have such a powerful physiological impact that simply stopping the use of the drug can, in and of itself, result in death. So (depending on what you're addicted to) it's very possible you'll need professional help. Especially with substance addiction, you need direct medical guidance because you cannot handle it on your own. This isn't because you don't have the strength or the willpower. It's because recovering from an addiction or any other chronic medical disease doesn't come easy. And specifically, there are some drugs—such as antidepressants, mood stabilizers, and antipsychotics—that, if you go off of them cold turkey, you could put your health and life in jeopardy.[18]

  Quitting any substance that your body is used to getting can be dangerous—for instance, research has shown that abruptly quitting something as innocuous as aspirin or a mild antidepressant after taking it regularly may increase the risk of having a heart attack or stroke.[19] You need a medical supervisor for these things, and the help of people who specialize in detoxification and rehabilitation on these substances. This can take the form of inpatient intervention, outpatient intervention, a combination of the two, or support groups.

In some cases, medication may be prescribed to help prevent relapse. According to the National Institute on Drug Abuse (NIDA),[20] "medications are an important element of treatment for many patients, especially when combined with counseling and other behavioral therapies." For example, heroin addicts may be given buprenorphine, a narcotic drug that blocks cravings as well as the pleasurable effects of heroin and other opiates, to help them taper off. Alcoholics can ask their doctor about naltrexone, di-sulfiram, or acamprosate—three medications that the National Institute of Alcohol Abuse and Alcoholism (NIAAA)[21] has found to help alleviate the symptoms of withdrawal. Naltrexone now comes in a shot form that lasts for thirty days at a time. No matter the combination, successful treatment depends on you. You must recognize that there is a problem, choose to change, and commit to the process as a permanent life decision.

It's well known that once you have been addicted to a substance, you can never ingest that substance again. If you are an alcoholic, you can *never* drink again—not in five years, not socially, not in any way. Another thing to keep in mind is that once you've been addicted to one substance, you are much more susceptible to being addicted to something else. So once you've stopped using drugs, you can't start drinking. There are a lot of informative websites such as www.enterhealth.com and those of the National Institute of Alcohol Abuse and Alcoholism (NIAAA), the National Institute on Drug Abuse, and the National Council on Alcoholism and Drug Dependence (NCADD), and there are organizations such as Alcoholics Anonymous that can help you.

If Your Loved One Is the Addict

- **Choose to Assist—But Not Enable—the Person You Are Trying to Help**
  Your first inclination when you find out that someone you care about has an addiction is probably to help them—especially if it's a spouse, parent, or child. Like most people, you probably feel that you'd do anything humanly possible to protect and save them from harm. There's nothing wrong with that; it's human nature. The problem, though, is that this can actually make matters worse with an addict. Your love, something strong and positive, can enable them. A good metaphor is HIV-AIDS. In this disease, the virus takes hold of the immune system, a part of us that is normally there to protect us, and turns it against the body. For an addict, your love can create an enabling effect, and unfortunately, you may discover you are not supporting them so much as supporting their addiction when you go into denial over their situation, give them money that goes straight to their habit, cover up and make excuses for their irresponsibility, or in any way prolong their ability to continue in their addiction through your own misguided and dysfunctional behavior.

- **Set Up an Intervention**
  I disagree with the popular myth that an addict must "hit bottom" before they can be helped. In my opinion, this is absolutely untrue; you need to get help now for someone you love who is fighting a substance addiction, because bottom may be six feet under. Although you cannot make the decision for someone to turn their life around, a structured intervention (if done properly) can lead the dependent person to the help needed to begin recovery. My recommendation is that you use a professional, but I also have included an intervention guide below as well as additional information included in the Resource Guide.

  If you decide to set up an intervention, you should keep the following points in mind when you are ready to confront the chemically dependent person.

- **Set Your Team**
  Get concerned people around who will help. Each person has to be willing to look the addict in the eye and say, "You have a problem, and you need help." If anyone on the "team" feels uncomfortable about that, you have a weak link who should not be involved in the process.

- **Confront Factually, but with Love, Care, and Concern**
  Bring a written list of data to the intervention that describes in detail the evidence that your loved one is using drugs. Confront him or her with content, not argument.

- **Remember That You Are Talking to the Drugs, Not the Person**
  Any time someone is addicted to drugs, the substance takes over their reasoning and problem solving and creates all types of paranoia and anger.

- **Create a Crisis for the Troubled Person**
  Remember that arguments are a comfort zone for a person on drugs because they allow him or her to stay in denial. Bring things to a head by giving him or her a choice to get treatment or face the undesirable alternative, such as being jailed, being kicked out of the house, having no contact with family, and so on.

- **Focus Only on Chemically Related Issues**
  Keep things focused on the fact that the addict has a disease for which he or she needs professional help. Be

specific about when, where, and with whom a chemically related incident happened. Stay on point without emotions or distractions. It's not about yelling, screaming, or your opinions, it's about facts.

- **Get a Commitment from the Addict to Go to Treatment or Be Prepared to Break Contact**
  You have to be prepared for the hard decision of letting the person go if treatment is refused. It doesn't just affect the addict; it takes a toll on the entire family.

- **Have a Firm, Immediate Plan**
  You don't want to waste time after you get a commitment. If the person agrees to get help, have a treatment center set up to admit him or her immediately. If the person does not agree to get treatment, know in advance how you will respond.

Remember that, despite every good intention and plan, your love and desire to help are not the deciding factors in someone else's recovery. The one thing you must face is the harsh reality that no matter how much you want to make things better for the loved one, ultimately there is nothing you can do to control another person. I'm not saying this is an easy fact to face. It's not. It's awful, and I can't think of anything worse than watching your child, parent, partner, spouse, or anyone else you love destroying their body and their life. You'll want to believe that you can save them or make them better, but when an addict's demand for a drug is stronger than his ability to choose (or not to choose), he'll stop at nothing to get it. Again, the only way that any change will happen is if the addict not only needs help but wants to get help.

You will find more information about dealing with addiction in the Resource Guide at the end of this book.

FINAL THOUGHT

Addiction is one of the worst diseases out there. A true addict will sell their soul to the Devil or anyone else who will take it in order to get their substance of choice. This one-track mind is dangerous because they'll stop at nothing. But even though this may be one of the worst wars you'll ever have to fight, there is hope, whether you're the addict or your friend or family member is. Many people do recover, and you can too. But like most things that require life changes, it isn't easy. It takes love, courage, and patience. It takes time and it takes work. There will be some really tough, low days, but you can come through it. You just need to make the choices that have to be made regardless of what others choose to do. If you'll do that, I'm telling you that you *will* get control of your own life back, and in the end, that's the only part you are responsible for.

Look, you know I don't sugarcoat things, so I hope you believe me when I say that alcohol and drug addiction *is* treatable. You can get it under control, you can put it behind you, and you can start on the path toward a wonderful, healthier, happier life. We know so very much more about treatment now than we did even a generation ago. Have hope, have commitment, be honest with yourself, and trust me when I say *you can do this*!

Have hope, have commitment, be honest with yourself, and trust me when I say *you can do this*!

If it's you who has an addiction to drugs or alcohol, recognize that you cannot deal with it yourself, that you cannot moderate it and bring it back under control again by yourself. There is no alternative but to get help and quit completely and forever. You may have to do it one minute, one hour, or one day at a time, but one way or another, it has to happen.

10

Existential Crisis

The Day You Have Lost Your Purpose and Have No Answer to the Question "Why?"

He who has a why to live can bear almost any how.

—FRIEDRICH NIETZSCHE

I think there is a time in just about everybody's life when you stop and seriously ask yourself, "What's the point? Why am I scrambling around doing what I do all day, every day? Nobody appreciates it, it doesn't change the world, I have no impact, I have no voice, and I'm just beating my head against the wall." If you don't have answers to those questions, you may become hopeless, questioning to the core of your soul what the meaning or purpose of your life is. It goes beyond playing the victim or feeling sorry for yourself. It goes beyond posing these questions to others just for effect, sympathy, or reassurance or in anger; that's what most people call whining. What I'm talking about here is when it gets to the point where you ask *yourself* these questions and sincerely do not have an answer. The opposite of the Friedrich Nietzsche quote above is also true: if you have no *why* to live, then you can not bear any *how* even if how you are living is by external standards comfortable or even enviable. Having no why to live can make every task seem overwhelming and make every minute feel like an hour and every day feel like a year. It can be a gut-wrenching emptiness.

Sometimes it is easier to recognize pain and problems in others than in yourself. If you observed this attitude in one of your children you would be highly concerned, and rightly so. You would do anything to help them feel that they mattered, belonged, and made a real difference. For a child to feel otherwise is a horrible existence. I have spoken to so many children of neglect who feel that if they died or disappeared, no one would care or miss them. Maybe you feel that way too, like an abandoned, lonely, and scared child. The day I am writing about now is the day that you or someone you deeply love hits a brick wall and cannot begin to find an answer, a meaning, or a purpose for going on. It may feel that the reason you can't find an answer is because there just simply isn't one.

After all, as some admittedly pessimistic, whiny, naysaying people are happy to rant, "We just kick, fight, scratch, bite, and struggle, yet, in the end we're just going to end up as worm food." Perhaps the more eloquently stated point of view is that nothing seems to really matter at all because in the end we all just die and, as has long been said, "You can't take it with you." Sometimes that statement can make you want to live for the moment. But on this day, it might make you ask yourself, "What's the point?"

Okay, if you are not currently depressed, lost, or feeling majorly empty, you may be thinking that all of this is a real "downer" point of view and a huge oversimplification. But the truth is that most people sometimes in their journey find that those daily and often overwhelming struggles can pile up, drag you down, drain your energy, and make the "fight" called life just seem pointless. There can be days when you feel as though you take one step forward and ten steps backwards, with everything seeming to be without meaning or purpose. So we ask, "What difference does it or do I really make?" We ask, "Why do I put myself through all of this when in the final analysis maybe it doesn't really matter?"

When you look at a hamster running endlessly in place on one of those wheels, you might think, "Stupid hamster." Well, the reason I wanted to address this subject is that I think an awful lot of people, maybe you some day, do reach a point in their lives when this world feels a lot like a big ol' hamster wheel. Most people talk about this in abstract, philosophical terms. But if you or someone you love is now experiencing this dilemma or find yourself there at any time in the future, I want to talk to you about it in ordinary, common sense, nonpsychobabble, day-to-day terms. What we are talking about here is what philosophers across the ages have referred to as existential anxiety or the existential crisis.

WHAT IS AN EXISTENTIAL CRISIS?

Obviously I'm not talking about a bad mood or a passing funk. Existential crisis or existential anxiety is a fancy name for the age-old search for meaning in life, taken from the phrase "the reason for existence." It can be triggered by an event, or it may just come on after years of wandering aimlessly in the world without purpose or passion. It can happen at any age; if it happens halfway through life, it is often referred to as a midlife crisis. But in truth what I am talking about here is so much more than something that a red sports car or a face-lift can fix. This day is not to be confused with a passing midlife crisis. Existential anxiety is really the deeply rooted pain that comes largely from failing to make sense of or find purpose in a world that sometimes just seems like nonsense. You can't have existential anxiety if you don't at least *want* to care about something or at least want to matter. If you truly had no "energy" or investment in your life, you would just kick back and rock along to nowhere. And the very fact that you've bothered to ask these questions means that you are someone who, at some level, does care.

You can't have existential anxiety if you don't at least *want* to care about something or at least want to matter.

We are all familiar with Shakespeare's famous line "To be or not to be, that is the question." Maybe a slightly tweaked version fits here. The question that I want to prepare you to deal with now is not just "to be or not to be" but also *why to be* and *how to be.* Be here in a way that is defined in the *why* of your purpose. And that's exactly what you'll be asking yourself on this most challenging day: not *who* you are but *why* you are. Why are you here? Why do you do what you do?

Before we go even one step further I just have to put one issue right up front because everything else I have to say is predicated on this truth: like it or not, you don't have a choice about being here. I say that because I flat-out reject self-destruction and suicide as a rational, viable option. In my view suicide is immoral, selfish, and cowardly because you leave behind people who will forever feel guilty (however irrationally) about a choice that *you* made. Maybe you didn't choose to be born into the place or situation that you're in, and maybe that doesn't seem fair. But fair or not, you do not get to choose when or how you die. What you *can* choose is how you live. You can choose the attitude you have about your life and what's in it, and there is great power in that ability. The great psychiatrist and former prisoner of war Viktor Frankl, who is largely responsible for bringing the concept of existentialism into the modern era, taught us that you can and should strive to find meaning even in your suffering. Without that meaning, the tough times of life can just be a painful penalty. Yet if meaning is found, that pain can at least become purposeful. That's part of the nobility of life and the moral compass and consciousness that we humans possess.

When you fail to identify what matters to you, what you are passionate about and what gives you some personal gratification, you are struggling in the search for meaning. When you fail to define yourself in a way that makes you feel vitally involved in your life and engaged in what's going on, you can run straight into this state of existential anxiety. In fact, it is this very lack of connection and involvement that makes this day so painful. Everyone needs to know they matter, and you are no exception. Everyone needs to feel that they are part of something and to have a strong sense of belonging. The ultimate in existential crisis is if you accept your life as meaningless and, more important, don't do anything about it. Sometimes we run from, or try to distract ourselves from, the lack of true meaning by trying to busy ourselves in a workaholic frenzy.

I know many workaholics who have sacrificed a lot to make a lot of money or to achieve a certain level of career status only to wake up one day and wonder, *Is this it?* This is even more true if, by the time they wake up, they've burned through a few marriages and their kids barely talk to them because they've been emotionally absent for so many years. I've also known people who sacrifice everything for their careers and then one day they go to work and find that the locks on their office doors have been changed. Instead of heading up a department, they're heading to the unemployment office.

Then there are people who think they are putting on the breastplate of martyrdom to deny their own needs and sacrifice their entire life, marriage, and existence for their children. That's what happened to Martha, a former advertising executive with an MBA. When her children were born, she gave up her fast-paced career to stay at home and raise them. Like the high achiever she was, she threw herself into motherhood. She spent hours arranging play dates, painstakingly sewing costumes for school plays, baking for fund-raisers, and driving her three kids from one activity to the next. Though she missed the adrenaline rush of her old job and the feeling of accomplishment she had had there, she enjoyed watching her children grow and believed that sacrificing everything for them was the right thing to do. Her children never seemed to quite "get it" or appreciate that their mother had chosen to forgo her own life in order for them to be happy. *They'll understand one day,* Martha would tell herself after another rude outburst from her daughter or one too many hours sitting in a hot car waiting for soccer practice to finish. But they never did. The emptiness set in when those now-grown children turned and walked into their own lives, leaving Martha behind. The people who had taken up almost every waking hour of her day and had once given her a purpose in life simply became voices on the other end of the phone line or a terse e-mail once or twice a week. It was as if she had been in a deep sleep while the rest of the world had been moving along at breakneck speed. She had nothing else that made her feel good or defined her because she'd given up all her hobbies, hadn't stayed on top of what was going on in the world of advertising, and let many of her friendships slide because it took her focus away from her kids. Even her husband seemed like a stranger without the one thing they had had in common: their children. She felt helpless and panicked and fell into a depression so deep that she considered suicide. Why stay on this planet and in this world, she wondered, when it would be no different without me? Martha had lost her purpose and her passion, in part, because she had defined herself as a function of her role in someone else's life. It was time to redefine herself in her own terms based on what mattered to her.

So What Is the Answer? What Is It All About?

The question of why we exist has been asked by millions of people across the ages. If you are a spiritual person and you're not in the middle of a crisis of faith, then to a great extent you have answers to that question. Though I am a Christian, I know that in a great country like ours there are many people who practice many faiths and paths that they feel lead them to God. I respect and understand the choice of others who seek religious fortification through other expressions. However, the commonality is that faith in general has a positive impact and decreases some levels of anxiety. I think any religion or belief system that believes in a supreme being and some kind of other life—such as an afterlife or reincarnation—does give its followers some meaning to their struggle and suffering. After all, if you believe that you are in transition into the life that really matters and what you do will determine your position or access to the next one, that does give you some purpose each day. Religion can also give you a sense of being part of something greater than yourself, and that in and of itself can help you discover a deeper part of life.

But even for some people of faith, that may not be enough. It may help to calm the soul about the hereafter, but religious practices do not always arrest emotional psychological tensions about the challenges of life in the here and now. You may still find yourself wondering *why*. What else is the point besides this other life? This feeling is actually quite typical—although way underreported by people for fear of being judged. Or maybe you judge yourself. I find that many times, people will not face their own questions about life in an attempt not to betray their belief systems in the face of what appears to them to be uncertainty. If you are a person of faith, I think it is very important that you do not feel that you have betrayed your faith if you have questions or need help coping with problems. Remember the man described in Mark 9:24 of the Bible who cried out to Jesus, saying "I do believe, help my unbelief." He is a clear and absolute depiction of the fact that we can be sure about some things but still have questions about them.

If you feel as though your life has no meaning, then you can't be passive and simply think that this is what God intended for you. No. I believe that God intended for you to be alive and to do your best. God intended for you to use all the resources that he gave you to live your best life. This is a significant subject for people of faith and it gives them permission to further fortify their existing faith with counseling and supplementary reading or counseling materials without feeling that they have betrayed the value of what they have in the faith they have chosen.

The good news is that this search for meaning—and the pain that comes along with it—is a very powerful motivation to make some changes in your life. It's like when I was just a kid and my friends and I walked barefoot across a scorching blacktop highway on a hot Texas summer day. We were young and pretty obviously not too bright. I learned really quickly, in fact it was one trial learning, that it was so hot that the blacktop was sticky and it hurt big time and I sure was not going to just stand still in the middle of the road and melt! When something hurts—and I mean *really* hurts—people move away from the pain. They do something different. Pain can truly be a great motivator. So can reward.

People move and make changes for both reasons. Sometimes they move away from pain, and sometimes they move toward rewards. As I said earlier, currencies are the rewards or payoffs you get when you engage in certain behaviors. Whether you're conscious of them or not, we all have them. It's just a simple fact of human nature that we tend to do things based on the payoff that we'll get in exchange. By the way, that doesn't make us selfish, it just makes us human. This may be something tangible such as money, food, or a new pair of shoes, or it may be intangible, such as achievement, contribution, attention, praise, privileges, or time spent with a loved one or helping another person.

It's just a simple fact of human nature that we tend to do things based on the payoff that we'll get in exchange.

Living your "why" is important, and I believe that if you're not doing something that furthers *your* currency, you need to stop what you're doing and start doing something that does. You can choose to use the gifts, skills, and abilities that God gave you. You will like having the sense of self-determination and the sense of being able to make a choice. You will like being able to affect your journey through this life and will get personal satisfaction from that.

One thing that's important to remember is that what's right for you may not be right for everybody. But that's what makes the world go round. What matters to me may not matter to someone else and vice versa. For another person it may be building a great bridge or coming up with a new seed that may increase the harvest. I know people who take great pride and find deep meaning in putting out pads, pencils, name plates, and refreshments for a big meeting; or drivers who get immense satisfaction from bringing people to those meetings. They feel that they play a crucial role, and they do. The challenge is to find what makes *you* feel most alive and purposeful. One person's currency isn't any more or less important than another person's.

Words like "meaning" and "significance" make it sound as though you need to do something huge and grand to find a purpose in your life. Of course, you can do big things, but size by other people's "yardsticks" does not matter when it comes to giving your life purpose and meaning. You don't have to scale Mount Kilimanjaro or build houses for the homeless to find what matters to you. I have done neither of those things and feel a great sense of purpose. I felt that purpose when I coached basketball for young boys year after year, sometimes without ever winning a single game. Some may think that the boys' basketball team I coached is trivial in the grand scheme of things. But I felt really good when I saw how much joy my team got from playing well and improving. They were joyful and so was I. For me, that was a great accomplishment. The point is you always have a choice to create meaning and purpose for your life, because it is not the activity that you seek, it is the feeling that comes from doing it.

On a lighter note, I once counseled a husband who was unfaithful to his wife and never came through for his kids. I told him that he could at least be the best bad example anyone could ever find! Kind of a smart-aleck approach, but I think that even though I was joking it actually shamed him into some changes! Who knew?

Living for—and in—the Moment

None of us is immune to losing our way at some point. Even right now, when I absolutely love what is going on in my life on many different levels, there are still times when I question why or how God could or would allow certain things to happen. It's the age-old question, why do bad people thrive and good people often suffer and die? There are also times when I look around at my world and realize that even with all my efforts, skills, and abilities, I'm just a renter. I'm just passing through this world. Old sayings become old sayings because they're profound, and, as I said earlier, "You can't take it with you" is one of them. So is the old Indian saying that "You can't leave a footprint in a moving stream." In other words, somebody will live in my house after I die. Somebody will produce in my studio after I'm gone and somebody will influence others after I finally choose to stop talking and talking and talking! So what's the big deal? In those moments, what gets me through is recognizing that helping people now and making someone else's experience better, in the moment, is enough for the moment. I also very strongly believe in the ripple effect. If, for example, I can get one person to control their anger and impulses, and therefore stop abusing their child, that effect can ripple through many generations to come.

It can be exhausting to live in this world without meaning and in what I call assigned roles, which are those given to you by other people that are disconnected from your authentic self. I remember how draining that was, and though I was close to 40 years old when I finally made that realization, I had to do something about it. That's because living that way robs you of energy. Denying your true purpose on this earth is like when you were a child and you'd try to hold a beach ball under the water. I've used this analogy before, but I do so because it's so appropriate. The beach ball's natural tendency is to pop up from beneath the surface, and so you'd need to use a lot of strength to fight and hold it down. Often, you had to use your whole body to do so. Eventually, you'd become exhausted and drained. (Besides, living that way is stressful, and chronic stress has a huge impact on your physical and emotional well-being, as I talked about in chapter 3.)

However, when you figure out why you exist, you have the energy, passion, and motivation to handle your life—even the obstacles. You don't need all your energy just to get out of bed each day so you can put that effort into things you love. You feel uplifted and empowered. You feel inspired, as though you can do anything, and the whole world looks different. Each day is no longer a burden; it is a gift.

Existential Crisis Audit

To figure out if you may be experiencing an existential crisis, take this audit. Read the descriptions of specific thoughts and feelings below, and then choose which one of these four responses fits your situation best.

Never: These emotions or thoughts have not been present or you have not been aware of them.

Occasionally: You have been aware of them, but they have not interfered with your life as it is.

Significantly: You have experienced these emotions or thoughts every day and your social relationships, personal quality of life, or work has been significantly influenced.

Severely: You have been severely limited in how you can embrace your present relationships, personal life, or work in the same attitude.

1. **I'm worried that I have a set number of years left in my life and I have yet to start truly living.**

   Never __ Occasionally __ Significantly __ Severely __

2. **I realize that I have a special mission in life, yet I don't know what it is and have no clue how to discover it.**

   Never __ Occasionally __ Significantly __ Severely __

3. **I am depressed about the things that I promised myself that I'd do but haven't done.**

   Never __ Occasionally __ Significantly __ Severely __

4. **I find myself worrying what my life is supposed to be about or who I am supposed to be.**

   Never __ Occasionally __ Significantly __ Severely __

5. **If I achieved everything I set out to do, I wonder what importance it would really accomplish for anyone.**

   Never __ Occasionally __ Significantly __ Severely __

6. **I doubt whether my life is worthwile.**

   Never __ Occasionally __ Significantly __ Severely __

7. **I am examining the values that I have lived by and wonder how I could know the truth of life.**

   Never __ Occasionally __ Significantly __ Severely __

8. **I wonder who I am and what would be left of me if I had no name or family background.**

   Never __ Occasionally __ Significantly __ Severely __

9. **I wonder why we exist and why we are here.**

   Never __ Occasionally __ Significantly __ Severely __

10. **I wonder, if I could, what I would choose as my name, my culture, or my family.**

    Never __ Occasionally __ Significantly __ Severely __

Scoring

If you checked mostly "Never" and "Occasionally," it's unlikely that you're experiencing an existential crisis. (However, some of the tips below can still help you in your life, so you may want to read on.)

If you checked "Severely" four or more times, you may be experiencing an existential crisis. In that case, you may need to evaluate your values and clarify the meaning you have for your life—something that may require a retreat from your present demands.

If you checked "Significantly" at least five times or "Severely" up to four times, it's likely that you're dealing with some moderate but significant levels of existential crisis. You should pay extra attention for some self-help ways of dealing with this struggle.

If you checked "Significantly" five times, you may be dealing with some temporary anxiety related to integration of behavior into your core values and self-authenticity. As a result pay close attention to the self-help recommendations that follow so that you can begin to control your life more efficiently.

WHAT TO EXPECT

One thing that's pretty common on this day is an overwhelming sense of helplessness. If you feel this, trust me, you are not alone. The psychological term for these emotions—perceived lack of control over your life or an apparent inability to escape from distressing pain—coined by the psychologist Martin E. P. Seligman, is learned helplessness (you shut down your learning process, where you can no longer process new information that might give you relief; your brain has said there is no help, no hope, and it closes the "window" through which new information would flow), and is a state in which you feel as if you have no control over what happens to you. You may feel trapped and believe that any efforts to help yourself are futile. Many people who attempt suicide report this sense of helplessness and say that their action was a result of feeling that they had no other solution. After all, if you feel as though you have no ability to control or influence your future, it can be overwhelming. This lack of direction, despair, and hopelessness can be a huge component of this crisis.

Other emotions you may experience are self-hatred, anger, paralyzing anxiety, emptiness, emotional numbness, a lack of self-respect, and a sense of irrelevance. You may become cynical. You may question everything from your values to your family. If you believe in God, you may now question why you do. You may also find yourself withdrawing socially and isolating yourself from other people. That's because your whole world has been rocked—

the part of you that is questioning your purpose in life is also questioning other people's motives for caring about you. Or you may view them as foolish and having no point in *their* lives.

If you start talking about this topic, don't be surprised if some friends and family members pull away. They simply may not want to ask themselves the question or deal with the deeper issues of life. They may urge you to just go with the program rather than rock the boat. All this may be extremely frustrating when you're trying to examine the very foundations of your existence.

GETTING BACK TO BETTER DAYS

On this day of existential reckoning, when it's *your* crisis, *you* need to figure out what gives your life meaning. And don't think that time will stop until you figure it out. Today, the average life expectancy in this country is 78 years.[1] That means that if you're 38 years old today, you've got about 40 years left. That's 480 months, or 14,600 days. What are you going to do with that time? How are you going to give it meaning? Do you have a plan for how you're going to spend the days that you have left and the significance of your life? On the one hand, 480 months probably doesn't seem very long. But if you spend it sitting on the fence instead of living with passion, it can be a very, very, long time. You must strive to find your fit, your meaning, your purpose.

Now before we move on to how you'll actually do that, there are a few key points that I need to make clear. As I have said earlier, in the chapter discussing the day you realize that fear dominates your life, your authentic self—complete with purpose and passion—is inside you and has always been there. You just need to find it. The problem is that most of us don't let our true selves and desires come out and take center stage in our lives. For whatever reason, other things crowd them out. Life is a series of interactions with both the external world and your internal world. This means that though you start with certain traits and characteristics, your journey through this world and subsequent interactions and reactions change who you are. If your life experiences have generated outcomes you believe are negative and pain-producing, and you feel as if you are powerless to prevent them, your true and authentic self and your real purpose in life can get buried as you try to just "get by" instead of living with purpose. After a while, you become so used to that quiet fictional person that you aren't sure who the real you is. But the good news is that the authentic you is in there and always has been; you can find and reconnect with these characteristics and traits when you are ready to look for them.

If You Want Meaning, Create Meaning

One way to move toward a sense of sanity in a crisis of meaning, a crisis of pain and emptiness, is to commit to not only *finding* but in fact *creating* meaning and purpose in your day-to-day life. Life can hurt; there is no question about that. But it is not a process that has to be in vain. You can make it matter, make it mean something. Earlier I mentioned Viktor Frankl, who survived three years of the Holocaust in four different concentration camps. He could have had a meltdown from the horror of the daily brutality and death that surrounded him, but instead he chose to find meaning in his struggles and the shocking conditions of his world. Without finding that meaning, without creating hope in his mind, I don't see how he could ever have survived. The meaning he "found" was in part to survive in order to share his realization with others: no matter what your circumstances in life are, no matter how much others may try to control your behavior, you always have the right and the ability to choose the attitude you take about it. By the way, *you* and *I* are among those he survived to tell.

Chances are, you won't have to find meaning in as horrible a suffering as Dr. Frankl did to make sense of your life, but the process is basically the same. I've always liked and believed in the passage from Ecclesiastes 3:11 that says, "God has made everything beautiful for its own time. He has planted eternity in the human heart, but even so, people cannot see the whole scope of

God's work from beginning to end." Whether or not you are a Christian, you have to acknowledge that those are profound words. They go along with my belief that there are no accidents and that things in life happen for a reason, even if we can't initially understand why.

Now, I've had experiences that were not fun (to put it mildly) when they were happening. But without them (as clichéd as it sounds) I have to admit that I wouldn't be who I am today. Just like everybody else, when something goes wrong I wrestle with questions such as, "Was this supposed to happen?" "Is this my fault?" "Did I cause this?," so I know that there's little use in telling you not to go through that mental exercise because you probably will—if you haven't already. The point is, if you are going to ask yourself those questions, *answer* them. Own your bad choices if you have made them, but then find the strength and maturity to forgive yourself. The way that the past becomes your future is if you spend all your time looking over your shoulder. Sure, maybe you really screwed up, maybe you made some really bad decisions, but not dealing with the guilt and regret and putting it behind you by forgiving yourself (and others for that matter) means you will forever be a prisoner of your past. Not even God can change what *has* happened. Forgive yourself and others for whom you harbor anger, resentment, or hatred and move on.

Are you accountable for your choices? Of course you are. Do you deserve a sentence of punishment in which you bear the burden of guilt forever? No. It is time to take whatever lessons you can from those mistakes or bad choices and get real busy moving on to the next chapter of your life.

When you're faced with an existential crisis, it may be hard for you to know what's right for you today. Even if you did know, you probably wouldn't feel like doing it. You might not have the confidence. But our values are deeply rooted and have not been erased by this existential crisis. They may not be center stage in your mind, but they are there and it is these values that tell us what is right and wrong. Even though you may be struggling to find or create meaning in your existence and may feel that your compass has gone haywire, you have the ability to look back at your life and recognize what *have been* your guiding principles in better times. Below we will look at the values in your life that you may have taken for granted and that you may have never really articulated even to yourself. That's why now, more than ever, it's important to think about and identify what you believe is important in your life and what your currency really is. You need to define what matters to you. There are questions later on in this section that can help you figure this out.

But our values are deeply rooted and have not been erased by this existential crisis.

None of your negative emotions—anger, bitterness, despair, loneliness, emptiness, or depression is not just the result of anything that has or has not happened in your life. As I've discussed earlier in this book, all of those emotions are a product of what you have said to yourself, based on your perceptions and labels for whatever happened or didn't happen in your life. As we progress further on this quest for meaningfulness, pay close attention to how you're talking to yourself about yourself and the events of your life.

Clearly, your history and your perceptions of that history help you figure out your future. The first part of discovering your value currency is for you to select the most positive events in your life (meaning those that you have labeled in a positive way through your internal dialogue) and record the feelings that made those times so gratifying. Remember, it is not the external object or goal but the self-generated, rewarding feelings that are important here. In psychology we describe self-generated feelings as intrinsic values and the one that we see in our external world as extrinsic values. For example, one of the events might have been choosing and buying your first car. The intrinsic feelings you probably experienced were elation about owning such valuable property and pride in your ability to purchase it, while the extrinsic sources of feelings might have been the admiration of your friends or even feeling more attractive when you were behind the wheel. If this was a really positive feeling, then you were labeling this event with really positive thoughts. Another example might be when you got married or graduated from school. You might have had the feeling of becoming an adult who makes your own decisions and pride in the accomplishment of doing something so significant. Even the time you made a sick friend laugh as she sat in her hospital bed, if labeled positively, can create a real feeling of contribution. Understand, I'm not saying that all you have to do is lie to yourself about an event to generate positive feelings. You know when you're telling yourself the truth, so it's your job to put things into context, not to overreact to and catastrophize about whatever happens, but to find meaning and purpose in all the days of your life. You have that power because you have the power to control what you say to yourself about what happens in your life.

I want to help refocus you on a couple of things that may have fallen off the radar screen for you so that you can have an answer to why we bother in this struggle called life—I want to help you define (or reconnect with) your core values. If you or someone you love is feeling meaningless, pointless, and directionless on this day, you are probably starting to get confused right about now. That's okay. I know that whenever we start talking about lofty things such as "core values" and "intrinsic and extrinsic feelings" it's easy to wind up with confusion and a knitted brow. So, I want to get back to the basics here. I am going to walk you through some important concepts and suggest some ideas to help guide you through this process. These aren't just concepts that I am going to invent for you today—in this moment—they are tried and true guideposts that I have seen other people use successfully in defining meaning in their lives. Here are a few things that I want you to have a discussion with yourself about.

Do you value things such as integrity, love, and accountability? What does each of those things mean to you?

- What does integrity mean to you? To me, having integrity means doing the right thing when nobody is watching except me.

- What does love mean to you? Maybe it means that you care about another person's well-being more than your own.

- What does accountability mean to you? For me, it means taking responsibility for the choices I have made and not playing the victim and blaming others.

Think of other values and qualities that are important to you. The three I listed above are just a start, so make your own list now. Nothing is too small if it matters to you and defines you.

If you recognize that you have any of the three qualities that I listed above, then hopefully you've found part of the answer to "Why bother?" You make this world a better place for everyone else in it. You're a good force in this world. A force that is felt by those around you. To be a person—a citizen, a father, a brother, a son, a wife, a mother, a husband, or a daughter—who lives with those qualities means that you make other people's lives better; you make your family better, you make your community better, and you make your own life better. If you don't have those qualities, perhaps that is something you should strive to embrace or rekindle.

Now that we have identified some of your core values that create the filter through which you look at the world, let's talk about what's important to you in your life with some greater specificity. The next thing you would want to do if you are feeling as if your life is pointless is to identify what your priorities are for your life.

I wrote a book back in 1998 called *Life Strategies,* and in it I asked people to do an exercise that I think was very important then and is very important now. I am going to walk through that same exercise right now. I want you to make a list of what really matters to you in your life. I'm not talking about traits and characteristics. I'm talking about the things, the activities, the people and parts of your life that matter to you or have mattered to you at one time. In the left-hand column list these priorities; the things you value and hold nearest and dear to your heart. List your top five priorities, beginning with the most important one. Begin by writing in space number one that which you hold to be the most important thing in your life. Then list that which you consider to be the second most important thing in your life, and so on, through number five. For example, my number one priority is providing safety, shelter, security, and comfort for my family, and my second is to, along with my wife, Robin, prepare our children to survive and thrive in this world on their own. Third might be to have a positive impact on the world I live in. Those are just some examples to get you started; what are your priorities? I understand that there may not be much separation between some of these values, but force yourself to order them one through five, nonetheless. Give it careful thought, and truly search your heart for what is important to you.

After you list your priorities, use the right-hand column to list your time allocations in descending order. In space number one, list the activity or pursuit that you spend the highest percentage of your waking hours on. Be honest and accurate, because this is a *quantitative* exercise. For example, how much time in each day do you really spend with your family? Think about it: you get up at 6:00 a.m., you race around, you get ready for work, you go to work—it's an hour commute, so you leave at 7:00 a.m. and get there at 8:00 a.m., you work until 5:00 p.m., you have an hour commute back, so you get home about 6:00 p.m., the kids are doing their homework and dinner is being fixed, and then you watch television—how much, no kidding, eyeball-to-eyeball quality time do you spend with those you love? Take a moment to fill out your own time allocations, honestly and accurately, in the space provided here.

Priorities	**Time Allocation**
1.__________________	1.__________________
2.__________________	2.__________________
3.__________________	3.__________________
4.__________________	4.__________________
5.__________________	5.__________________

Having performed all of your assigned steps, let's examine what you've just written down. Ask yourself if you have neglected some of your priorities. I suspect that if you are feeling the way you are, you're probably not being true to your priorities. Pay attention to these incongruencies. If God and family are at the top of your priorities but work is at the top of your time allocation, you have a problem. How much time are you spending on what you care about? For example, how much time are you spending with your family? If you're in a busy workaday world like so many people, it's probably going to be a fraction of the time you spend at work and probably less than the time you spend watching television. So if that's the case, based strictly on your time allocation, television must be more important to you than your kids.

I'm not saying that you should quit your job and risk becoming homeless so that you can spend more time with your family. But it does tell you that you may want to balance these things more. It may mean getting out from under some car payments so you can work less. It may mean turning off the television so that you have actual conversation time. It may mean taking the video controller out of your kid's hands when he is playing video football, going out into the backyard, and throwing a *real* football around. It may mean creating meaning, purpose, and value by actively changing how you are living your life. To create meaning, you have to change how you've been living your life, because based on the results, it's not doing it for you, and I'm just trying to give you some suggestions on where you might start looking to make some changes.

Be honest with yourself in this audit. If you realize that you're actually spending an hour and a half with your family, ten hours working, and four hours watching TV—then your reaction may be "Whoa, wait a minute, maybe I need to get rid of these cars, quit that second job, and spend time with my kids." I guarantee you that they would rather ride to school with you in a '98 Honda than watch you pull away in a new Lexus. They would rather spend time with you in the backyard of a modest house than never see you while they sit alone in a grand house. If that is the trap you're in, you may well feel meaningless, because you're not being consistent with what's important to you. You *are* doing the things that are meaningless and neglecting things that are meaningful. That can lead to powerful feelings of frustration and meaninglessness in your life. The fix I talked about above—downgrading your material life—may sound like a sacrilege, but that may be exactly what you need to do. It may mean dumping some *things* in order to be able to focus on people and purpose. Maybe you need to move somewhere where you are not house-poor so you can become family-rich. Maybe you need to just buck the trend and get back to something that allows you to pursue what's really important to you. If you do that, you may just start feeling more payoff from your life. I say all of this to you because so often we can feel so far down that we don't really know where to start. I have had people say to me, "Dr. Phil, I *do* want to create meaning in my life, but I don't know where to start, I don't even know where to begin!" Well if you are in that position, now you have a suggestion as to where to begin.

The next year is going to go by whether or not you are comforting yourself and generating currency that makes you feel better or you're just dropping out and sitting on the curb.

Now I Ask You, "Why Not?"

If none of the philosophies and strategies I've laid out in this chapter resonates with you, let me pose another question. During this challenging day of feeling empty and purposeless, you ask, "Why am I struggling? Why am I going on when it doesn't seem to matter?" Maybe one simple answer to your question is found in another question: "Why not?" Even if you believe that your life is pointless and meaningless and you can't justify your existence on this planet, why not *try*? Why not struggle and *try* to achieve? What else do you have to do? As I said before, if you're 38 years old and experiencing this existential crisis, what will you gain by sitting around pouting and complaining for the next 40 years or 480 months?

Your only alternative is working to create some satisfaction, some self-reward, some peace and security. At least identify your currency. What do you value? What makes you feel better today? Figure that out and then work to create a little bit of it today. You worry about tomorrow, tomorrow. Be selfish right now and create some self-satisfaction. Why? Because it feels better when you do this than it does when you don't. Wouldn't you rather feel better than not? Generate something that makes you feel better today. And by the way, that is not *totally* selfish, because when you feel better, you do better, not just for you but for everyone. At the very least, you want to be warm and dry or be well fed. The next year is going to go by whether or not you are comforting yourself and generating currency that makes you feel better or you're just dropping out and sitting on the curb. There may not be a purpose to this life that you can identify right now, but at least care for yourself and at least cushion your existence in some way. And who knows, "Why not?" may be your first step in your journey to figuring out why.

FINAL THOUGHT

One last important note: this search for meaning and purpose in your life should not be taken lightly. Think about it, in the entire history of the world there has been only one you. Others may share your name. There are lots of Bobs, Bills, Karens, and Susans, but each one is unique. You are unique, and it is up to you to find your place in the world, create the impact that only you can create, and define your existence in a way that truly is distinctively yours. I urge you not to look at reality as a burden or problem, but as something that can change your life in ways you can't imagine, if you will just have an appreciation for the opportunity that is *you*. You may not feel that you are some special being right now, and you can roll your eyes if you must, but stick with it and, eventually, I think you'll agree. Because with effort, patience, and dedication you can begin to define your role in the journey through this life and your role in the lives of those making the trip with you.

It is absolutely okay to question things until you are satisfied with the answers. The key is to keep questioning until you get the answers. You do not want to get frustrated and quit the quest. We have benefited as a society and culture from the collective questioning that occurs. There has definitely been a movement of thinking across time. Asking the hard questions is a good thing, stopping the pursuit for answers is not. Our sensitivities as a human race seem to have grown into a new appreciation for life in general. We even seem to be coming closer to a deeper gratitude for the earth on which we live and our responsibilities in connection with it. There is clear evidence that we, as a whole, derive our levels of consciousness from the cumulative existential questions that arise and the answers that we find individually and together. Everyone has a part, which can be scary. After all, it takes courage and wisdom to create and, more important, own your life experience.

11

The Next Step

If you are going through hell, keep going.
—WINSTON CHURCHILL

Okay, we have taken a hard look at the realities of the seven most challenging days of your life. Boy oh boy, wasn't that fun! A lot of detail, and probably way more than you think you would ever want or need to know. But I can assure you that *when*, not if, you or someone you love wakes up to one of these most challenging and unwanted days, you will be glad you did the work to prepare yourself for that challenge.

Life is anything but formulaic, and seven is no magic number of days. I'll bet you could add some to the list that I didn't write about here. You may experience only four or five of them; you may have to go through all seven; and, unfortunately, you may have to go through some of them more than once. Either way, hopefully you get my point that forethought, planning, and realistic expectations are crucial to how you will react to these or any other crises. There may be nothing you can do about whether or not they occur, but you have now done something to get ready for when they do.

Despite good choices and high-ground intentions, neither you nor I can avoid *all* of the pitfalls. We can live right, choose well, be smart and alert, and avoid problems that reckless living brings, but there is a whole other category of problems that simply come with being human and the cycle of life. The question isn't whether or not it's fair or unfair because much of our experience in life is not fair. The point is that it just *is*. As I said when we started this conversation, I do believe that you, me, all of us have within us, or can certainly acquire, the intellect, strength, depth, moral compass, and determination to survive and, in fact, successfully deal with any challenge we'll encounter in our lives. Now, this doesn't mean that you don't have to learn certain skill sets or techniques. It also doesn't mean that you will like these challenges or that they won't hurt you and change your life. But you have the depth to get through these challenges and to find a way to exist with value and purpose. It is the finding of that way that we have been working on here.

You have the depth to get through these challenges and to find a way to exist with value and purpose.

What I have done with this book is endeavor to do at least two things: one, I want you to believe in yourself enough to know that these days might make you bend but not break—that you do have within you that strength and fortitude I described; and two, I wanted to provide you with certain specific skill sets and mental and emotional strategies to make the most of your God-given gifts, traits, and characteristics. You have what you need to survive and thrive, but like most of us, including me, you may have needed a wake-up call. This is your reminder that life is about choices and that you do have the privilege and the ability to choose. Choosing well in the fire of chaos can be difficult if not impossible. Things happen too fast, emotions run too high, and the distractions can be mentally paralyzing. That is precisely why you need to prepare *in advance*.

Even the professional airline pilots who fly you and your family rely on this approach. They rely on "placards," boldfaced bullet points printed in bright red and posted right in their sightline on the instrument panel. These placards outline the immediately required steps in the event of an emergency such as an engine failure or fire. That is certainly on their list of most challenging days!

These professionals recognize that the ability to think under pressure is greatly enhanced by preplanning and having something to prompt them in the moment. I hope that this book becomes part of your "boldfaced placard" for the seven most challenging days of your life. I hope that there is information here that you have learned from and can refer to when needed. It won't be your only resource, but hopefully it can help. As I have said throughout the book the good news is that many of the strategies are lifestyle-based and centered on your thoughtful choices—choices as to attitude, approach, emotionality, and expectations, all of which come from within you and are therefore common from one crisis day to the next.

I talk about this from experience because I have had many crises in my own life. I've experienced financial turmoil and dire straits. I have lived through the painful loss of my own father, the sudden death of both my mother-in-law and father-in-law, and something that had perhaps an even more powerful impact on me, the tremendous pain that these deaths caused my wife. Watching her suffer had, perhaps, an even more powerful impact on me. All those things were demanding and difficult, but I learned from each experience. I observed myself in those difficult times and discovered that, while I was vulnerable, I "chose" to survive. You can make that choice too, and what's more, you will get better with practice. I guess that's what we call maturity. I wish I had known during that first crisis in my life what I knew by the time I faced the most recent crisis. My hope is that this book has "fast-forwarded" some of that important knowledge to you.

When I think about how lost and frail my mother looked the day my father died, I distinctly remember wondering how she'd get through it all. What would life be like for her? Would I ever see her vivacious spirit again? Would I ever hear her laugh? I'm not going to say that those first few months and even years weren't difficult. Because they were—for all of us. But in time, my mother found the rhythm for her new life. She moved to a smaller home, tended her lawn, and made friends with her neighbors. I'm not saying she forgot her husband. Not by a long shot. She simply found another way to live her life. She blossomed in this unexpected chapter of her life. She got through the piercing pain. And so can you.

I obviously can't guarantee that you'll be happy for the rest of your life, and you wouldn't believe me if I did—neither of us is that foolish. What I *can* promise is that as you deal with the darkest

You can find your way back to a life of joy and purpose after any of these seven or more days. You can find your way back to a hopeful and loving life.

moments of your life, you will be changed; you will be wiser and, I'm betting, more appreciative of the smooth times in your life. You can find your way back to a life of joy and purpose after any of these seven or more days. You can find your way back to a hopeful and loving life. It is a cliché to say that hard times build character, so I won't say it. What I will say is that you are smart and you will learn. You will emerge and hopefully live with passion and purpose. Tim McGraw sang it well: "Live like you are dying."

THE CONTINUITY OF LIFE

Madeleine L'Engle very profoundly said, "The great thing about getting older is that you don't lose all the other ages you've been." I think that it is critically important that we maintain a continuous relationship between who we are today and who we were when we were 10 years old, 12 years old, 15 years old, 20 years old, 30 years old, even as recently as your forties or fifties. This is especially crucial on those seven days, because you need to remember and stay in touch with who you were *before* that day happened. When a crisis hits, we get wrapped up in it and can literally forget who we are. We can lose sight of what has uniquely identified us over the years because we are emotionally overwhelmed, scared, and confused—maybe even in panic mode—so much so that we forget our own history of strength and success. We can begin to question everything we thought we knew, every strength we thought we had, and even the value of every resource and loving person around us. It is really, really easy to feel very lost and alone in our darkest hours. But those dark hours don't take away who we were before they occurred—that is, unless we let them. Bottom line: I'm telling you to stand up in the face of adversity and be a player, be a survivor in this game of life. You made it this far, and you can choose to make it further. Think about it: by the age of two to three, you mastered walking and talking, and in the first five years of life your personality was well along the road to being shaped. By the eighth grade, you beat the majority of deadly diseases that kill huge numbers of children around the world with a fine-tuned immune system. You've accumulated large quantities of information and established some level of problem-solving skills that got you this far in a complex world. Your development is a cumulative process, and you have been paying tuition as you go.

I don't believe that crises make heroes. I believe that crises just give heroes yet to be discovered a place to shine. Every one of these seven days needs a hero to step up, and that hero can be you. I know for sure that the same things that got me through life when I was 15 years old, on my own, and actually living on the street with only a few—if any—cents in my pocket are the same things that got me through every crisis I've been through since then. I often say that the best predictor of future behavior is relevant past behavior. I know that I survived all of that because I saw myself do it, and as long as I remember that, I know I will survive whatever the future holds. You need to know that, too.

Life is a movie, not a snapshot. Therefore, if you pause the movie of your life at any one moment, you will not have a true picture of who you are. If you pause it at your most victorious moments, you will have a distorted view of who you are and what your life is like. And if you pause it at the worst moments of your life—such as one of these seven days—you will also have a distorted view of who you are and what your life is all about. It is only if you look at the whole movie to date and the continuity of it that you get a true sense of who you are. On the flip side, if you lose your continuity, you lose your identity.

I personally feel a greater sense of power and self-determination because of that continuity. One way that I stay in touch with my identity and the personal truth of who I really am is through music. I listen to oldies music a lot. So much so that I can't tell you the number of times my two boys have said, "Hey, Dad, your oldies are really getting old." But when I'm alone and particularly want to focus on who I am and where I've been, oldies music has strong emotional power. It's not because I'm living in the past or want to go back to that time. I don't. I like my life now better than I have at any other point in the past. But I listen to that music to remember what my life was like at that time, and I use that as an anchor to who I am. I remember how I felt when I was hurt, disappointed, or alone or when I was victorious and on top of the world. Music is an effective "time machine" because songs are actually processed in the same parts of our brain as our emotions. As a result, hearing one of these songs reconnects us with the feelings of the time it represents. For example, "Amazing Grace" is one of the most beloved and important gospel songs for a great number of people. In fact, most of them can tell you the day—even the moment—when that song became meaningful for them. That's the same mechanism that causes music from a victorious time in our past to inspire us and bring out the best of who we are in the present. Once you understand and are aware of this continuity, however you may connect with it, you realize that roots grow deep. And the deeper the roots grow, the harder it is to get knocked over.

My point here is that it is critically important to stay focused on your *whole* life, not just who you are or what you're going through today. You are more than today. You're more than this week. You are the sum total of all the years of your life. Your past is a big body of evidence of who you are. I have fifty-seven years' worth of evidence that shows me who I really am. As a result, even if something awful happened yesterday or something difficult happens today or tomorrow, it is not going to define however many years I've got left on this planet or alter the years I have already lived. For the most part, I like the guy I've been observing for the last fifty-seven years. I would be his friend if I met him somewhere along the way, so I need to be his friend now, especially in difficult times. I'm okay with him and the choices he's made in his life and what he's done. Sure, he's made mistakes, but I have compassion for him and the places where he's messed up. He *can* and *will* strive—learn and grow—but in the meantime and along the way, he's a pretty good egg. Doesn't it make sense to be your own best friend?

LOOKING FORWARD

In order to see your life in context and with balance, you also have to look at the blessings. I know that you have a lot of great things ahead of you, so let's look into the future for a moment. I believe that you're going to experience *at least* seven miracles—moments unlike any other—and you will know them when they arrive. Yes, we have predictable frictions and turns in our lives that can bring us to our knees. But there are also miracles that can occur any day of your life. And what's really wonderful is that if you look for them, the joy that comes from these miracles can outweigh the pain of your crises. Here are those that I can almost assure you will happen in your future.

The miracle of life. It's likely that you're going to witness the unique moment of a baby being born—either your own or someone else's. Words can't even describe this, but the feeling you get inside is proof that you are in the midst of something truly miraculous and beyond our own understanding. There are times when we get egotistical and self-centered, but then there are other times when we realize that we are a small but unique part of a much larger picture. We don't have a clue as to how to create the life of even the simplest flea. We're extremely primitive in the dynamics and mechanics of how this three-pound organ that we call our brain functions. I am totally shocked when I read books that question the existence of God and the origins of life, especially when we have very infinitesimal knowledge of even a single cell. We're just arrogant to presume that we can define life.

The miracle of love. Love is stronger than death because it is something that stays with us even after a loved one passes away. Love is a healing force that's physical as well as mental, and love binds us. What's amazing is that it's one of the few things that we have an infinite amount of; our capacity to love never shrinks but only expands. Even after someone dies, we are able to find love again—maybe not the same love, but somehow we open our hearts again. There are times when you're going to feel loved—even when you think you don't deserve it. I know this firsthand because I'll be the first to admit that in more than three decades of marriage, there have been times when even *I* didn't believe I deserved the love that Robin offered. I truly believe that this kind of unconditional emotion, and the fact that you can be loved in spite of yourself, is a true miracle.

The miracle of forgiveness. Forgiveness is a gift, and I mean that whether you are the person being forgiven or doing the forgiving. When someone hurts you deeply, it is all too easy to get fixated by emotions that keep you from moving forward. This anger and need for revenge and attempts to hurt in order to satisfy your own pain eat away at any joy that you can have. It's an act of ill will that can bind both people into a vortex of destruction both physically and mentally. The miracle occurs when you have the ability to let go of that emotional debt, because it can truly transform your life.

The miracle of beauty. You're going to see something so beautiful that it's going to take your breath away. Maybe it will be a gorgeous sunset, an awe-inspiring mountain range, or an amazingly tender moment between your child and spouse. You're also going to hear something of a similar magnitude. This could be a lullaby, the words of a poem, a hymn, a wedding song, or the first time your child says, "I love you."

The miracle of compassion. You're going to witness true altruism from somebody who unselfishly gives of himself or herself. Maybe it's a soldier putting his life on the line for yours, or maybe it's witnessing people reaching out to help total strangers in tragedies as they did after Hurricane Katrina and 9/11. But these moments should remind you that you are never ever alone.

The miracle of healing. Yes, the seven most challenging days of your life are full of pain, both mental and physical, but even though the events that we've just discussed are so dark—the *real* miracle is that we are blessed with healing. We're not machines, where once a part is broken it is always broken. Our bodies and minds are programmed to heal. Think of people who experience the worst trauma you can imagine as children or young adults—trauma that could easily incapacitate them—yet they survive.

The miracle of awareness. You have an awareness that you are not alone but part of something greater than yourself. Most people feel isolated and separate in their suffering, especially when they experience emotional or physical pain. Perhaps the basis of that is because the root of the word pain comes from the Latin word for "punishment." After all, it's very common to believe that good people are rewarded while the not so good are punished. Consequently, this sense of pain tends to isolate us and cause immense shame. In contrast, sharing that pain and realizing that you are part of something greater than yourself can save you. You become connected. You transform. Alcoholics find a great deal of comfort and bond when dealing with other alcoholics who like themselves are struggling to manage their disease. Deaf people have been known to find tremendous strength when they bond with other deaf people—even to the point that they refuse to have surgery that will give them their hearing back.

Observe Your Own Life

I want you to try something for me. For as many nights as it feels right, before going to bed, write down at least one miracle or blessing that you experienced that day. Maybe it's something as amazing as seeing your best friend's baby when she is just hours old or as small as a neighbor helping you carry your groceries when the bags are about to break. Write these down in one place—a notebook or journal. At the end of each month I want you to go through each day and see what's happened. See if you recognize any of the seven that I've mentioned above. It will feel good, I promise.

In addition to observing your life and noticing all of the blessings, it's key to be proactive and make the rest of your days the best they can be. In earlier chapters, you figured out about how many days you have left on this earth. It's good to spend some quiet time thinking about what you will do with those days and even write down those things that you want to achieve in the same place you wrote your blessings. It won't take five minutes a day, and you deserve that quiet, personal time.

The result can be empowering. Franklin D. Roosevelt said, "There is nothing to fear but fear itself." I couldn't agree more. Fear is often the greatest barrier to joy and peace. After all, nobody wants their obituary to talk about how they didn't stand up for their values or take a leap because they were afraid. Fear is at the seat of every limitation in the human experience, yet it yields only a destructive end. Do your best to push past it. As I have said over and over, in reality, there's nothing you can't bear.

By the way, that doesn't mean that you have to go through all of your struggles or climb all of your hills alone. In fact, it's often hard to take the first step (or even the fifth or sixth step) toward getting through difficult times on your own. It's okay to feel this way—many people do. You also shouldn't feel weak, inadequate, or bad about yourself if you want to seek professional help from a qualified psychologist, psychiatrist, or pastoral counsel for any or all of these tough moments in your life. Time spent with an objective mental health care provider can be invaluable as you deal with these seven crises or any of the other days of your life. No one gets extra points in life for going it alone.

THE END . . . FOR NOW

I've spent chapters talking about stuff no one wants to talk about, the dark, difficult days that can bring us to our knees and make us wonder how we'll get through the next minute. But life is also filled with beauty and richness that you can't even predict, and now that you've prepared for some of the most challenging days, I believe you will see the best even more clearly. In your journey through this book, I hope that you have changed the attitude that you take to the process of your life. Sitting on the sidelines with sweaty palms is a waste of precious time. Letting other people or events drive your decisions is just wrong. You have been given the gift of choice, and hopefully you now have some additional ideas about how to choose well. Taking responsibility for your actions and knowing that you create your own experience is an empowering reality that helps you live with a sense of calm, peace, and security. Remember, if you get into the middle of a dark day or even a longer crisis and you feel that you need a miracle—be that miracle.

Appendix A

1. Desensitization and Cognitive Therapy

Desensitization is a process in which the emotional attachment of an event or image can be removed to allow an individual to focus more rationally. The premise of the procedure is basically that you cannot experience fear and relaxation at the same time (be in a sympathetic and parasympathetic state simultaneously) because the mind simply is not wired that way. The process is to relearn a relaxed association instead of a fear-related association.

There is more than one protocol, but I will give you an example. Suppose you had a very fearful experience when you first attempted to drive a car; you had an accident or you heard a horrific story that you identified with, and since then you have been afraid of touching a steering wheel. The therapist might start the relearning by helping to identify the specific factors with the association. Then there would be steps to dissolve the fear and reassociate the events with rational relaxation, such as having you learn to breathe and relax your muscles while you imagine and then eventually drive a car.

Cognitive therapy is an approach that looks at your irrational thoughts that produce your fear and helps change your thinking patterns. This works by teaching you that you can actually *choose* your thoughts—meaning that you can choose your reactive thoughts to the events that confront you. And if you have the freedom to change your thoughts, you can change your fears. You can make better choices—choices not motivated by fear but by your true desires. Instead of living with unchallenged thoughts—for example, that you're unlovable or undeserving—you can change your thoughts to the truth that you are deserving of good things regardless of what anyone else thinks.

Appendix B

Note: This information is not offered for you to self diagnose, but for you to recognize the presence of certain traits, characteristics, or thought patterns that should suggest to you to seek out professional help.

1. Types of Mood Disorders

- **Major depressive disorder:** Characterized by one or more severe depression periods lasting at least two weeks.
- **Dysthymic disorder:** Characterized by a lack of enjoyment and/or pleasure in life that occurs most days for at least two years. The symptoms are milder than those of major depression, and the affected person is able to function—at less than peak performance.
- **Bipolar I disorder:** Generally considered the "classic" form of the illness, it is characterized by extreme mood swings between high periods called "manic episodes" and low periods called "depression," which may alternate with periods of normal mood.*
    - Manic episode: A period of intense, euphoric highs occurring nearly every day for at least one week during which a person feels almost indestructible. They may talk more and/or faster than usual, have an overinflated sense of self-esteem, become easily excitable and/

* Depression usually follows on the tail end of a manic episode, when the person's mind finally slows down enough to recognize the consequences of their actions.

or distracted, have racing thoughts and more energy than usual, and need less sleep. These people may seem like the "life of the party," but mania can be dangerous, putting the affected person out of touch with reality and leading to impulsive spending or gambling, rash business and/or personal decisions, risky sexual behavior, and excessive use of drugs and/or alcohol.

- **Bipolar II disorder:** A less severe form than bipolar I in which the signature highs and lows are present, but instead of the highs being manic episodes they are hypomanic episodes.
    - Hypomanic episode: A high period with symptoms similar to those of a manic episode but not quite as severe. Does not warrant hospitalization or cause obvious impairment in the person's social or work life.
- **Postpartum major depression (PMD):** Characterized as serious depressive symptoms that occur after childbirth and last weeks or months. Women may be vulnerable to depression during this time because of the hormonal changes that follow childbirth combined with psychosocial stresses such as sleep deprivation.

2. Types of Disorders Related to Anxiety

- **Panic attack:** An unexpected burst of terror in which feelings of doom, apprehension, or fearfulness take over. May be accompanied by scary physical symptoms such as chest pain, dizziness, and/or shortness of breath.
- **Agoraphobia:** Fear of places and situations where escape might be difficult in the event of a panic attack, leading to an avoidance of normal activities outside the home.
- **Phobia:** Significant anxiety, usually irrational, provoked by a specific circumstance or object.

- **Obsessive-compulsive disorder:** Characterized by repeated, unwanted thoughts (obsessions) and/or repetitive behaviors or rituals performed to prevent the thoughts or make them go away (compulsions).
- **Post-traumatic stress disorder:** High levels of anxiety in the reexperiencing of an extremely traumatic event or ordeal (that involved physical harm or the threat of it) through associated imagery or exposure to similar circumstances or cues.
- **Generalized anxiety disorder:** Long-term excessive anxiety that is unprovoked and causes exaggerated worry and tension (at least six months).

3. Types of Severe Mental Disorders

- **Schizophrenia:** A disorder lasting at least six months that is characterized by hallucinations, disorganized behavior, delusions, and/or thought disorders.

  Subtypes of schizophrenia:

  - Paranoid: Characterized by delusions and hallucinations that typically share a common theme, such as persecutory fears or grandiose, arrogant emotions.
  - Catatonic: Disturbed movement, body, and language that may be displayed through extreme negativism, muteness, the striking of odd poses, and echoing others' remarks.
  - Disorganized: Disorganized speech and a severe reduction in emotional expressiveness that may be demonstrated through things such as poor personal hygiene or silliness and laughter unrelated to the topic of conversation.
- **Schizoaffective:** The combination of schizophrenia and a mood disorder.

- **Schizophreniform:** A moderate form of schizophrenia that is temporary (one to six months).
- **Brief schizophrenia:** A schizophrenia behavior that lasts one to thirty days.
- **Delusional disorder:** A disorder characterized by nonbizarre delusions without other aspects of schizophrenia.

Appendix C

Note: If you recognize the presence of some or all of these thought patterns, traits, or characteristics, let that be your cue to seek professional help.

LEARN HOW TO RECOGNIZE WARNING SIGNS

Where there's smoke, there may well be a fire. And the earlier you get to the source, the quicker you can do something about it and the less chance you have of it escalating into a five-alarm fire that burns everything down, including your future.

Here are some warning signs that things may be getting out of hand for you or someone you love.

Signs of Depression

For each of the following signs, decide if any of these emotions or feelings has severely restricted your social relationships, personal life, or work:

- Feeling sad and empty about what you haven't accomplished in life or what you may accomplish in the future.
- Feeling that the world would be better off without you.
- Having no energy or motivation to do anything that might make you feel better emotionally.
- Having no interest in activities that you used to enjoy or participate in.
- Can't sleep or sleeping all the time.

- Feeling fatigued.
- Feeling worthless.
- Having a cloud of guilt that prevents you from enjoying anything.
- Can't concentrate or focus attention on anything.
- Having recurrent thoughts of death and thinking about suicide.
- Feeling alone, even when people are around.

Signs of Anxiety Disorders

For each of the following signs, consider if any of these emotions or feelings has severely restricted your social relationships, personal life, or work:

- Having excessive stress and apprehensive expectations (worries) about events and activities (work, school, marriage, family, etc.).
- Cannot control apprehension and stress, so it continues until someone or something else disrupts it.
- Finding yourself restless and feeling on edge (more often than not).
- Feeling fatigued and tired, regardless of what you have done, for the majority of the time.
- Having difficulties concentrating on something for the majority of the time.
- Frequently irritable, impatient, and short-tempered with others.
- Experiencing great muscle tension in the shoulders, legs, and neck—so much that these areas ache.

- Experiencing great difficulties falling asleep or waking up soon after and being unable to go back to sleep.
- Having irrational fears regarding the environment (outside the home, people, heights, etc.).
- Having irrational fears about controlling things that relate to health issues (gaining weight, contamination, serious illness, etc.).

Signs of Schizophrenia/Psychosis

For each of the following signs, consider if any of these emotions or feelings has severely restricted your social relationships, personal life, or work:

- Hearing voices that tell you to hurt yourself or others.
- Often having delusions and hallucinations that no one else experiences.
- Feeling overwhelmed with the challenges in your life and not having the coping skills to deal with it.
- Having severe problems in knowing where you are and your reality is totally different from the actual reality.
- Living in a world of great suspicion and being afraid of invisible or distorted objects as out to get you physically.
- Being afraid of everything about life.
- Experiencing great difficulties in having good relationships with family or having good long-lasting intimate relationships.
- Having poor mental health and displaying inappropriate behavior that costs you good job experiences.
- Having thoughts that are confusing and disorganized.

Notes

Chapter 3: Stress: The Days Between the Peaks and the Valleys

1. Quoted in Vince Fox, *Addiction, Change, and Choice* (See Sharp Pr, 1993).
2. Harvey Simon, "Stress," University of Maryland Medical Center, October 25, 2006, http://www.umm.edu/patiented/articles/what_health_consequences_of_stress_000031_3.htm (accessed May 27, 2008).
3. Rick E. Luxton, and David D. Ingram, "Vulnerability-Stress Models," in *Development of Psychopathology: A Vulnerability-Stress Perspective*, ed. Benjamin L. Hankin and John R. Z. Abela (Sage Publications, 2005), 520.
4. D. S. Charney, and H. K. Manji, "Life Stress, Genes, and Depression: Multiple Pathways Lead to Increased Risk and New Opportunities for Intervention," *Sci. STKE* 2004, re5 (2004).
5. David R. Imig, "Accumulated Stress of Life Changes and Interpersonal Effectiveness in the Family," *Family Relations*, July 1981: 367–371.
6. Lyn W. Freeman and G. Frank Lawlis, *Mosby's Complementary and Alternative Medicine: A Research-Based Approach* (St. Louis, Mo.: Mosby, 2001).
7. Harvey Simon, "Stress," University of Maryland Medical Center, October 25, 2006, www.umm.edu/patiented/articles/what_health_consequences_of_stress_000031_3.htm (accessed May 27, 2008).
8. Ernest Lawrence Rossi, *Psychobiology of Mind-Body Healing: New Concepts of Therapeutic Hypnosis* (New York: W.W. Norton & Company, 1993).
9. J. C. Coyne and A. DeLongis, "Going Beyond Social Support: The Role of Social Relationships and Adaptation," Journal of Consulting and Clinical Psychology, 54: (1986): 454.
10. J. D. Wilson, E. Braunwalk, K. J. Issenbacher, et al., *Harrison's Principles of Internal Medicine*, 12th ed. (New York: McGraw-Hill, 1991).
11. Janice K. Kiecolt-Glaser, Laura D. Fisher, Paula Ogrocki, Julie C. Stout, Carl E. Speicher, Ronald Glaser, "Marital Quality, Marital Disruption, and Immune Function," *Psychosomatic Medicine*, 1987: 13–34.
12. Janice Kiecolt-Glaser, Laura D. Fisher, Paula Ogrocki, Julie C. Stout, Carl E. Speicher, Ronald Glaser, "Marital Quality, Marital Disruption, and Immune Function," *Psychosomatic Medicine*, 1987: 13–34.
13. The American Institute of Stress, "Job Stress," http://64.233.167.104/search?q=cache:RuhgnCNhFKYJ:www.stress.org/job.htm+1+million+people+call+in+sick+to+work+each+day+due+to+stress&hl=en&ct=clnk&cd=1&gl=us (accessed May 27, 2008).

14. Jeanna Bryner, "Job Stress Fuels Disease," LiveScience.com, November 2006.
15. S. Melamed, A. Shirom, A.S. Toker, and L. Shapira, "Burnout and Risk of Type 2 Diabetes: A Prospective Study of Apparently Healthy Employed Persons," *Psychosomatic Medicine* 68(2006): 863–869.
16. C. Aboa-Eboule, C. Brisson, E. Maunsell, et al., "Job Strain and Risk of Acute Recurrent Coronary Heart Disease Events," *Journal of the American Medical Association* 298(2007): 1652–1660.
17. J. K. Kiecolt-Glaser, W. Garner, C.E. Speicher, et al., "Psychosocial Modifiers of Immuno Competence in Medical Students," *Psychosomatic Medicine* 46, no. 1 (1984): 7.
18. L. D. Kubzansky, I. Kawachi, A. Sprio, et al., "Is Worrying Bad for Your Health? A Prospective Study of Worry and Coronary Heart Disease in the Normative Aging Study," *Circulation* 95(1997): 818.
19. J. Denollet and D. L. Brutsaer, "Personality, Disease Severity, and the Risk of Long Term Cardiac Events in Patients with a Decreased Injection Fraction after Myocardial Infarction," *Circulation* 97(1998): 16.
20. J. Milam, "Post-traumatic Growth and HIV Disease Progression," *Journal of Consulting and Clinical Psychology* 74, no. 5(2006): 317.
21. *Americans Report Stress and Anxiety On-the-Job Affects Work Performance, Home Life: Almost Half of Employees Say Their Anxiety Is Persistent, Excessive, 2006 Stress & Anxiety Disorders Survey* (Silver Spring, Md.: The Anxiety Disorders Association of America, 2006).
22. The British Council and Richard Wiseman, "Pace of Life Project," *Pace of Life: A Quirkology Experiment*, August 22, 2006, www.paceoflife.co.uk (accessed July 10, 2008).
23. Centers for Disease Control and Prevention, "Physical Activity," *Department of Health and Human Services Centers for Disease Control and Prevention*, March 26, 2008, www.cdc.gov (accessed July 10, 2008).
24. Mayo Clinic Staff, "Aerobic Exercise: What 30 Minutes a Day Can Do: Need Inspiration to Start a Fitness Program? Explore the Many Benefits of Aerobic Exercise, from Increased Energy and Improved Stamina to Disease Prevention," *MayoClinic.com*, February 16, 2007, www.mayoclinic.com/health/aerobic-exercise/EP00002 (accessed July 10, 2008).
25. G. F. Lawlis, D. Selby, and D. Hinnan, "Reduction of Postoperative Pain Parameters by Presurgical Relaxation Instructions for Spinal Pain Patients," *Spine*, 1985: 649–651.
26. Radha Chitale, "You Feel What You Eat: Certain Foods May Have Direct Impact on Emotional State," *ABC News*, March 5, 2008, www.drgeorgepratt.com./main_reviews_article_abc-20080305.html (accessed July 10, 2008).
27. "Stress from Foods," *Stressinfo.net*, 2005, www.stressinfo.net/Foods.htm (accessed July 10, 2008).
28. Frank Lawlis and Maggie Greenwood-Robinson, *The Brain Power Cookbook* (New York: Plume, 2008).
29. "Prevent Stress Setbacks," *MayoClinic.com*, July 20, 2006, www.mayclinic.com/health/stress-management/SR00038 (accessed June 24, 2008).
30. Michael Braunstein, "Humor Therapy Part 2: The Few, the Proud, Funny." Heartland Healing Center, 1999, www.heartlandhealing.com/pages/archive/humor_therapy_pt2/index.html (accessed June 24, 2008).

Chapter 4: Loss: The Day Your Heart Is Shattered

1. Martha Tousley, *Understanding the Grief Process*, 1999–2000, www.griefhealing.com/column1.htm (accessed June 25, 2008).
2. Richard H. Steeves, R.N., Ph.D., "The Rhythms of Bereavement," *Family Community Health*, 2002: 1–10.
3. Karen Kersting, "A New Approach to Complicated Grief: Better Assessments and Treatments Lead to a Brighter Outlook for People with Severe Grief, According to a Report from an APA Group," *Monitor on Psychology*, 2004: 51–54.
4. Cathy Meyer, "Supporting Yourself After Divorce," www.divorcesupport.about.com/od/lovethenexttimearound/a/support_divorce.htm (accessed July 10, 2008).

Chapter 7: Health: The Day the Body Breaks Down

1. Andrew Steptoe, ed., *Depression and Physical Illness* (New York: Cambridge University Press, 2007).
2. Patricia Blakeney Creson and Daniel Creson, "Psychological and Physical Trauma." *Journal of Mind Action: Victim Assistance*, 2002.
3. J. K. Kiecolt-Glaser, J. R. Glaser, S. Gravenstein, et al., "Chronic Stress Alters the Immune Response in Influenza Virus Vaccine in Older Adults," *Proceedings of the National Academy of Sciences USA* 93 (1996): 3043.
4. National Institute on Alcohol Abuse and Alcoholism (NIAAA), "The Genetics of Alcoholism," *Alcohol Alert*, 18 (Rockville, Md.: 1992).
5. American Diabetes Association, "The Genetics of Diabetes," www.diabetes.org/genetics.jsp (accessed July 11, 2008).
6. American Heart Association, "Heredity as a Risk Factor: Can Heart and Blood Disease Be Inherited?" July 11, 2008, www.americanheart.org/presenter.jhtml?indentifier=4610 (accessed July 11, 2008).
7. Martin L. Rossman, *Guided Imagery for Self-Healing* (Tiburon, Calif.: H. J. Kramer, Novato, CA: and New World Library, 2000).
8. Jeanne Achterberg and G. Frank Lawlis, *The Health Attribution Test*, (Champaign, Ill.: IPAT, 1979).
9. Jeanne Achterberg and G. Frank Lawlis, *Bridges of the Bodymind: Behavioral Approaches to Health Care* (Champaign, Ill.: Institute for Personality and Ability Testing, 1980).
10. World Health Organization, "World Health Organization Assesses the World's Health Systems," June 21, 2000, www.who.int/whr/2000/media_centre/press_release/en/index.html (accessed May 22, 2008).
11. Barnaby Feder, "New Priority: Saving the Feet of Diabetics," *The New York Times*, August 30, 2005.
12. Ibid.
13. Lyn Freeman and G. Frank Lawlis, *Mosby's Complementary and Alternative Medicine: A Research-based Approach* (St. Louis, Mo.: C. V. Mosby, 2000).

Chapter 8: Mental Health: The Day the Mind Breaks Down

1. National Institute of Mental Health, *Depression: What Every Woman Should Know* (U.S. Department of Health and Human Services, 2000).
2. William Glasser, *Defining Mental Health as a Public Health Issue* (The William Glasser Institute, 2005).

3. "Mental Health: A Call for Action by World Health Ministers," *Ministerial Round Tables 2001 54th World Health Assembly* (Geneva: World Health Organization, 2001), pp. 43–45.
4. DuPage County Health Department, "Mental Health Matters," www.dupage health.org/mental_health/stigma.html (accessed March 3, 2008).
5. (Some material taken from the) Canadian Mental Health Association (MHA), *Understanding Mental Illness*, 2008, www.cmha.ca/bins/contents_page.asp?cid=3 (accessed June 27, 2008).
6. Virginia Aldige Hiday, Marvin S. Schwartz, Jeffrey W. Swanson, Randy Borum, and H. Ryan Wagner, "Criminal Victimization of Persons with Severe Mental Illness," *Psychiatric Services: A Journal of the American Psychiatric Association*, 1999: 62–68.
7. National Institute of Mental Health, "The Number Count: Mental Disorders in America," June 26, 2008, www.nimh.nih.gov/health/publications/the-numbers-count-mental-disorders-in-america.shtml#Anxiety (accessed June 27, 2008).
8. American Psychiatric Association, *Diagnostic and Statistical Manual of Mental Disorder: DSM-IV-TR*, Washington, D.C.: American Psychiatric Association, 2000.
9. C. Mazure, "Life Stressors as Risk Factors in Depression," *Clinical Psychology: Science and Practice* 45 (1998): 867–872.
10. webMD, "Depression Caused by Chronic Illness," May 4, 2008, www.webmd.com/depression/guide/depression-caused-chronic-illness (accessed June 27, 2008).
11. Noreen Cavan Frisch, and Lawrence E. Frisch, *Psychiatric Mental Health Nursing: Understanding the Client as Well as the Condition*, 2nd ed. Albany (Delmar Publishers, 2002), 456.
12. "*Depression: What Every Woman Should Know*," National Institute of Mental Health, (Washington, D.C.: U.S. Department of Health and Human Services, 2000).
13. "Mayo Foundation for Medical Education and Research (MFMER)," CNN.com., February 14, 2006, www.cnn.com/HEALTH/library/DS/00175.html (accessed May 6, 2008).
14. National Institute of Mental Health, "The Numbers Count: Mental Disorders in America," June 26, 2008, www.nih.gov/health/publications/the-numbers-count-mental-disorders-in-america.shtml#Anxiety (accessed June 27, 2008).
15. Whitney Matheson, "Pop Candy: Unwrapping Pop Culture's Hip and Hidden Treasures: A Q&A with . . . Alan Alda," *USA Today*, November 9, 2005, www.blogs.usatoday.com/popcandy/2005/11/a_qa_with_alan_.html (accessed July 2, 2008).
16. Graham K. Murray, Luke Clark, Philip R. Corlett, Andrew D. Blackwell, Roshan Cools, Peter B. Jones, Trevor W. Robbins, and Luise Poustka, BMC Psychiatry, "Lack of Motivation in Schizophrenia Linked to Brain Chemical Imbalance, *Science Daily*, May 8, 2008, www.sciencedaily.com/releases/008/080508075216.htm (accessed June 27, 2008).
17. Thomas W. Heinrich and Garth Grahm, "Hypothyroidism Presenting as Psychosis: Myxedema Madness Revisited," *The Primary Care Companion to the Journal of Clinical Psychiatry*, 203: 260–266.
18. American Art Association, "About Art Therapy," www.arttherapy.org/about.html (accessed July 19, 2008).
19. American Music Therapy Association, "Frequently Asked Questions About Music Therapy," 1999, www.musictherapy.org/faqs.html (accessed July 9, 2008).

20. Robert Fried with Joseph Grimaldi, *The Psychology and Physiology of Breathing: In Behavioral Medicine, Clinical Psychology and Psychiatry*, The Springer Series in Behavioral Psychophysiology and Medicine (New York: Springer, 1993).

Chapter 9: Addiction: The Day Addiction Takes Over

1. C. W. Nevius, "Meth Speeds Headlong into Suburbs." *San Francisco Chronicle*, March 5, 2005, B-1.
2. Michael D. Lemonick, "The Science of Addiction (How We Get Addicted)" *Time*, December 2007: 42–48.
3. National Council on Alcoholism and Drug Dependence, "Facts: America's Number One Health Problem," July 20, 2007, www.ncadd.org/facts/numberoneprob .html (accessed May 3, 2008).
4. Ibid.
5. "Traffic Safety Facts: Data," (Washington, D.C.: National Center for Statistics and Analysis, 2005).
6. "Facts: America's Number One Health Problem," *National Council on Alcoholism and Drug Dependence*, June 2002, www.ncadd.org/facts/numberoneprob.html (accessed June 26, 2008).
7. "Addictive Behaviors," Psychologist 4therapy.com, May 2, 2008, www.4therapy .com/consumer/life_topics/category/566/Addictive+Behaviors (accessed May 3, 2008).
8. Charles N. Roper, "Myths and Facts About Addiction and Treatment," www .alcoholanddrugabuse.com/article2.html (accessed July 14, 2008).
9. "CBC News Indepth: Drugs," CBC, September 19, 2006, www.cbc.ca/news/ background/drugs/crystalmeth.html (accessed May 2, 2008).
10. Eric J. Nestler, "The Neurobiology of Cocaine Addiction," *Science & Practice Perspectives*, 2005: 4–12.
11. National Institute of Alcohol Abuse and Alcoholism, "A Family History of Alcoholism," September 2005, http://pubs.niaaa.nih.gov/publications/FamilyHistory/ famhist.htm (accessed May 3, 2008).
12. Dr. Barry Starr, "Ask a Geneticist," May 12, 2006, www.thetech.org/genetics/ asklist.php (accessed July 14, 2008).
13. National Institute on Drug Abuse. *NIDA InfoFacts: Understanding Drug Abuse and Addiction*, January 2, 2008, www.nida.nih.gov/infofacts/understand.html (accessed June 28, 2008).
14. Darryl S. Inaba, "Discoveries in Brain Chemistry," January 30, 2008, www.cnspro ductions.com/drugeducationblog/category/in-the-news/ (accessed July 13, 2008).
15. "Cocaine and Meth Information," *Inpatient-Drug-Rehab.info*, 2007, www.inpatient-drug-rehab.info/cocaine-meth.php (accessed July 14, 2008).
16. "Fergie's New Fight," *Marie Claire*, April 2008, www.marieclaire.com/world/make-difference/fergie-fights-aids (accessed May 2, 2008).
17. Amanda J. Roberts, Ph.D., and George F. Koob, Ph.D., "The Neurobiology of Addiction: An Overview." *Alcohol Health and Research World*, 1997: 101–106.
18. American Psychological Association, "Monitor on Psychology: Empty Pill Bottles," March 2007, www.apa.org/monitor/maro7/emptypill.html (accessed May 2, 2008).
19. Faculty of the Harvard Medical School, "Aspirin: Quitting Cold Turkey Could Be Dangerous," August 21, 2006, www.body.aol.com/conditions/aspirin-quitting-cold-turkey-could-be-dangerous (accessed May 3, 2008).

20. "InfoFacts—Treatment Approaches for Drug Addiction," National Institute on Drug Abuse, August 2006, www.nida.nih.gov/infofacts (accessed June 26, 2008).
21. "Helping Patients Who Drink Too Much," National Institutes on Alcohol Abuse and Alcoholism, 2005, www.pubs.niaaa.nih.gov/publications/Practitioner/CliniciansGuide2005; shguide.pdf (accessed June 26, 2008).

Chapter 10: Existential Crisis: The Day You Have Lost Your Purpose and Have No Answer to the Question "Why?"

1. "Life Expectancy Average United States," www.data360.org (accessed June 29, 2008).

Resource Guide

The information provided in this resource guide reflects a variety of viewpoints and subject matters, and many are from sources other than the author. The inclusion of an organization or service does not imply an endorsement of the organization or service, nor does the exclusion imply disapproval. It is up to you, the user, to determine what organizations or services might be best for you and your particular situation. If you believe you need immediate assistance, please call your local emergency number or a crisis hotline listed in the following pages or in your local phone book's government pages.

STRESS: THE DAYS BETWEEN THE PEAKS AND THE VALLEYS

Websites

The American Institute of Stress
www.stress.org
(914) 963-1200

The American Institute of Stress is a nonprofit organization dedicated to advancing Americans' understanding of the role of stress in health and illness, the nature and importance of mind-body relationships, and how to utilize the potential for self-healing. It serves as a clearinghouse for information on all stress-related subjects.

The site contains information on job stress and the relationship between stress and diseases/disorders, information and resources on stress, a constantly updated library of information, and reprints on all stress-related topics culled from scientific and lay publications from which informational packets can be ordered, a monthly newsletter that reports on the latest advances in stress research and relevant health issues, and information on consultation services.

To evaluate your own level of stress online, go to:

The Perceived Stress Scale
www.macses.ucsf.edu/Research/Psychosocial/notebook/PSS10.html

The PSS was designed for use for people with at least a junior high school education. It is easy to understand, and the results are simple to grasp.

Online stress test:
www.helenjarvis-aromatherapy.co.uk/stresstest.html

This site combines the well-known Holmes-Rahe Stress Rating Questionnaire with the Hanson Scale of Life Stress Resistance to help you rate your overall stress level.

For information on how Americans deal with stress, see:

"Americans Reveal Top Stressors, How They Cope: Century-Old Movement Launches New Era of Mental Wellness." www1.nmha.org/newsroom/system/news.vw.cfm?do=vw&rid=903

This NMHA news release reveals information on what is stressing Americans most and how they cope with stress.

For more information on stress and disease, go to:

Stress and Diseases
www.medicalmoment.org/_content/risks/dec04/279555.asp

This article from the National Institute of Child Health and Human Development (NICHD) gives an overview on stress and how it relates to disease.

Stress
www.umm.edu/patiented/articles/what_health_consequences_of_stress_000031_3.htm

This article was reviewed by Harvey Simon, M.D., editor in chief, associate professor of medicine, Harvard Medical School, and physician, Massachusetts General Hospital, and gives an in-depth report on the causes, diagnosis, treatment, and prevention of stress.

Reading References

Blonna, Richard. *Coping with Stress in a Changing World*, 4th ed. New York: McGraw-Hill Humanities/Social Sciences/Languages, 2006.

———. *Seven Weeks to Conquering Your Stress.* BookSurge, 2006.

Childre, Doc, and Deborah Rozman. *Transforming Stress: The Heartmath Solution for Relieving Worry, Fatigue, and Tension.* Oakland, Calif.: New Harbinger Publications, 2005.

Ellis, Albert, and Robert A. Harper. *A Guide to Rational Living*, 3rd rev. ed. Chatsworth: Wilshire Book Company, 1975.

Freeman, Lyn W., and G. Frank Lawlis. *Mosby's Complementary and Alternative Medicine: A Research-Based Approach.* St. Louis, Mo.: Mosby, 2001.

Lawlis, G. Frank. *The Stress Answer: Train Your Brain to Conquer Depression and Anxiety in 45 Days.* New York: Viking, 2008.

Maultsby, Maxie C. *You and Your Emotions.* Appleton, Wisc.: Rational Self-Help Books, 1974.

Wheeler, Claire Michaels. *10 Simple Solutions to Stress: How to Tame Tension and Start Enjoying Your Life (10 Simple Solutions).* Oakland, Calif.: New Harbinger Publications, Inc., 2007.

LOSS: THE DAY YOUR HEART IS SHATTERED

Websites

Association for Death Education and Counseling
www.adec.org/coping/index.cfm
(847) 509-0403

ADEC is one of the oldest interdisciplinary organizations in the field of dying, death, and bereavement. Its nearly two thousand members include a wide array of mental and medical health personnel, educators, clergy, funeral directors, and volunteers.

The Grief Recovery Institute
www.grief-recovery.com
(818) 907-9600

This website has invaluable resources for those dealing with death, a divorce, or other major losses, particularly if you have become aware that you do not know what to do to help yourself deal with the emotions you are experiencing. It also has information for those who wish to train to help others deal with loss and for those seeking information on grief and recovery for their organization. For example, you can learn about sponsored programs for your social service organization, health care facility, religious or spiritual group, large corporation, or small business.

Grief Healing
www.griefhealing.com

This site is for those who are anticipating or coping with a significant loss in their life and wish to better understand the grief that accompanies such loss—this includes pet loss as well. The site is run by a certified hospice bereavement counselor, Martha Tousley.

The U.S. Department of Health and Human Services
www.hhs.gov
(877) 696-6775

Devoted to improving the health, safety, and well-being of America. Use this site to search many different grief articles and resources.

Rivendell Resources, Inc.
www.griefnet.org

GriefNet.org is an Internet community of persons dealing with grief, death, and major loss with almost fifty e-mail support groups and two websites. It is directed by Cendra Lynn, Ph.D., a clinical psychologist and certified traumatologist, has an integrated approach to online grief support, and provides help to people working through loss and grief issues of many kinds.

Reading References

Botwinick, Amy. *Congratulations on Your Divorce: The Road to Finding Your Happily Ever-After.* Deerfield Beach, Fla.: Health Communications, 2005.

Bustanoby, Andy. *But I Didn't Want a Divorce.* Grand Rapids, Mich.: Zondervan, 1978.

Deits, Bob. *Life After Loss: A Personal Guide Dealing with Death, Divorce, Job Change and Relocation.* Tucson, Ariz.: Fisher Books, 1992.

Kübler-Ross, Elisabeth. *On Death and Dying.* New York: Touchstone, 1969.

Kushner, Harold S. *When Bad Things Happen to Good People.* New York: Avon Books, 1981.

Neuman, Gary. *Helping Your Kids Cope with Divorce the Sandcastle Way.* New York: Times Books, 1998.

Rando, Therese A. *How to Go On Living When Someone Dies.* Lexington, Ky.: Lexington Books, 1998.

———. *Understanding Grief, Dying, and Death: Clinical Interventions for Caregivers*. Champaign, Ill.: Research Press, 1984.

Shriver, Maria, and Sandra Speidel. *What's Heaven?* New York: St. Martin's Press, 1999.

Tousley, Martha. *Finding Your Way Through Grief: A Guide for the First Year.* Phoenix, Ariz.: Hospice of the Valley, 2000.

FEAR: THE DAY YOU REALIZE YOU HAVE LIVED YOUR LIFE AS A SELLOUT

Websites

For more on cognitive therapy, go to:

The American Institute for Cognitive Therapy
www.cognitivetherapynyc.com
(212) 308-2440

This site provides extensive reading material and information on cognitive-behavioral therapy—a practice that can help you choose your thoughts, change your fears, and make better choices.

For more on self-administered desensitization, go to:

www.guidetopsychology.com/sysden.htm

This site provides information on self-administered systematic desensitization, a procedure in which events that cause anxiety are recalled in imagination and then the anxiety is dissipated by a relaxation technique.

For more on mental and emotional health, go to:

www.mental-emotionalhealth.com

This site allows you to explore mental and emotional health issues and learn how to cope in difficult times.

For information on Emotional Freedom Techniques (EFT), go to:

www.eft-therapy.com

This site provides information on EFT, a technique that uses the end points of the twelve major meridian channels and the two governing vessels found in Chinese medicine to help foster a release, thus clearing the physical or emotional pain being worked on.

For information on emotional intelligence, go to:

www.eqi.org

This site provides information on emotional intelligence (the innate potential to feel, use, communicate, recognize, remember, describe, identify, learn from, manage, understand, and explain emotions) and other related topics such as emotional abuse.

Reading References

Adams, Kathleen. *Journal to the Self: Twenty-two Paths to Personal Growth—Open the Door to Self-Understanding by Writing, Reading, and Creating a Journal of Your Life.* New York: Warner Books, 1990.

Ellis, Abert. *Overcoming Destructive Beliefs, Feelings, and Behaviors: New Directions for Rational Emotive Behavior Therapy.* Amherst, Mass.: Prometheus Books, 2001.

Fiori, Neil A. *Awaken Your Strongest Self: Break Free of Stress, Inner Conflict, and Self-Sabotage.* New York: McGraw-Hill, 2007.

Luciani, Joseph. *The Power of Self Coaching: The Five Essential Steps to Creating the Life You Want.* Hoboken, N.J.: Wiley, 2004.

McGraw, Phillip C. *Self Matters: Creating Your Life from the Inside Out.* New York: Free Press, 2003.

Roberts, Mark D. *Dare to Be True: Living the Freedom of Complete Honesty.* Colorado Springs: WaterBrook, 2003.

Staples, Walter Doyle. *In Search of True Self: 21 Incredible Insights That Will Revitalize Your Body, Mind, and Spirit.* Gretna, La.: Pelican, 1996.

ADAPTABILITY BREAKDOWN: THE DAY YOU REALIZE YOU ARE IN WAY OVER YOUR HEAD

Websites

For more on Abraham Maslow and the hierarchy of needs, go to:

http://webspace.ship.edu/cgboer/maslow.html

This site provides information on the psychologist Abraham Maslow and the hierarchy of needs, a famous model that rates and categorizes human needs.

For more on irrational beliefs, go to:

www.coping.org/growth/beliefs.htm

This site offers tips on how to recognize irrational beliefs and steps for refuting them.

For more on job searching, changing careers, and career planning, go to:

Thejobsolution.com
www.thejobsolution.com

This site provides a listing of online job opportunities, job search links that can help you identify local job listings, links to online job applications, links to résumé services and employment searches, and much more.

CareerPlanner.com
www.careerplanner.com

This site offers career testing, links to the Myers-Briggs Personality Test, a free job search tool, job listings, salary calculator, career counseling, and online access to the Dictionary of Occupational Titles at www.careerplanner.com/DOTindex.cfm

For more on meditation and breathing techniques, go to:

www.meditation-techniques.net/breathing-meditations.htm

This site provides a variety of breathing and meditation exercises and techniques designed to help you calm yourself and feel better.

Reading References

Glasser, William. *Reality Therapy* A New Approach to Psychiatry New York: First Perennial Library, 1990.

Heywood, John. *Learning Adaptability and Change*. Thousand Oaks, Calif.: Paul Chapman Educational Publishing, 1989.

Maultsby, Maxie C. *You and Your Emotions*. Appleton, Wisc.: Rational Self-Help Books, 1974.

McGraw, Phillip C. *Self Matters: Creating Your Life from the Inside Out*. New York: Free Press, 2003.

Payne, John W., James R. Bettman, and Eric J. Johnson. *The Adaptive Decision Maker*. New York: Cambridge University Press, 1993.

Rathus, Spencer A., and Jeffrey S. Nevid. *Psychology and the Challenges of Life: Adjustment in the New Millennium*. Hoboken, N. J.: John Wiley & Sons, 2002.

Steckle, Lynde C. *Problems of Human Adjustment*. New York: Harper & Brothers, 1949.

HEALTH: THE DAY THE BODY BREAKS DOWN

Websites

EMedicine
www.emedicine.com

The original open-access comprehensive medical textbook for all clinical fields. 10,000 contributors, 6,500 articles.

Family Doctor
http://familydoctor.org

This site is operated by the American Academy of Family Physicians (AAFP), a national medical organization representing more than 93,700 family physicians, family practice residents, and medical students. All of the information you will find has been written and reviewed by physicians and patient education professionals at the AAFP.

Mayo Clinic
www.mayoclinic.com

The Mayo Clinic's three main websites provide information and services from the world's first and largest integrated, not-for-profit group medical practice. Using the expertise of Mayo's 2,500 physicians and scientists, you will find information and tools to help you manage a chronic disease or condition. You can also learn how to access medical services, find information on keeping you and your family healthy, and gain access to Mayo's medical research and education offerings.

MedlinePlus
www.nlm.nih.gov/medlineplus

Medline Plus, updated daily, brings together authoritative information from NLM, the National Institutes of Health (NIH), and other government agencies and health-related organizations. Preformulated MEDLINE searches are included in MedlinePlus and give easy access to medical journal articles. MedlinePlus also has lists of hospitals and physicians, clinical trials, extensive information about drugs, an illustrated medical encyclopedia, interactive patient tutorials, and latest health news.

Merck and *The Merck Manuals*
www.merck.com/mmpe/index.html

The Merck Manuals are a series of health care books for medical professionals and consumers. As a service to the community, the content of the *Manuals* is now available in an enhanced online version as part of the Merck Manuals Online Medical Library. The Online Medical Library is updated periodically with new information and contains photographs and audio and video material not present in the print versions.

National Center for Complementary and Alternative Medicine (NCCAM)
www.nccam.nih.gov
(888) 644-6226

The National Center for Complementary and Alternative Medicine (NCCAM) is the federal government's lead agency for scientific research on complementary and alternative medicine (CAM). It is one of the twenty-seven institutes and centers that make up the National Institutes of Health (NIH) within the U.S. Department of Health and Human Services.

The National Institutes of Health (NIH)
www.nih.gov
(301) 496-4000

The National Institutes of Health (NIH) is part of the U.S. Department of Health and Human Services and is the primary federal agency for conducting and supporting medical research. Among other things, the website contains an A–Z directory of health topics and access to a wide variety of toll-free health information hotlines on topics ranging from AIDS/HIV and cancer to osteoporosis and aging.

U.S. Department of Health and Human Services
www.dhhs.gov
(202) 619-0257

The Department of Health and Human Services (HHS) is the U.S. government's principal agency for protecting the health of all Americans and providing essential human services, especially for those who are least able to help themselves. On this website you can find health tips, use the A–Z index, test your health IQ, and find links to the resources you need; for example, the Health Resources and Services Administration (HRSA), which is the primary federal agency for improving access to health care services for people who are uninsured, isolated, or medically vulnerable.

Reading References

Remen, Rachel Naomi. *The Will to Live and Other Mysteries*. Louisville, Colo.: Sounds True, 2001.

Segal, Irma. *The Secret Language of the Body: The Essential Guide to Healing*. Melbourne, Victoria, Australia: Glen Waverley: Blue Angel Gallery, 2007.

Siegel, Bernie. *Love, Medicine, and Miracles: Lessons Learned about Self-Healing from a Surgeon's Experience with Exceptional Patients*. New York: First HarperPerennial, 1990.

Simonton, Carl, James Creighton, and Stephanie Simonton. *Getting Well Again: The Bestselling Classic about the Simontons' Revolutionary Lifesaving Self-Awareness Techniques*. New York: Bantam, 1992.

Simonton, Carl, Brenda Hampton, and Reid Henson. *The Healing Journey*. Bloomington, Ind.: Author's Choice Press, 2002.

MENTAL HEALTH: THE DAY THE MIND BREAKS DOWN

Hotlines

National Adolescent Suicide Hotline
(800) 621-4000

National Institute of Mental Health
(888) ANXIETY (269-4389)

Suicide & Crisis Hotline
(800) 999-9999

Websites

American Psychiatric Association
www.psych.org
(888) 357-7924

American Psychological Association
www.apa.org
(800) 374-2721

The American Psychological Association seeks to advance psychology as a science and profession and encouragement psychology in all its branches. This site helps users find information, find a psychologist, find research, and so on.

Help Guide
www.helpguide.org

Help Guide is made up of a dedicated team of talented people who have collaborated to create a free, noncommercial resource for people in need. Its mission is to empower you and your loved ones to understand, prevent, and resolve life's challenges.

Internet Mental Health
www.mentalhealth.com

A free encyclopedia of mental health information created by a Canadian psychiatrist, Dr. Phillip Long.

Mayo Clinic
www.mayoclinic.com (see page 302)

MedlinePlus
www.nlm.nih.gov/medlineplus (see page 302)

Mental Health America
www.nmha.org
(800) 969-6642

Formerly known as the National Mental Health Association, it is the country's leading nonprofit organization dedicated to helping *all* people live mentally healthier lives. Its message is simple: good mental health is essential to the health and well-being of every person and of the nation as a whole. Get up-to-date information by audience, by issue, or by disorder and treatment.

Mental Help Net
www.mentalhelp.net

Selected as the "Forbes Favorite" mental health website, Mental Help Net is an established and highly regarded website designed and maintained by clinical psychologists and dedicated to educating the public with up-to-date coverage about mental health, wellness, and family and relationship issues and concerns while maintaining an independent editorial stance. On the site you will find news, articles, reviewed links, interactive tests, book reviews, self-help resources, therapist, and job listings and videos.

National Alliance for the Mentally Ill (NAMI)
www.nami.org
(800) 950-NAMI

NAMI is the nation's largest grassroots mental health organization and is dedicated to improving the lives of persons living with serious mental illness and their families. There are NAMI organizations in every state and in more than 1,100 local communities across the country, and you will find information, support, and ways to take action on this website.

National Institute of Mental Health (NIMH)
www.nimh.nih.gov
(301) 443-4513

The National Institute of Mental Health is the largest scientific organization in the world dedicated to research focused on the understanding, treatment, and prevention of mental disorders and the promotion of mental health.

National Mental Health Information Center, SAMHSA, HHS
www.mentalhealth.org
(800) 789-2647

The Substance Abuse and Mental Health Services Administration (SAMHSA)'s National Mental Health Information Center provides information about mental health via the toll-free telephone number above, its website, and more than 600 publications. It was developed for users of mental health services and their families, the general public, policy makers, providers, and the media and includes helpful resources, a mental health dictionary, a mental health services locator for your area, and much more.

National Suicide Prevention Lifeline
www.suicidepreventionlifeline.org
(800) 273-TALK (8255)

A 24-hour, toll-free suicide prevention service available to anyone in suicidal crisis.

Psych Central
http://psychcentral.com
(978) 992-0008

The Internet's largest and oldest mental health social network, created and run by mental health professionals to guarantee reliable, trusted information and support communities for more than twelve years. The site features psychological tests and quizzes, resources, and an "ask the therapist" section, a medication library, blogs, news, books, chat rooms, and more.

Suicide Prevention Resource Center
www.sprc.org
(877) 438-7772

The Suicide Prevention Resource Center (SPRC) provides prevention support, training, and resources to assist organizations and individuals to develop suicide prevention programs, interventions, and policies and to advance the National Strategy for Suicide Prevention.

More on Anxiety Disorders

Call (866) 615-6464 to get free information about panic disorder.
Call (866) 615-NIMH to have free information about OCD mailed to you.
Call (888) ANXIETY to get free information about anxiety.

Anxiety Disorders Association of America
www.adaa.org
(240) 485-1001

The Anxiety Disorders Association of America (ADAA) is a national nonprofit organization dedicated to the prevention, treatment, and cure of anxiety disorders and to improving the lives of all people who suffer from them. Among other things, the site has information on finding a therapist near you, clinical trials, self-tests, support groups, stories of hope, message boards, tips on helping family members, and much more.

National Center for Posttraumatic Stress Disorder
www.ncptsd.va.gov

The National Center for PTSD (NCPTSD) aims to advance the clinical care and social welfare of U.S. veterans through research, education, and training on PTSD and stress-related disorders. This site is an educational resource on PTSD and traumatic stress, for veterans and also for mental health care providers, researchers, and the general public.

More on Mood Disorders

Call 1-800-421-4211 for more information on depression.

Bipolar World Web Site
www.bipolarworld.net

Provides many resources for people with bipolar disorder and their families, including an "ask the doctor" link, information on diagnosis, treatments, and self-injury, personal stories, information on disabilities and stigma, community and family support, relevant books, a bipolar message board, and chat rooms.

Child and Adolescent Bipolar Foundation
www.bpkids.org
(847) 256-8525

The Child and Adolescent Bipolar Foundation (CABF) is a parent-led, not-for-profit, Web-based membership organization of families raising children diagnosed with, or at risk for, pediatric bipolar disorder.

Depression and Bipolar Support Alliance (DBSA)
www.ndmda.org
(800) 826-3632

The Depression and Bipolar Support Alliance (DBSA) is the leading patient-directed national organization focusing on the most prevalent mental illnesses with a website written in language the general public can understand. DBSA helps when people need it most: before diagnosis, when first diagnosed, and when treatment isn't working. Each month it distributes nearly 20,000 educational materials free of charge to anyone requesting information about mood disorders and living with mood disorders. Its educational materials are hopeful, have no medical or scientific jargon, and are reviewed by patients to ensure that the contents are targeted to patients and their families.

Men Get Depression National Educational Outreach Campaign
www.mengetdepression.com
www.depresionyloshombres.com

This campaign seeks to increase knowledge of, reduce the stigma of, and promote screening and treatment for male depression, including a national PBS television broadcast of "Men Get Depression" and an extensive community outreach nationwide with a specific focus on reaching men and their families within the Latino and African-American communities in spring 2008. The Web site includes materials in English and Spanish,

PSI: Postpartum Support International
www.postpartum.net
(805) 967-7636
Helpline: (800) 944-4PPD (4773)

PSI is a nonprofit organization whose mission is to eradicate the ignorance related to pregnancy-related mood disorders and to advocate, educate, and provide support for maternal mental health in every community, worldwide.

More on Severe Mental Disorders

Schizophrenia.com
www.schizophrenia.com

Schizophrenia.com is a leading nonprofit Web community dedicated to providing high-quality information, support, and education to the family members, caregivers, and individuals whose lives have been impacted by schizophrenia.

Reading References

American Psychiatric Association. *Diagnostic and Statistical Manual of Mental Disorders (DSM-IV-TR)*. Washington, D.C.: American Psychiatric Association, 2000.

Bourne, Edmund J. *Beyond Anxiety and Phobia: A Step-by-Step Guide to Lifetime Recovery*. Oakland, Calif.: New Harbinger Publications, 2001.

C., Roy. *Obsessive Compulsive Disorder: A Survival Guide for Family And Friends*. New York: Hazelden, 1999.

Castle, Lana R. *Bipolar Disorder Demystified: Mastering the Tightrope of Manic Depression,* with a forward by Peter C. Whybrow. New York: Marlowe & Company, 2003.

DeLisi, Lynn E. *100 Questions & Answers about Schizophrenia* Sudbury, Mass.: Jones and Bartlett, 2006.

Fast, Julie A., and John D. Preston. *Loving Someone with Bipolar Disorder*. Oakland, Calif.: New Harbinger Publications, 2004.

Gardner, James, and Arthur H. Bell. *Phobias and How to Overcome Them: Understanding and Beating Your Fears*. Edison, N.J.: Castle Books, 2008.

Glasser, William. *Defining Mental Health as a Public Health Issue*. The William Glasser Institute, 2005.

Golant, Mitch, and Susan K. Golant. *What to Do When Someone You Love Is Depressed: A Practical, Compassionate, and Helpful Guide*. New York: Holt Paperbacks, 1996, 2007.

Goulston, Mark. *Post-Traumatic Stress Disorder for Dummies.* Hoboken; N.J.: Wiley, 2008.

Hilliard, Erika B. *Living Fully with Shyness and Social Anxiety: A Comprehensive Guide to Gaining Social Confidence.* New York: Marlowe & Company, 2005.

Jamison, Kay Redfield. *Touched with Fire: Manic-Depressive Illness and the Artistic Temperament.* New York: Free Press, 1996.

Kingdon, David G., and Douglas Turkington. *Cognitive Therapy of Schizophrenia (Guides to Individualized Evidence-based Treatment).* New York: Guilford Press, 2004.

Knaus, William J., and Albert Ellis. *The Cognitive Behavioral Workbook for Depression: A Step-by-Step Program.* Oakland, Calif.: New Harbinger Publications, 2006.

McLean, Richard. *Recovered, Not Cured: A Journey through Schizophrenia.* Crows Nest, NSW, Australia: Allen & Unwin, 2003.

Miklowitz, David J. *The Bipolar Disorder Survival Guide: What You and Your Family Need to Know.* New York: Guilford Press, 2002.

Mueser, Kim T., and Susan Gingerich. *The Complete Family Guide to Schizophrenia: Helping Your Loved One Get the Most Out of Life.* New York: Guilford Press, 2006.

National Institute of Mental Health. "Depression: What Every Woman Should Know." Washington, D.C.: U.S. Department of Health and Human Services, 2000.

Newman, Cory F., Robert L. Leahy, Aaron T. Beck, Noreen Reilly-Harrington, and Gyulai Laszlo. *Bipolar Disorder: A Cognitive Therapy Approach.* Washington, D.C.: American Psychological Association, 2001.

Schwartz, Jeffrey M., and Beverly Beyette. *Brain Lock: Free Yourself from Obsessive-Compulsive Behavior.* New York: HarperPerennial, 1996.

Strauss, Claudia J., and Martha Manning. *Talking to Depression: Simple Ways to Connect When Someone in Your Life Is Depressed.* New York: New American Library, 2004.

Temes, Roberta. *Getting Your Life Back Together When You Have Schizophrenia.* Oakland, Calif.: New Harbinger Publications, 2002.

Torey, E. Fuller. *Surviving Schizophrenia: A Manual for Families, Patients, and Providers*, 5th ed. New York: Collins, 2006.

White, John R. *Overcoming Generalized Anxiety Disorder—Client Manual: A Relaxation, Cognitive Restructuring, and Exposure-based Protocol for the Treatment of GAD*. Oakland, Calif.: New Harbinger Publications, 1999.

Yapko, Michael D. *Breaking the Patterns of Depression*, New York: Doubleday, 1997.

ADDICTION: THE DAY ADDICTION TAKES OVER

Hotlines

24 Hour Cocaine Hotline
1-800-992-9239

Al-Anon/Alateen Hotline
1-800-344-2666

Al-Anon Family Group Headquarters
1-800-356-9996

Alcohol/Drug Abuse Hotline
1-800-662-HELP

Cocaine Help Line
1-800-COCAINE (1-800-262-2463)

Marijuana Anonymous
1-800-766-6779

National Drug Abuse Hotline
1-800-662-HELP (1-800-662-4357)

Poison Help Hotline
1-800-222-1222

Websites

Mothers Against Drunk Driving
www.madd.org
(800) 438-MADD

MADD is one of the most widely supported and best-liked nonprofit organizations in America. Its mission is to aid the victims of crimes performed by individuals driving under the influence of alcohol or drugs, to aid the families of such victims, and to increase public awareness of the problem of drinking and drugged driving.

National Association for Children of Alcoholics
www.nacoa.org
(888) 554-COAS

The National Association for Children of Alcoholics (NACoA) is the national nonprofit 501(c)3 membership and affiliate organization working on behalf of children of alcohol- and drug-dependent parents. It has affiliate organizations throughout the country and in Great Britain, publishes a bimonthly newsletter; creates videos, booklets, posters, and other educational materials to assist helpers to intervene and support children; hosts this Internet site with information about and ways to help children of alcoholics and other drug-dependent parents; sends information packets to all who ask; and maintains a toll-free phone number available to all.

National Association of Addiction Treatment Providers
www.naatp.org
(717) 392-8480

Dedicated to promoting, assisting, and enhancing the delivery of ethical, effective, research-based treatments for alcoholism and other drug addictions, NAATP represents nearly 275 not-for-profit and for-profit providers (free-standing and hospital-based programs, which offer a full continuum of care from outpatient to partial hospitalization and inpatient rehabilitation regimes)

National Clearinghouse for Alcohol and Drug Information
www.ncadi.samhsa.gov
(800) 729-6686

The nation's one-stop resource for information about substance abuse prevention and addiction treatment.

The National Council on Alcoholism and Drug Dependence (NCADD)
www.ncadd.org
(212) 269-7797

One-stop shopping for consumers and their families, students, the media, the medical community, medical researchers, public health professionals, educators, children, teenagers, and their parents who want objective information, including statistics, interviews with medical/scientific experts, and recommendations about drinking from leading health authorities. Provides "Awareness Activities" such as sample press releases, public service announcements, and suggested activities for raising awareness in your community. Has links to prevention and treatment programs and a Registry of Addiction Recovery (ROAR).

Or call its toll-free 24-hour affiliate referral:
Hope Line: (800) NCA-CALL

The National Institute of Alcohol Abuse and Alcoholism (NIAAA)
www.niaaa.nih.gov
(301) 443-3860

Provides the latest information and publications on alcoholism and alcohol abuse. Provides pamphlets, brochures, fact sheets, and posters. Offers a list of current and upcoming NIAAA workshops, meetings, and events. A comprehensive site with informative publications, research information, clinical trials, and resources.

National Institute on Drug Abuse (NIDA)
www.nida.nih.gov
(301) 443-1124

Provides information, publications and news releases on drugs of abuse, education resources and materials on drug abuse for students and young adults, and a variety of resources for parents and teachers, researchers, and medical health professionals, including clinical trials, curriculum guides, and links to NIDA Centers of Excellence.

If You Suspect Your Child Is Using . . .

Children Now. "Talking with Kids About Alcohol and Drugs." *Talking with Kids.* http://www.talkingwithkids.org/drugs.html (accessed July 2, 2008).

The National Council on Alcoholism and Drug Dependence. "How to Tell if Your Child May Be in Trouble With Alcohol." The National Council on Alcoholism and Drug Dependence. http://alcoholism.about.com/gi/dynamic/offsite.htm?zi=1/XJ&sdn=alcoholism&cdn=health&tm=84&gps=135_1532_1020_637&f=11&su=p726.2.152.ip_p284.8.150.ip_&tt=2&bt=0&bts=0&zu=http%3A//www.ncadd.org/facts/parent2.html (accessed July 2, 2008).

The Partnership for a Drug-Free America. *11 Points for Parents to Protect Their Kids.* June 9, 2005. http://www.drugfree.org/Parent/KeepingTabs/11_Points_for_Parents (accessed July 2, 2008).

———. *What to Do if Your Child Is Using Alcohol or Other Drugs.* May 28, 2008. http://www.drugfree.org/Parent/WhatToDo/What_to_Do_if_Your_Child_is_Using (accessed July 2, 2008).

Support Groups

Adult Children of Alcoholics
www.adultchildren.org
(310) 534-1815

Adult Children of Alcoholics is a twelve-step, twelve-tradition program of women and men who grew up in alcoholic or otherwise dysfunctional homes. They meet with one another in a mutually respectful, safe environment and acknowledge common experiences with the purpose of gaining freedom from the past and improvement of the present. This site provides literature, online forums, special event information, and ways to find meetings in your area.

Alcoholics Anonymous
www.alcoholics-anonymous.org
(212) 870-3400

Alcoholics Anonymous is a group of men and women whose purpose is to stay sober and help others stay sober. The only requirement for membership is a desire to stop drinking. There are no dues or fees for AA membership, and the group is not allied with any sect, denomination, politics, organization, or institution. This site provides media resources, member services, and tools for locating the group nearest you that suits your needs best.

Treatment Centers/Intervention

Hacienda del Lago
www.haciendadellago.com
(800) 713-7144

Provides inpatient treatment to chemically dependent individuals whose primary language is Spanish.

Hazel Street Recovery Center
www.hazelstreetrecoverycenter.com
(903) 791-0385

Provides an affordable residential care option in Texarkana, Texas, developed specifically for adolescent males age 14 and older in early recovery who are willing to commit to a three-month minimum stay and be actively involved in a twelve-step program, and who are medically stable. One of its main goals is to support the individual through the beginning stages of recovery while assisting with the development of initial educational and vocational choices and decisions.

La Hacienda Treatment Center
www.lahacienda.com
(800) 749-6160

La Hacienda has been providing inpatient treatment to the chemically dependent and their families since 1972. The 32-acre treatment center is located 75 miles northwest of San Antonio on the Guadalupe River in the Texas Hill Country. It offers patients a peaceful, natural environment conducive to the full recovery of body, mind, and spirit. The facility is fully licensed by the Texas Department of Health and by the Texas Department of State Health Services (DSHS) Substance Abuse Services. La Hacienda is accredited by the Joint Commission on the Accreditation of Healthcare Organizations and is approved by most major insurance carriers. This site provides links to a variety of treatment centers all over the country.

Love First
www.lovefirst.net
(888) 220-4400

Intervention for alcoholism and drug addiction. It has interventionists all over the United States and in Europe who travel nationally and internationally to help with an intervention or a crisis.

Urschel Recovery Science Institute
www.recovery-science.com
(214) 905-5090

One of the nation's leading centers for addiction treatment that specializes in helping you understand and fight addiction through personalized treatment that won't disrupt your everyday life. Offers a wide range of leading-edge services including chemical dependency and psychiatric evaluations, counseling, and psychopharmacology for addiction and psychiatric illnesses.

Or go to Dr. Urschel's online addiction therapy affiliate:

Enterhealth
www.enterhealth.com

An online addiction therapy service that combines the latest medicines and best-in-class therapies with eLearning and coaching support.

Reading References

Alcoholics Anonymous. *Alcoholics Anonymous—Big Book 4th Edition*. New York: Alcoholics Anonymous World Services, Inc. 2001.

Riggs, Randy. *From Darkness to Light: An Inspiring Story of One Man's 25 Year Struggle and Victory over Drug and Alchohol Addiction*. Fairfield, Calif.: 1st Books Library, 2003.

Tate, Philip, and Albert Ellis. *Alcohol: How to Give It Up and Be Glad You Did*. Tucson, Ariz.: Sharp Press, 1997.

Tyler, Bob. *Enough Already! A Guide to Recovery from Alcohol and Drug Addiction*. Parker, Colo.: Outskirts Press, 2005.

EXISTENTIAL CRISIS: THE DAY YOU HAVE LOST YOUR PURPOSE AND HAVE NO ANSWER TO THE QUESTION "WHY?"

Websites

For more on existentialism as a philosophical/literary movement, go to:

The Existential Primer: A Guide to Nothing in Particular
www.tameri.com/csw/exist/index.html

This site provides a basic introduction to existentialism, the major literary and philosophical figures associated with it, and the related Continental philosophies.

For more on Viktor Frankl, go to:

http://webspace.ship.edu/cgboer/frankl.html

This site provides information on the psychiatrist and former POW Viktor Frankl, who is largely responsible for bringing the concept of existentialism into the modern era.

Reading References

Jakes, T. D. *Reposition Yourself*. New York: Atria, 2007.

Keen, Ernest. *Three Faces of Being: Toward an Existential Clinical Psychology*. New York: Irvington Publishing, 1970.

Lev, Julian, and Zara Kriegstein. *The Meaning of Life: A Child's Book of Existential Psychology*. Tijeras, N. Mex.: Trans-Limbic Press, 2007.

May, Rollo. *Love and Will*. New York: W. W. Norton, 1969.

McGraw, Phillip C. *The Discovery of Being: Writings in Existential Psychology*. New York: W. W. Norton, 1983.

———. *Life Strategies: Doing What Works, Doing What Matters*. New York: Hyperion, 1999.

———. *Self Matters: Creating Your Life from the Inside Out*. New York: Free Press, 2003.

Park, James. *Becoming More Authentic: The Positive Side of Existentialism*, 3rd ed. Existential Books, 1996.

———. *Our Existential Predicament: Loneliness, Depression, Anxiety, and Death*. Existential Books, 2000.

Pausch, Randy, and Jeffrey Zaslow. *The Last Lecture*. New York: Hyperion, 2008.

Yalom, Irvin. *Existential Psychotherapy*. New York: Basic Books, 1980.

———. *Momma and the Meaning of Life: Tales of Psychotherapy*. New York: HarperCollins, 1999.

———. *When Nietzsche Wept: A Novel of Obsession*. New York: Basic Books, 1992.

For More Advanced Reading

Chirban, Dr. John. *True Coming of Age*. New York: McGraw-Hill, 2004.

Evans, C. Stephen. *Existentialism: The Philosophy of Despair and the Quest for Hope*. Grand Rapids, Mich.: Zondervan/Probe, 1984.

———. *Soren Kierkegaard's Christian Psychology: Insight for Counseling and Pastoral Care*. Vancouver, BC, Canada: Regent College Publishing, 1995.

Frankl, Viktor E. *The Doctor and the Soul: From Psychotherapy to Logotherapy*. New York: Alfred A. Knopf, 1983.

———. *Man's Search for Meaning: An Introduction to Logotherapy* (I. Lasch, trans.). New York: Washington Square Press, 1963.

———. *Psychotherapy and Existentialism: Selected Papers on Logotherapy*. New York: Simon and Schuster, 1967.

———. *Viktor Frankl: Recollections: An Autobiography* (J. and J. Fabray, trans.). New York: Plenum Publishing, 1996.

Jaspers, Karl, Edith Ehrlich, and Leonard H. Ehrlich. *Great Philosophers, Volume IV: The Disturbers: Descartes, Pascal, Lessing, Kierkegaard, Nietzsche: Philosophers in Other Realms: Einstein, Weber, Marx*. New York: Harcourt, 1995.

Kierkegaard, Soren. *The Sickness unto Death: A Christian Psychological Exposition for Upbuilding and Awakening.* Princeton: Princeton University Press, 1980.

May, Rollo. *Existential Psychology.* New York: Random House, 1988.

Mullen, John Douglas. *Kierkegaard's Philosophy: Self Deception and Cowardice in the Present Age.* Lanham, Md.: University Press of America, 1995.

Tillich, Paul. *The Courage to Be.* New Haven, Conn.: Yale Nota Bene, 2000.